CONTEMPORARY ANTHROP
A series published with t
Anthropology of
Laurel Kendall, Series Editor
Curator, Division of Anthropology, America Museum
of Natural History

Published by Palgrave Macmillan:

Body/Meaning/Healing
By Thomas J. Csordas

The Weight of the Past: Living with History in Mahajanga, Madagascar
By Michael Lambek

After the Rescue: Jewish Identity and Community in Contemporary Denmark
By Andrew Buckser

Empowering the Past, Confronting the Future
By Andrew Strathern and Pamela J. Stewart

Islam Obscured: The Rhetoric of Anthropological Representation
By Daniel Martin Varisco

Islam, Memory, and Morality in Yemen: Ruling Families in Transition
By Gabrielle Vom Bruck

A Peaceful Jihad: Negotiating Identity and Modernity in Muslim Java
By Ronald Lukens-Bull

The Road to Clarity: Seventh-Day Adventism in Madagascar
By Eva Keller

Yoruba in Diaspora: An African Church in London
By Hermione Harris

Islamic Narrative and Authority in Southeast Asia: From the 16th to the 21st Century
By Thomas Gibson

Evangelicalism and Conflict in Northern Ireland
By Gladys Ganiel

Christianity in the Local Context: Southern Baptists in the Philippines
By Brian M. Howell

Missions and Conversions: Creating the Montagnard-Dega Refugee Community
By Thomas Pearson

Gender, Catholicism, and Morality in Brazil: Virtuous Husbands, Powerful Wives
By Maya Mayblin

Direct Sales and Direct Faith in Latin America
By Peter S. Cahn

Shamans, Spirituality, and Cultural Revitalization: Explorations in Siberia and Beyond
By Marjorie Mandelstam Balzer

Spirits without Borders: Vietnamese Spirit Mediums in a Transnational Age
By Karen Fjelstad and Nguyễn Thị Hiền

The Halal Frontier: Muslim Consumers in a Globalized Market
By Johan Fischer

Faith in Objects: American Missionary Expositions in the Early Twentieth Century
By Erin L. Hasinoff

The Christianity of Culture: Conversion, Ethnic Citizenship, and the Matter of Religion in Malaysian Borneo
By Liana Chua

Communitas: The Anthropology of Collective Joy
By Edith Turner

Communitas

The Anthropology of Collective Joy

Edith Turner

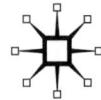

COMMUNITAS
Copyright © Edith Turner, 2012.
All rights reserved.

First published in 2012 by
PALGRAVE MACMILLAN®
in the United States—a division of St. Martin's Press LLC,
175 Fifth Avenue, New York, NY 10010.

Where this book is distributed in the UK, Europe and the rest of the world, this is by Palgrave Macmillan, a division of Macmillan Publishers Limited, registered in England, company number 785998, of Houndmills, Basingstoke, Hampshire RG21 6XS.

Palgrave Macmillan is the global academic imprint of the above companies and has companies and representatives throughout the world.

Palgrave® and Macmillan® are registered trademarks in the United States, the United Kingdom, Europe and other countries.

ISBN: 978–0–230–33908–8 (paperback)
ISBN: 978–0–230–33905–7 (hardcover)

Library of Congress Cataloging-in-Publication Data

Turner, Edith L. B., 1921–
　　Communitas : the anthropology of collective joy / Edith Turner.
　　　p. cm.
　　ISBN 978–0–230–33908–8 (alk. paper)—
　　ISBN 978–0–230–33905–7 (alk. paper)
　　1. Experience. 2. Ethnology—Philosophy. 3. Ethnology—Methodology.
4. Symbolic anthropology. 5. Collective behavior. 6. Experience. I. Title.

GN345.T87 2011
306.01—dc23   2011024723

A catalogue record of the book is available from the British Library.

Design by Newgen Imaging Systems (P) Ltd., Chennai, India.

First edition: January 2012

10 9 8 7 6 5 4 3 2 1

Printed in the United States of America.

To Rose Wellman

Previous Publications

Image and Pilgrimage in Christian Culture: Anthropological Perspectives (with Victor Turner), 1978.

The Spirit and the Drum, 1987.

Experiencing Ritual: A New Interpretation of African Healing, 1992.

The Hands Feel It: Healing and Spirit Presence Among a Northern Alaskan People, 1996.

Among the Healers: Stories of Spiritual and Ritual Healing around the World, 2005.

Heart of Lightness: The Life Story of an Anthropologist, 2006.

Contents

Preface ix

Acknowledgments xiii

Introduction 1

Chapter 1
Contrasts: Communitas and False Communitas 13

Chapter 2
Festivals: July 4th, Carnival, and Clown 23

Chapter 3
Music and Sport: Being in the Zone 43

Chapter 4
The Communitas of Work: Surprising Conclusions 55

Chapter 5
The Communitas of Disaster 73

Chapter 6
The Sacredness of the People: The Communitas of
    Revolution and Liberation 85

Chapter 7
The Communitas of Nonviolence 111

Chapter 8
The Communitas of Nature 143

Chapter 9
Rites of Passage: Communitas in Times of Change 167

Chapter 10
Alignment: Turn the Key and the Door Opens   197
Conclusion   219

Notes   225
References   239
Index   253

Preface

He who binds to himself a joy
Doth the winged life destroy
But he who kisses the joy as it flies
Lives in eternity's sunrise.
— William Blake. Eternity. 1770

The Power of Communitas

I was conducting research in the snowy north of Alaska. This was in 1990, in a village where the tradition of whale hunting has continued for many centuries as a way of providing food in a harsh climate. In late April, a warm current was coming up the Bering Strait. I found the whale men looking anxiously out of their windows toward the favored south shore, hoping for "water cloud," the sign of open water in the long-frozen ocean. They needed a north wind to blow the ice out to sea and open the waterway. But the weather was too warm and muggy and a southerly wind was blowing the ice against the south shore. As there was no water through which a whale could come, there would be no whales, and no food source.

The wind was still blowing from the south after church on Sunday. That afternoon I was out visiting my neighbor Annie Kasugaq when a call came through on the citizens' band. There was going to be a Rogation (prayer for whales) in the church at 3:00. I knew I had to go. I remembered how the sons of the preacher had brought their whaling boat into the church the first year I was there, and how the preacher blessed it and all the village crews, and prayed for whales. I left Molly's house and wandered outside in the snow to watch. Over a stretch of snow beside the preacher's house, I saw men collecting around a sixteen-foot skin boat that still rested on its high rack. The men manhandled it down onto a sled, which was hitched to a snowmobile. I had to run to keep the boat in view as the snowmobile, sled, and boat glided around the streets and to the side of the church. I came up panting behind the boat and saw the captains with five of their young sons heaving the boat off the sled. They took the sled and deftly passed it into the church and parked it up in the aisle in the sanctuary. Then they lifted the boat itself through the church entrance, sideways, banging and slipping until they could finally get it through the door. The boat was set up on the sled as if it were ready to go down to the sea, but this was in church—where the altar boy was in the act of changing the colored altar cloth for a white one. Whales like white. The preacher wore white. The paddles were all scoured white and set upright in the boat, which is a signal to other boats at sea, meaning "a catch."

The church was now filling quickly. All twenty-two whaling captains, including the hunter with the greatest catch, Robert Nashanik, stood in a crowd on each side of the boat. The preacher took up his station at the prow and began. We all sang: "The whales and all that move in the waters," "The sea is his and he made it," and, "When I in awesome wonder consider all the worlds"; songs that brought tears to the eyes of many of us—Annie Kasugaq, Robert's wife, Dora, myself. Then the captains stepped forward and put their hands on the gunwale all around, and their wives came behind them and put their hands on their husbands. The congregation went up and put their hands on the wives until we were all touching. Then we all began to pray for the wind to change. The sound rose until my eyes were starting out of my head. I prayed hard—and weird cries came from the crowd and arms whirled high in the air. The clamor grew and grew and grew.

I had never participated in a religious event like this before. I looked over at Robert's face in the crowd. It was calm—and faintly happy. I knew he was a shaman, and I calmed down, too. Soon the uproar was over. We finished with one more hymn. By this time I had goose bumps. As the congregation started to leave, I stayed to watch the men take the boat down and out of the door. I ventured gingerly over the snowy step to find my friend Annie waiting to walk back with me.

When we reached the end of the church and faced the open, the realization came to me. The wind had changed to the north. It blew icy and fresh at ten degrees Fahrenheit, and fell freely on our cheeks and the south shore. It would blow the ice away—there would be water, a passage for the whales.

No one said a word. This was their way of life. The next day there was open water near the south beach, and the men went down on the ice to break trail over the ice ridges for the snowmobiles. By Tuesday, many crews had come down to the water. They caught their quota of three whales.

The people's call to the wind was an act of communitas, inspired fellowship. The villagers had made contact with the shamanic powers. They were aware that the whale was a spirit animal. Clem, a whaling captain, used to tell me, "The whales know and they control the wind and the weather. They have senses that are much more than ours." He spoke deeply of the Iñupiat vision: "When things are right, our friendship covers all of us like a tent." I could see that. Down on the ice, we wore our mammalian warm-blooded skins and our fur parkas, and over us all was the friendship that made any environment possible. So it was not a matter of degrees of comfort, or of just accepting the weather: degrees of friendship overrode these by far. We had gotten on a certain wavelength in the church, and it carried us away up yonder where the power was, the power easily connecting through to the outside of the church and the welter of changing wind pressures, to big movements of air ceasing to pour from the south and now arising from the top of the world, strong enough to push the ice away from the south shore and open a water channel for the whale.

The village was sited on a liminal place, perched on a strip of land betwixt-and-between the sea and a lagoon, dependent on the vagaries of the sea for food. The unpredictable nature of the sea kept things unsteady, sometimes stressful. But these people were at home with prayer, that is, shamanic power in which they were skilled. So they brought the boat and its sacred whale's symbolism into the church, they Eskimoized the church, and there they sang their lives in harmony. Music can be pure communitas, and the voices in flow started the communitas. Moreover, having moved forward, we were all touching each other, with the whale boat in the center, in alignment each-with-each, a sense that grew, like a tower, a fountain, in the midst of us. Communitas arose, a tower of the senses, fierce with spirituality. The whole event lasted only half an hour; it was peculiarly nested in time. Everyone knew when it started—with the songs, tears, and cries. The very pleasure of communitas grew, too, as our voices rose to the rafters. As soon as the people came out and saw the north wind, the communitas was transmuted into a sense of siblinghood throughout the village.

For the Iñupiat this event was embedded in a long history of land problems, frustration, and insult from racist whites. It was an example of a powerful ability that would sometimes come over them—in this instance, to alter the weather with their whirling arms as they stood in a thick crowd. This and other seeming impossibilities—healing, second sight, sensing the dead—occurred with communitas, with me there to see, a researcher who witnessed and experienced it. I had been seeking the phenomena since the end of my collaboration with Victor Turner. It was he who established the term "communitas" during our fieldwork together. After his death, I traveled widely to develop a further understanding of the concept.

The communitas elements I experienced were numerous. This kind of power had nothing to do with the other kind of power, that of the oil industry, for example. Commercialization and oil exploitation were of a different order from the whale hunt. No one in the village would ever sell whale meat. Individual ownership of it was unthinkable. They would only give, give, give the meat.

When anthropological research enters a culture for the purposes of fieldwork, it may exist as a strange seed inside the womb of that culture. It grows and strains against its flesh, producing something entirely new—a combination of that culture's own truth, and the gift of a vision of what that society is really like. This book describes scenes where light dawns for all kinds of groups, times, and places, where people stumble on "the best time they've ever had" "—the time of communitas, unexpected and extraordinary. I not only describe these experiences but also show the distinct nature of communitas, the way it behaves, where it is found and not found, its very probable optimal conditions, and the curious and startling facts about its shyness and its untouchability by commercialization or institutionalization. Moreover I show that the moment of its inception can be noted, and the time it takes for it to develop or "kick in" among a group of strangers can be measured. This book is an opportunity for the reader to get a purchase on the elusive nature of communitas, the overlooked moment of memorable experience. When communitas emerges, one feels it; it is a fact of everyone's experience. That being so, once we become familiar with its properties, it can be recognized as necessary for survival.

Acknowledgments

My greatest thanks are due to Victor Turner whose book this ought to have been. Then to Irene Wellman, Rose Wellman, and Joshua Bergst, who in 2005 collectively decided I should write it. Since then, our daughter, Irene, and I have been in deep discussion at every stage of the writing. And Rose, our granddaughter, has been my continual help and steady backing. She set the tone in the first place by saying that I needed to show communitas by what it is not. She was right.

The book owes much to the stimulus of the political scientist Ari Zolberg and his paper, "Moments of Madness: Politics as Art" (1971), a paper on the communitas of revolutions that Zolberg sent to Turner and which still bears Turner's delighted margin notes.

A major help was to be found in students. Once I had planned the book, I gathered a University of Virginia anthropology class together that I called "Communitas and Humanism," so that the students could "do the work" for me. A couple of them, Kelli Nash and Courtney Stafford-Walter, did just what Rose prescribed, and collectively wrote for me a long essay on the contrast between true communitas and false. Some of it is here in the book—as are essays by other students. I was ostensibly teaching the students communitas, while they were all busy teaching it to me. Thus, regarding acknowledgments, the debt I have to them is impossible to assess. So with all my heart I thank those students whose passages are in the book or have influenced it: Katherine Megear, Kelli Nash, Courtney Stafford-Walter, Ashleigh Shepherd, Van Griffiths, Mana Anandsongkit, Laura Scherberger, Matt Bierce, Scott Osborne, Laura Cannon, Diana Collins, David Azzam, Theodora Biney-Amissah, and Joseph Whelan.

Countless anthropological colleagues have helped with the understanding of communitas—which makes me glad because of their skill in handling new ideas: I mention mainly Roy Wagner, George Mentore, Tenibac Harvey, Mieka Brand, Paul Stoller, Matthew Engelke. Colwyn Trevarthen, Laura Scherberger, Roy Willis, Stephen

Friedson, Don Handelman, Peter Ochs, and Ter Ellingson. I have referred to work of many of these here.

Helping in discussion were my sons, Fred, Bob, Alex, and Rory Turner; also Claudette Bethune, Cindy Murray, John and Elaine Bunch, Dorothea Anthony, Mary-Ellen Bambrick, Theresa Davis, and Nadine Ellero; as well as Deborah Bhatti, Peter and Vanessa Ochs, Ann and Edward Chambers, and my mentor, Chester Michael. Then I warmly thank my helpers and mentors in field research, Manyosa Kajima, Fideli Benwa, Singleton Kahona, Rex Tuzroyluk, Molly Oktollik, Dorcus Rock, Ernest Frankson, Eileen and Timothy Whooley, John and Mary Sullivan, Sharon Myers, and many others. This book was collectively written.

I am grateful to others, people often volunteering from my classes, who gave me much needed help in researching and editing for the manuscript—Van Griffiths, Kate Adamson, Erin Golden, Lauren Jones, Sharon Stein, Hannah Trible, Michael Mahoney, Kate Hofstra, Charity Donnelly, Daisy Rojas, Booton Lee Barnett, Brigitte Shull, Samantha Hasey, and Deepa John. Special thanks go to the professional editor Dawn Hunt, who took the manuscript in hand in the first place and got rid of many of the bugs. She actually wrote some of the passages. No one knows more about communitas than she does. I thank these patient people more than I can say. Those who gave more general help were Joyce Christmas, Sharon Myers, and John Kiser, "without whose help"—as the old male scholars said of their wives in their acknowledgments—"this book would never have been written," This was so true.

I owe warm thanks also to the Wenner-Gren Foundation for Anthropological Research which supported much of my early fieldwork in Zambia and Alaska; also to James and Mary McConnell and the University of Virginia for grants; and the Teaching Resource Center of the University of Virginia, which helped to fund copyediting assistance from 2007 to 2008. I am grateful to the Department of Anthropology at the University of Virginia for its encouragement and its share of the research expenses of the writing.

What meant everything to me was the steady encouragement of Laurel Kendall. Heartfelt thanks to you, Laurel. Finally I thank my family, every one, for their patience and love.

Introduction

What is communitas? The characteristics of communitas show it to be almost beyond strict definition, with almost endless variations. Communitas often appears unexpectedly. It has to do with the sense felt by a group of people when their life together takes on full meaning. It could be called a collective *satori* or *unio mystica*, but the phenomenon is far more common than the mystical states. Communitas can only be conveyed properly through stories. Because it is the sense felt by a plurality of people without boundaries, there are numberless questions as to its form, provenance, and implications. To answer these, this book explores the findings among many branches of human activity and types of relationships.

How does communitas relate to the field of mainstream anthropology? Anthropology already concerns itself with humanism, the study of which "seeks to bring out the intricate and contradictory processes of life in other cultures—including that of the anthropologist... [It] evokes the human condition in all its messiness, glory, and misery... and is thus able to promote cross-cultural understanding," according to the mission statement of the journal *Anthropology and Humanism*.[1] This statement implicitly refers to the concept of the "naked unaccommodated human being," giving a sense of a free soul who can link unreservedly with others.

Communitas fountains up unpredictably within the wide array of human life. Still the documentation of its occurrences requires their classification, and from that comes more understanding—which leads to its recognition, the faculty with which we may grasp what might be called the "ineffable." The classifications given here are mainly grouped into communitas scenes in our common everyday life, in history, and in nature. Recognition says more than analysis and is not destructive of the truth and spontaneity of the experience.

Communitas occurs through the readiness of the people—perhaps from necessity—to rid themselves of their concern for status and dependence on structures, and see their fellows as they are. Why it comes is unanswerable, except through the mercies of the energy of nature and through spirits. One can answer with a functionalist explanation, but the randomness of the events renders this ineffective. Besides, experiencers of communitas will say, "There is more to it than that."

Many circumstances can produce communitas. It often comes in the direst moments of the life of a person or society. Communitas appears in the visit of a spirit bringing healing and salvific gifts, or in the coming of a prophet such as Moses leading the Hebrews to the promised land; in the vision of Pohjola's daughter (as in Sibelius's music); or in the appearance of the mother of God at Knock in starving Ireland. Spontaneous communitas may arise in disasters: the Dunkirk spirit in World War II. Or it may happen during the rise of oppressed peoples producing activists and revolutionaries such as Mahatma Gandhi and Nelson Mandela. It may arise in movements such as Methodism in its day, and in liberation theology; in conversion, as in the case of Thomas Merton, or those in Alcoholics Anonymous; or in a near-death experience. Communitas dwells with the powers of the weak. The Universal Declaration of Human Rights shows that ethic today; the idea of democracy is founded on the value of the simple human being as undifferentiated, beyond the bailiwick of social-structural rules and status-made distinctions.

Communitas is a group's pleasure in sharing common experiences with one's fellows. This may come into existence anywhere. This book explores communitas where it is found in festivals, in music, in work situations, in times of stress, in disaster, in revolution, and in nature. Victor Turner, in "Betwixt and Between" (1964) and his book *The Ritual Process* (1969), made a connection between the joy of communitas and rites of passage, moments of change freed from the regular structures of life. Also because of this joy, this sense of the unaccommodated human being, we may link these connections up with the sense of community Martin Buber rediscovered in the 1940s, with his "I–Thou" and "I–We." These may touch on the early Karl Marx and his social idealism in our age of greedy capitalism. That idealism grew in parallel with the Gospels, so that these two teachings, social idealism and the Gospels, led to both violent and nonviolent progressive revolutions, each with a hidden communitas. The book *Communitas* keys in with the twentieth century Mikhail Bakhtin, writing from within communist Russia while he was condemned by Stalin, telling of his understanding of the joys of the people—which link with their festivals and clowns. Here, too, can be found instances from the various folk religions, and so, through to the sacredness of the land, to nature.

When communitas appears, one is conscious that it overrides psychological and sociological constructs. This is a big claim. Even within the time frame of a rite of passage, its provenance appears as the whole universe, because communitas knows no boundaries. Spirits enter in. Turner drew attention to the "unused evolutionary potential of communitas, a potential not yet externalized and fixed in structured form."[2]

Not yet externalized—this puts a finger on both the conundrum of the futuristic component of communitas and on its invisibility. Our present findings show communitas to be further still from strict definition than in Turner's time, with innumerable variations.

In the book, we will come across communitas as the deep, rich substance of the thing it is. It does not merge identities; the gifts of each and every person are alive to the fullest. It remains a spring of pure possibility, and it finds oneness, in surprise. That is, it has agency, and seems to be searching. It has something magical about it. There appear to be innumerable threads of crisscrossing lines of meaning, *flows* of meaning, in my words on communitas. That is its nature. It comes unexpectedly, like the wind, and it warms people toward their fellow human beings. It arises when people let go into negative capability, which itself is a condition of creativity, a readiness without preconceived ideas.

It resides in the poor and those considered inferior in their culture, a gift coming up from below.[3] In concrete circumstances, communitas may be found when people engage in a collective task with full attention—often a matter of ordinary work. They may find themselves "in flow." That is, they experience a full merging of action and awareness, a crucial component of enjoyment. Once in flow, there is no need for conscious intervention on their part.

In communitas there is a loss of ego. One's pride in oneself becomes irrelevant. In the group, all are in unity, seamless unity, so that even joshing is cause for delight and there is a lot of laughter. The benefits of communitas are quick understanding, easy mutual help, and long-term ties with others.

Communitas and the Study of Anthropology

Turner ventures into that land of spiritual unity in *The Ritual Process*, Chapter 3, "Liminality and Communitas." Spiritual unity has also been finely documented in African life by Colin Turnbull,[4] Stephen

Friedson,[5] and Roy Willis;[6] in Native American life by Tenibac Harvey,[7] Joan Koss-Chioino and Philip Heffner,[8] and William Powers;[9] and in European life in Turner's own examples of Saint Francis and Leon Tolstoy. When developing the Zambians' theme,[10] Turner laid open the inner liminal stage of initiation. Initiation is the entry into a more mature stage of life, of spiritual awareness, of something beyond. Initiation rites are bodily, breaking down personal superiority and pride, creating comradeship from person to person; creating bonds that are undifferentiated, egalitarian, direct, spontaneous, concrete, and unmediated. The rites become regular customs, ways to deal with one's friends' sudden biological changes, such as in birth, adolescence, marriage, illness, and death—customs that are rites of passage that take people through a liminal "gateway." The participants are all in the same boat, as it were; they are all going through a change. Teenagers, students, trainees, travelers, those with new jobs, those in disaster conditions develop this unlikely sense, which seems to be jogged into being by the circumstances. Communitas is thus a gift from liminality, the state of being betwixt and between. During this time, people find each other to be just ordinary people after all, not the anxious prestige-seeking holders of jobs and positions they often seem to be. And people like feeling this in themselves. People see each other face to face. All the little details matter. People's personalities stand out in 3D, and they are somehow likeable, gifted. No one bothers about regulations, though they may follow old customs with relish. Thus, liminality and the state of people in the midst of change gives a framing—that is, some recognizable conditions—for communitas, a kind of flowerbed ready, waiting for it. The people have found innumerable ways to celebrate this unexpected increment that happens from mere change. These are often rituals.

Communitas is togetherness itself. Why people like to be together is because of the bubbling up of communitas that comes with it. Communitas has given them this gift, just as goodness is now thought to be biological, as shown below in Chapter 8. Communitas is exciting; it makes people able to organize and work together. With this power, they will eventually develop organizational habits, structures, and rules of behavior, and ranks and positions. These often work well, if they remain on the human level; yet if they become overly law-bound, communitas will bubble up again from below and question the old system. Turner quotes Jean-Paul Sartre in "Itinerary of a Thought," who put it this way: "I [agree] that social facts have their own structure and laws that dominate individuals, but I see in this the reply of worked matter to the agents who work it. Structures are created by activity which has no structure, but suffers its results as structure."[11] Turner saw liminality as a phase in social life in which this confrontation between "activity which has no structure" and its "structured results" produces in humans their greatest moments of understanding of who they are. Even syntax and logic are *problematic* and not *axiomatic* features of liminality, he said. Therefore we have to see for ourselves whether syntax and logic exist in liminality, or in what respect they matter to the concept.

Communitas should be distinguished from Émile Durkheim's "solidarity," which is a bond between individuals who are collectively in opposition to some other group. In "mechanical solidarity," unity in one group depends on the opposition of the alien group for its strength of feeling. This is the "in-group versus out-group" opposition. But in the way communitas unfolds, people's sense is that it is for everybody—humanity, bar none. In communitas moments in the heart of revolutions it is the same; see Chapter 6.

Communitas arises in many locations: in the rituals of Africa and other preindustrial cultures, and in churches, temples, mosques, and shrines all over the world, often brought on by collective prayer. Pentecostal and charismatic churches find moments of universal love, praying for the sick, and that "sweet, sweet peace and union that comes riding into a charismatic worship service on the wings of what they call 'singing in the Spirit,' a quiet communitas."[12] In Pakistan, and Afghanistan, Sufi brotherhoods in intense, collective, submissive chants to Allah find that sense of unity. Communitas seems to be the best word for the wide comity of Islam itself. It is very real in Jewish funerals, among the Hasidim of Chagall and in *Fiddler on the Roof*. It dwells with the Dalai Lama, and with the beloved gopis dancing around Krishna. It is there in the hands of the Native American healer, with her eyes near to tears. It is present in music, and the change of consciousness in religious and shamanic groups. Communitas is sought in the Olympic Games, where the possibility of a finely tuned human body is the one truly common factor among all humankind, open to all, whatever one's rank and class. The communitas spirit, or sporting spirit, is not limited to any one institution. It does not take sides; it does not rush to "in-group/out-group" competitiveness. Nevertheless it can be woefully prostituted to produce prejudice against an "enemy."

Communitas as a fieldworker's method has been unconsciously expressed in the publications of some of our greatest founding field anthropologists.[13] Surprisingly, it appeared in Bronislaw Malinowski's notes of the 1920s. He was discovering the now obvious fact that laboring with the natives is the way to understand them:

> At 10:30 they decided to go for a *polo* [fishing expedition] and I set out with them.... Rode in a boat. Many Observations. I learn a great deal.... I observe taboo. Technology of the hunt, which would have required weeks of research. Opened-up horizons filled me with joy.[14]

As for Turner, he also emerged from a school of thought that was new in its time, "process anthropology," developed in Manchester, England, under Max Gluckman. Turner set out the rituals he had documented, not as structured custom, but as moment-by-moment living situations. Gluckman, however, was surprised by Turner's later development, his unusual handling of the activity mode he called "liminality," and how the participants felt about it, which he called communitas. Anthropologists at that time were not ready to consider communitas. The apparent sense of solidarity and community of Hitler's Nuremberg rallies were often in the minds of social scientists in the forties and fifties. Indeed, Ernst Cassirer particularly warned against crowd feeling as a temptation to incite racism and mob violence, the in-group/out-group emotion of anger and competitive hatred.[15] Meanwhile, in the fifties, America was reaffirming triumphalist individualism. The historic root of American individualism came from self-made men, factory founders, businessmen, for-profit farmers, and slave owners who had forged the new country and pushed its rapid expansion. So when the idea of communitas was first broached in the twentieth century, it needed time to flower and develop as an acceptable concept.

The Experience of Communitas

Both Victor Turner and I had experienced communitas earlier. Before Victor ever did fieldwork, he knew what communitas was. He could identify it: he and I knew it as the basic unaccommodated human being. The basic being—seemingly a lonely figure—is actually gifted with an immediate and genuine sense of the other, the plural of beings. This is in accordance with the "other-tending" nature of the universe, which I explore in Chapter 8. Victor had a sense of it when he was in the British Army in World War II, as a conscientious objector loading food onto railroad wagons. The men, looked down on as they were, worked like demons and broke all records for the number of wagons loaded per day. He and the other conchies really liked each other, as in *A Day in the Life of Ivan Denisovich* by Aleksandr Solzhenitskin, in the marvelous scene of men in the prison camp in Siberia, finding joy—joy—in working together. Victor Turner then found communitas flourishing among the boys in the circumcision camp in Zambia. It was obviously the comradeship of those under ordeal together. He spent weeks with the men in the depth of the forest, with the uncles and fathers who had been ordered up by their own young nephews to hurt them grievously with a bare knife in the act of circumcision. The hidden magic side of fertility was that of the female. I on my side participated in much of what the women were doing and thinking during the women's proceedings. For instance, I was practically enveloped in their "childbirth contractions" performance during initiation—and we all knew communitas together (see Chapter 9).

Turner first wrote about liminality in 1964, when he gave a paper entitled "Betwixt and Between" at the annual meetings of the American Ethnological Society at Pittsburgh. In it, he expanded the non-Durkheimian notion of liminality using Arnold van Gennep's *Les Rites de Passage*,[16] identifying many of the liminal anomalous moments "in and out of time" that had no connection to normal social structures. He said in 1974, "Communitas is a fact of everyone's experience, yet it has almost never been regarded as a reputable or coherent object of study by social scientists."[17] One may comment that even now it is not treated seriously, not investigated experientially; its odd characteristics are not counted in the study of the realpolitics with which much of our discipline is concerned.

In spite of the avoidance of communitas in anthropology, this theme was being taken up by a number of religious studies scholars such as Urban Holmes[18] and Tom Driver.[19] After Turner's death in 1983, the concept of communitas was adopted slowly, almost unconsciously, by anthropological humanists. Without fanfare, anthropological humanists such as Edward Bruner,[20] James Fernandez,[21] Miles Richardson,[22] Barbara and Dennis Tedlock,[23] and later Tim Knab[24] and Duncan Earle,[25] explored religious anthropology when there was no religious anthropology. This work had the effect of freeing much of the discipline from its tight positivism, looking kindly, not critically, at the sincerity behind the religious experiences of those we study. In fact, these researchers often participated as practitioners in those religions—they were actual practitioners. It was the side of religion that the humanists had been picking up, Bruce Grindal,[26] also Don Mitchell,[27] Margaret Trawick,[28] Nadia Seremitakis,[29] the poets of anthropology, and more recently, Jean-Guy Goulet,[30]

Stephen Friedson,[31] Edith Turner,[32] Roy Willis et al.,[33] Stephen H. Sharp,[34] George Mentore,[35] Laura Scherberger,[36] Tenibac Harvey,[37] Mieka Brand,[38] Jill Dubisch,[39] Pedro Pereira,[40] Sónia Silva,[41] Joan Koss-Chioino,[42] and Jo Thobeka Wreford.[43] These studies proceed with methods of the greatest empathy. There is also a large body of anthropologists who are similarly interested in religious interactions that are hard to analyze in social science terms, scholars who reduce their accounts of the phenomena they encounter to the report, "It is alleged that," thus keeping their loyalty to rational social science. Benetta Jules Rosette returned to secular social studies after a religious experience among the African Apostles, as so did Larry Peters on Tamang shamanism. After a time, Peters went back to his original understanding and is practicing shamanism today. Lévi-Strauss in "The Effectiveness of Symbols," showed he knew the depth and power that were contained in what he called "myth." This was the other level of consciousness that the shaman of his story experienced, and Lévi-Strauss's words sang of it. Clifford Geertz positively staggered between the two stances.

Communitas keeps revealing itself. It has evolutionary potential—communitas, the very thing one cannot lay hands on. We anthropologists may have to use the estimating tools and measuring rods of communitas itself—that is, what we call the "human heart"—to study it. The heart has been mentioned in anthropology before. Of all social phenomena, communitas is most likely to turn into something else when watched. Researchers can only get a purchase on this slippery thing when they are right inside of it.

Now that we can place communitas within the field of anthropology—the field in which social communitas first became recognized—we can make cross-cultural comparisons of communitas occasions on a world basis. This book takes on the task of a full-length description of the phenomenon, particularly in its manifestation as a process, or a happening, or sometimes felt as a spiritual being. At present, communitas, empathy, altruism, sociality, and human permeability are better understood and are no longer out of our reach or a cause of bewilderment for the social scientist. We know how to recognize communitas, locate it, and handle it. Knowledge of the conditions that favor it makes it pleasantly easy and sometimes predictable, as with Christmas present giving. What is more, much is known about why communitas may be absent and about the results of attempting to construct it artificially. Even though businesses and government institutions would dearly like to be able to construct it artificially, and have tried, such attempts have been hampered because there is an important principle at the heart of communitas, the inversion of the structural order[43] and the abandonment of status and acquisition. Indeed, any hoped-for spreading of communitas for profit would ultimately fail.

The Method of "Showing through Stories"

This book advances its task of unfolding communitas by telling stories that show the phenomenon in action. These stories highlight communitas and its relevance in the book. Readers may spot the relevance themselves, but there is so much involved in the swing and flow of communitas (almost like a natural art form) that we need all the help we can get. Through these stories, these real events, we are able to reveal historic and ethnographic flash points sparking across the globe. The stories in this book stake a claim on the oneness in humanity, and I make claim on the story form as the speech of communitas, for it aptly fits.

In keeping with this, what runs through the book is mostly the work of students and colleagues in anthropology.[44] The fresh minds of students are well adapted to grasping communitas, for they are not long out of their childhood. For instance, in the first chapter, "Contrasts," appear extracts from an essay on that theme by two students. The two had been alerted to the difference between true communitas and fake communitas—and have told stories to highlight the contrast. The experiences of students, professors, writers, and ordinary people in the book have enabled us to grasp what genuine communitas is—ringing clear as a bell with spontaneity.

A serious word should be said about the social class of the writers of the stories. Almost all of these come from the well-to-do or professional classes, including myself, a doctor's daughter. All the student writers, for instance, are a very select group and literate, and almost all derive from the professional classes. However, the man I call Clem in my Iñupiat accounts was turned down from the University of Alaska Fairbanks for saying that his people remembered walking over the land bridge that is now the Bering Straits. Clem told me some of his own extraordinary experiences. Professor Ntumba, now of the University of Kinshasa, Congo, says that what he called "Us-ness," his way of expressing "communitas," had been in place "always, already, and necessarily"—in existence before all time. This idea is ordinary, for Africans, and sometimes called *ubuntu*.[45] It should be said that these two men, Clem and Ntumba, did gain formal education, but still spoke out. We are going to have to listen to the real people. It is these, people with minimum exposure to academic training, who can often tell us about communitas. It will sometimes be in religious language.

The chapters of the book unfold through what is easily recognized, and then move onto what may come as a surprise. At the outset in Chapter 1, "Contrasts," the neurobiologist Colwyn Trevarthen shows that babies possess an innate predisposition to true communitas. Then Jacqueline Kelli Nash and Courtney Stafford-Walter give examples that reveal true communitas by what it is not, that is, invented, imitation, or false communitas. Chapter 2 shows festivals and joyous occasions concerned with celebrations; the happiness is easy to recognize. Here, the rituals of the calendar—that is, the earth's movement around the sun—are celebrated, with enormous pleasure, with fun, with carnival, with transgressions of ordinary behavior—all are bursting with communitas. We are on a high. In Chapter 3, communitas is revealed through the flow of music and harmony, often the way the joy of the community is communicated. High spots in music are sometimes called "being in the zone." Because the zone effect also occurs in sport, I follow music with sport here, because the consciousness of communitas is so similar. As in music, skilled abilities such as sports have the power to draw people together. In both music and sport, the sense of an inner helping entity is strong.

At much humbler levels, communitas may also occur in work itself, as in Chapter 4, where the comradeship of labor is described as delight. In Chapter 5, the book takes a steep and scary step down to the communitas of disaster, showing events of great duress and bravery. This area of study widens from individual cases to nations in Chapter 6. Communitas, with the greatest of courage, brings about triumph and enormous benefits from the greatest misery—and this part is not about religion, but about revolution. The chapter gives irrefutable evidence of the communitas moments in revolutions. Chapter 7 reveals the path of new nonviolent revolutions and protests in many forms. One may trace an entire swing away from using force for the betterment of humanity to using nonviolence instead, the very statement of the humanist. In Chapter 8, the discussion flows out at last to nature, its humility and peace. Humankind has had communitas with nature itself and all the objects and life forms in it since the beginning of consciousness. In Chapter 9, nature takes us along to a discussion of rites of passage that arise during natural change. It was through rites of passage that anthropologists first understood the complex and profound power of ritual among indigenous people. And in those rites we see odd and unexpected visions of communitas in the same manner as they are found in revolutions. Chapter 10 gives the reader a key, "alignment," which is the process of clearly sensing the possible presence of communitas, then drawing closer to it, and aligning with it, until one actually receives the whole experience—as if one had hit the exact button to lift the barrier. These ten chapters reveal what it is that liberates communitas.

The book's conclusion likens communitas to the impossible electron—in keeping with the inversions that are found in it everywhere. It contends that if you know the stories, then you know the answer. Like music, you have to be in it, hear it, to join in: then you know. You cannot get it from "program notes." Ordinary communitas is natural, as natural as breathing.

As for anthropology, what I am doing, then, is examining an aspect of human life that is little studied, describing it in detail. Anthropology has given the world a great store of scientific understanding of society, its bones and muscles, and its illnesses, but it has not allowed itself to get mixed up in such matters as person-to-person feelings unless they are analyzable and unless the analysis shows some kind of objectivity about human identity or consciousness. This book, however, tackles communitas, togetherness itself, taking the reader to the edge of the precipice of knowledge—and beyond, over the barrier of the scientists' analysis and into experience itself. Light dawns on what the real thing is, and we feel lucky that it exists.[46] Then we can make discoveries.

Chapter 1

Contrasts: Communitas and False Communitas

Babies

Scientific studies confirm humankind's innate capacity to recognize a relationship of communitas. In the late 1970s, Colwyn Trevarthen, a child neurologist at the School of Neurobiology at Edinburgh University, found that babies at two months old can recognize their mothers in a live picture on two-way television, which provides warm interactive communication between baby and mother. The babies can distinguish between two things: seeing their mothers live, and seeing a delayed replay, a mere copy of the sight of their mothers in an "off the mark" communication. Many repeated tests involving two-way television and volunteer mothers with their babies have shown that babies can indeed distinguish the live image from the replay. Here are excerpts from two of Trevarthen's articles.

> In film studies in my own laboratories of infants from four weeks of age through the first year, we have obtained evidence of gestures of recognition. Infants smile, gesture, grimace, pre-speak and vocalize to persons, often tuning and grading their expressions to fit closely with the pattern expression of their partners. Disruption of the partner's acts, caused by inattention or external interference is, we have found, capable of producing strong indications of distress and withdrawal in an infant of two months who has been in communication just before. This proves both that infants are capable of close involvement in the complexity of normal "baby talk," and that they are emotionally dependent on its progress.[1]
>
> With these considerations in mind, two experimental studies were carried out to examine in detail the sensitivities and expressive capacities of infants under three months old. A double closed-circuit

television system was designed in which each partner sees a video image of the other that is full-face and life size, with eye-to-eye contact. The images of the two partners are replayed via video recorders to monitors, permitting the timing of the display of one partner to the other to be instantaneous, live, or in real time, OR delayed after a 30 second interval in which the tape was rewound.

During the period of normal interaction, the infants looked at their mother's face most of the time and smiled frequently. During the replay, the mother's behavior that the baby heard and saw was exactly the same as that which was successfully communicated with the preceding live sequence but, of course, the mother's behavior was unresponsive to the baby's.... When the mother, unaware that she was to view a replay, was presented with the video sequence of her infant recorded during the normal, live interaction from a few minutes previously, her baby talk systematically changed. Its affectionate tone was reduced, and she spoke of her infant as behaving in an odd way. Her utterances revealed that she felt her infant was strangely unaware and avoidant. Several mothers said that there must be something "wrong" in their own behavior that was disturbing the infant. The mothers expected their infants to be highly responsive to their own feelings in a positive or constructive manner. In the nonsynchronized video replay the infant displayed puzzlement, confusion, distress, and withdrawal.

Eighteen sessions were run with four infants, two boys and two girls, between the ages of 6 and 12 weeks old. These results suggest that infants of 6 to 12 weeks have the capacity to detect features of the mother's behavior that require a joined circle of emotional communication.... A non-reductionist interpretation should be made of these data (Trevarthen, 1983a, b). Infants are ready to engage in interpersonal contacts and form active emotional relationships with particular persons before they are ready to handle and manipulatively explore objects. To be able to discriminate the behaviors of persons, they must possess an innate set of processes by which the values of human emotions are formulated.[2]

We can picture what happens when the mother waves in the nonsynchronized showing. The child does not wave back. There is no eye contact. The timing is wrong and the baby becomes puzzled and distressed. What has happened is that the communitas of interaction between mother and child is lost. The baby has been presented with a false communitas—and apparently by its own mother. Babies can recognize the real thing when it comes, *and* its opposite. Trevarthen insists that a reductionist analysis will not do, because of the wealth and range of emotions involved and the sharp comprehension of the infant. He draws the conclusion that the faculty of recognition of the genuine is innate. Trevarthen is familiar with communitas, and has determined that it is communitas that the children recognize and transmit, on the one-on-one level.

It appears, then, that humans do have innate knowledge of genuine interactive communitas, and that we know it all our lives. In this chapter are some telling accounts of the working of true and false communitas in adult life, based on personal communications shared from Kelli Nash and Courtney Stafford-Walter. First, Courtney describes her educational guided tour.

Communitas and its Negation[3]

Up the Mountain

Courtney was looking forward. In front of her was the back of a fellow hiker. They were climbing, grabbing roots uncovered by rainforest downpours.

Her foot slipped! The loose, recently moistened soil crumbled under her feet and somersaulted down a steep valley to her left. She watched it fall. Before her eyes was a sea of ferns—the first opening in the rainforest canopy she had seen for two weeks. Her eyes shifted back to the mountain. She felt the weight of mother earth pulling her down, resisting ascent. Her breath was shallow; she could not go on. The top of the mountain was still not in sight. Her legs quivered as she continued to climb using all four limbs and all of her will, yet she was weak.

She could hear the gasps of her fellow hikers—like her own. The gasps became audible groans. Up and down the line, legs were weakening—just like her own. Their minds were pushing them forward in a rhythmic pattern, and she realized she too could do this, suspended in the fluid of the weakness of them all.

Then they were there. It was over!

Weakness turned into accomplishment, and they experienced a wave of communal joy like nothing she had ever felt before. They sat in the afternoon rain and ate avocado and burritos in silence. It was the perfection of human existence.

The rain pelted down on the tin roof of the shack where everyone lay outstretched on their sleeping bags, relaxing at last. Now Maureen, one of the guides, called them to come together for a meeting, ripping them from their individual reflections. These meetings, listed as "part of the experience," made Courtney feel a bit awkward. After a full day of trekking through the rain forest, the last thing she wanted to do was sit in a circle that was constructed by their two guides and go through a pre-arranged order of "reflection" tools.

"Okay, chicos, let's start with our 'highs' and 'lows' for the day," said Maureen.

"I'll start," said Courtney, just to hurry things up and get the process over with. "My high for the day was the first waterfall, where we stopped for lunch. That was pretty awesome." She paused and looked around at everyone's faces. They were all trying to think of something different to say, since she had taken the good "high" for the day.

She continued, "My low was probably crossing that last river where I hurt my hip." She felt silly talking about an event in which her fellow hikers stopped and took care of her, an event they survived together. They proceeded to go around the seated circle, each person coming up with something else that was a "high" or a "low."

Then Jackie asked, "What is everyone's favorite book?"—not spontaneously or out of curiosity, but because this was next on the agenda in the daily "question" list. They awkwardly went around in the circle and "shared" their answers. Then it was the turn of their two guides to spark a discussion about anything that went wrong. But somehow it was the guides telling them what was wrong, and Courtney often did not agree with them.

At last the group was able to sprawl out across the floor, hanging out together as they might have been doing the past hour.

Some time later Courtney heard about communitas and wondered what it was in this group interchange that clouded the communitas of climbing the mountain. She realized that it was the structured nature of the circle discussion. The predirected interaction had ruined it, by forcing the hikers to reflect on their communitas. She knew that a vital ingredient of communitas was the immediacy of the moment, and when the climbers were forced to try to define the indefinable, the spiritual freedom they had experienced drained away. They became irritated with the task they had to do within the circle, because the guides had suddenly switched from their previously equal status into persons with hierarchical social roles. The guides had become separate from them: it was a matter of "them" instead of "we, the hikers." The hikers had become trapped in a cycle of self-criticism, which destroyed the liberating interconnectedness. Attempts at counterfeiting the feeling were in vain, creating only awkwardness in a situation in which they did not know how to act.

The Corporate World

Courtney was now in a bank job in the corporate world. There she sat. She could feel a yawn coming. It tackled and overcame her, marking the beginning of the morning huddle. Ah, the morning huddle. How could she describe that painful ordeal? They were supposed to sit with their co-workers in a large circle of comfy chairs and listen to one another for about fifteen minutes each morning before the bank opened.

Her boss's voice, bubbly and counterfeit, rang around the circle. "Let's start this morning off with some recognition!"

Courtney shot an awkward glance at her co-workers beside her, who were shooting awkward glances back. After a moment of uncomfortable silence, Bill, one of the personal bankers, spoke up.

"I would like to recognize Cynthia for handling that grumpy customer so well yesterday. She recommended a checking account for him, and we also managed to open a savings account, and he applied for a credit card!" Bill said.

"Oh, it was nothing, but thank you," said Cynthia.

"Any more recognitions?" said the boss. "No? Well, let's go on to talk about numbers. We're gonna need to maintain our numbers in order to end the quarter with a bang. So if each teller gets two referrals today, we'll get the right number of checking accounts. So you guys can't leave without getting two referrals, okay? Make some calls if you have to, talk to your customers. Just get two referrals 'cause we all want to get paid, right? I'm just concerned about you guys getting paid for the quarter." She said this twice. "The teller who gets the most checking accounts this week will be rewarded with 250 spirit points! What do you think about that, guys? How does that sound to you?" No matter how many times the boss asserted that her worries were for the tellers' well-being, Courtney couldn't help but wonder if her real intention was to secure her end-of-the-year cruise.

"All right, guys, let's make this a great day!" The boss's exclamation marked the end of the morning huddle, the end of the forced communitas, and the beginning of the possibility for Courtney's connection with her fellow tellers.

For Courtney, as with the meeting in the shack, the event seemed to create awkwardness. The boss, the leader of the huddle, continued to maintain her difference in status. If she truly valued a favor from another, Courtney thought, why not express it naturally, at the moment when the good act occurred? The boss was trying to win a cruise, while the employees feared for their paychecks. This refuted all attempts for communitas. She realized—because the feeling of communitas was so good and much sought after—that attempts to force communitas were frequent and were encountered throughout the corporate world and throughout humanity.

Although the feeling of connectedness could never be found in the morning huddle, Courtney found that the opportunity for communitas did arise within the same work environment under a less structured situation, in the lunch-hour rush. When the tellers were working the drive-through and they could see cars in long lines, they had to work at a run inside the bank and concentrate on avoiding collisions with each other. Courtney's fellow bank tellers were quite competent. Most days when the drive-through got "slammed," that is, speeded up, they maintained quick and good service without screwing up any transactions or making any customers angry. Their speed of work was made possible by the communitas between them, which spread to all their customers. They handled each other's transactions, yelled advice across the room, and never failed to do anything that could help another person. Even throwing a purple lollipop across the room to get the soccer mom's transaction all wrapped up was something more than just that: it reflected their cooperation and sense of sharing during the lunch rush. After they finished up with the last car and pushed the send button on the tube, they all shared a sigh of relief. They were grateful to each other for so much assistance. Here, in the rush with the tellers, was where Courtney felt truly "recognized": she became an organic part of the bank system.

This communitas also appears during the lunchtime rush at diners where diner employees work in synch with each other. Good humor and work efficiency combine in an effort that is actually pleasurable.

Communitas as a Treatment Option?

The following story is from an employee in a treatment center for troubled teens (Courtney changed the employee's name to Susie to protect her identity). The organization Susie worked for utilized a combination of communal residence, schooling, and treatment as a recovery method for sexually reactive teenage boys. These boys had been pulled out of foster care for inappropriate actions toward other members of their foster families. This treatment facility was basically the last option that provided the boys with some sort of freedom instead of a strict, hospital-like institution. The idea here was that these boys could come together, become like a family, and help each other get better through mutual support. They went through group and individual therapy to help them cope with their issues, and the group setting was intended to help them see that they were not alone.

But in the cabin itself, Susie was in charge of getting the boys up, making sure their morning chores were done, and getting them ready for school. The chores and responsibilities of preparing food, cleaning, and basically taking care of themselves as a community were intended to bring them together and give them confidence and reassurance that they could all recover and live normal lives.

However, come morning time, if one of the boys refused to do his share of the work, Susie was the one who had to remind him that if he didn't pull his weight, all the others in his community would have to do his work for him and therefore suffer. Susie would have to write an individual report on him, and he would be reprimanded. Courtney wondered how this organization expected the boys to feel connected and experience communitas during these tasks when it was Susie, an employee of the organization, who told the boys they should feel communitas. And what was even more destructive of communitas was the policy that stated that the employees should not share with the boys any information regarding their own personal lives. If the boys could not identify with Susie as a real person with a real story, she could never actually be part of their healing community. She could get them punished. Moreover, the existence of the individual report forms made the noncompliant child feel separate from the community with whom he was supposed to feel at one.

In some situations, however, the "communal living" treatment option could be successful, bringing order and pattern to the lives of those struggling with personal issues. Courtney told the story of Mary, who was anorexic; she participated in a program for recovering anorexic girls. Structured interaction helped Mary get her previously chaotic life under control.

Many people who battle their disorders alone lose the fundamental connections with other people that allow for communitas. The structure of Mary's treatment facility, however, in combination with an environment of girls brought together by their own intentions to get better, formed such intense bonds that communitas was inevitable. Although they had to meet at a certain time and do certain activities imposed on them by authority figures, they grew and changed together and went through major healing during those communitas moments.

Camp 4

Sometimes the story is best not told too plainly if the communitas is to be allowed to survive. Such is the case of Camp 4, a site in Yosemite National Park where there exists an untidy but beloved resting point for climbers. It has become a kind of natural institution—a nest of communitas. The climber Kevin Kelly says this about the communitas of such a nest: "What Camp 4 illustrates is that the best you can do is *not kill it*. When it pops up, don't crush it. When it starts rolling, don't formalize it. When it sparks, fan it. But don't move it to better quarters. Try to keep accountants and architects and police and do-gooders away from it. Let it remain inefficient, wasteful, edgy, marginal, in the basement, downtown, in the 'burbs, in the hotel ballroom, on the fringes, out back, in Camp 4. When it happens, honor and protect it."[4]

Anticommunitas during the Katrina Hurricane[5]

Bernie Porch, one of thousands who had endured the flood trapped on New Orleans bridges and overpasses, spoke passionately about the need for others to know how the bridge people suffered in the face of cruelty and neglect. Bernie recounted the following:

"I'm telling you, you had dead bodies on the bridge. You had people with, I mean—people from different areas trying to survive the storm. Well, the storm was over—trying to survive this bridge action that's going on. And they had one black cop; he was the only black cop on the bridge. Everybody else was white, Hispanic, whatever. So, they had this one lady cop and she was a real b*****—and I hate to say it; she came on the bridge. She had a pump [gun]. She pumped it, and she looked at everybody, like everybody on the bridge was suspect, you know, like did a crime or something. So, I mean, kids watching this, I mean kids saying, 'Mommy, Daddy, she got a gun.' I mean, there was no need for her to act the way she did."

Bernie noted how, even during his days on the bridge, there were people who were trying to keep him and his fellow survivors from getting their story out.

"And that time, the news reporter...white man, came [onto the bridge], and he was coming towards the people, you know, I guess to interview them or something like that. So, what they did, the police officers, they made a circle around the...newsman, and he could never get close to nobody on the bridge...and when he left they kind of like escorted him off the bridge. Like you couldn't, you ain't going to talk to this man here, so that's why I say [that people] don't know what happened on the bridge." Seven months after leaving the bridge, Bernie was still looking in vain for evidence that the true story of the bridge was getting out.

"I bought two Katrina books; they have never stated nothing about a bridge. You know, they never stated nothing about what went on [on] the bridge 'cause they don't know...

"All I'm saying is that if there's any way possible that you can get this tape and let them hear it—because they need to know that what went on, on this bridge, was way beyond what happened at the Superdome."

The bridge scene, vividly told in the words of the black survivors—one can picture the scene—showed the basic innocence of the people. The account of the survivors showed the sharp distinction between communitas and anticommunitas, signaled by the gun. Facing the difference between true and false communitas enables one to grasp what the genuine article is—everything we love, ringing clear with spontaneity, like a bell. The antithesis is demonstrated in the bank "huddle" story: bastardized as real communitas, prostituted as real communitas, sold and used to feign a situation of sugary cooperation, a process by which institutions employ some "proven" method to win approval and literally to make money.

Worse than this is the force used with good intentions, as in the boys' home. What shines out, though, is the group of anorexic girls who voluntarily chose to undergo discipline for the sake of their health. Such is the fragile membrane between real communitas and its painful botching, and such is the horror at its criminal absence during Katrina's aftermath.

One of the great and holding principles of communitas is that it cannot be forced on anyone. One is not "socialized" into it—it is voluntary, spontaneous. Hence the gulf between this and "the social" of social science, the "social facts" of Émile Durkheim and anthropological analysis. The reader will need all the examples in this book to become fully familiar with the concept of communitas—although its simple form shows itself well through the shock of its contrast with our "socialized" lives.

Our reaction to true communitas is gratitude—surprised recognition, then gratitude. From the "Contrasts" accounts, we see groups knowing communitas where it really exists, and recognizing it. We see its elusiveness, its untamed nature, its spontaneity. You "get" it. Often, big free exertions of the human body set off communitas, as in the climb and in the rush hour. It is a very healthy phenomenon.

There, in those grand exertions, a generous common friendliness maintains, and rank does not matter. The sense cannot fully be put into words.

On the principle of "from what you know to what you do not know," the next chapter depicts the most obvious forms of communitas—that the crowds enjoy—festivals, celebrations, with communitas in plenty.

Chapter 2

Festivals: July 4th, Carnival, and Clown

The communitas of the crowd: lonely no more.

—*Pace*, David Riesman

A Deep Sense of Community

Victor Turner said that in a great celebration, a community is sending a proboscis out of itself, a long arm reaching up high with an eye on the end of it that turns around and looks at itself, fascinated. This is: "we the people" seeing the people as multiple versions of "each other," an entity that is entirely beneficial to gaze on and enjoy when the vision is upon us—and it is love, communitas.

We start the present chapter with celebrations.

At the Washington Mall: The Eye of Communitas

Turner, a Scotsman, was happy to respond to the invitation of the Smithsonian Folklife Center to experience the season of the United States Bicentennial Celebrations on the Washington Mall. At the Lincoln Memorial on July 4, 1982, he stood pondering in front of Lincoln's statue. He said: "When you look at one side of Lincoln's face you see a stern face, against all forms of hypocrisy and untruth; when you look at the other side you see a mild man, all for peace. So he somehow combines these two attributes, sweetness and force, like few other men have ever done."

Turner walked to the left and read from the inscription of the Gettysburg address on the wall: "The world will little note nor long remember what we did here."

He said, "Of course we did note it greatly and long, long remembered it."

He went on reading: "It is for us, the living, which we should rather be dedicated to the unfinished work for which they fought here so nobly, the proposition that all men were created equal." Turner responded, "And remember the words of the Scottish poet Rabbie Burns, 'A man's a man for a' that'—we find those words actually *attested*, actually *embodied* in a nation, in a constitution."

I saw for myself how the inhabitants of the mall were just—*the people*. I marked the way they came in vast companies that day, threading through the streets of Washington and flooding into the mall, to the heart of their democracy. I saw a gentle, liberated, slightly wild people in picnic clothes moving easily, so different from the British public among whom I was raised. The Americans seemed to be coming to the mall in families. The children went to the Air and Space Museum and said, "Coo-oo-l" to the Apollo 11 exhibit. We all want to hear that word of praise from our children.

The mall is not a place where one worships some spiritual figure as they do at Lourdes or Jerusalem. The mall is a space for democracy. That is the hidden secret of it. Neither is it a place for hero worship; it cannot be, because here the people create their own politicians. In this country of the United States, dictators are unacceptable, and if the people are made to feel powerless, they act.

Later that day we sat on a large picnic freezer in the middle of the grassy mall, surrounded by a mile of picnickers and baseball players. With the Capitol behind him, Turner commented, "All of them have 'gathered themselves to a greatness,' as Shakespeare said." They're trying to express something of the 200 years of American culture, with all its faults, with its mistakes of foreign policy. Nevertheless they're trying to communicate something special to humankind. Looking around here I see all these people, drinking colas, sitting in family groups, from Arkansas, Virginia, Georgia, wherever. They're happy. They're clapping their hands at a baseball win. I love this. If we were only able to cleave to the ordinariness, to the decency, to the humanism of this, we'd wipe out all the fears, the nonnecessities, the barbarities the great world powers are trying to inflict on a person. Let's be what we are in our picnicking selves! That is love, that is humanism. That is what, from the very beginning, America was all about. And as a Scotsman I endorse it!"[1]

It is hard to put into words the unconscious communitas Americans have for each other. One gets the sense of Lincoln, in a way *still here*, in his log cabin immortality. Also, one is astonished at the spreading quality of communitas. This was demonstrated on the grass of that very mall, a few years later, when people spread out the immense AIDS quilt. It radiated a sense of human dignity in three-by-six-feet pieces, each representing a deceased loved one—which makes you shiver. How does communitas do that? And, we can remember a moment further back in time on that same mall, when humanity heard the radiant words of Martin Luther King Jr.'s "I have a Dream." Indubitably the place is sacred.

In the next story of the communitas of festivity, I relate what is almost commonplace in America in many churches when celebrating Easter. It is a ritual of inversion, held on the Holy Thursday before Easter Day.

Washing Feet

In our church, on Maundy Thursday, Holy Thursday, we literally washed each others' feet with bowls of water at the evening mass. Shoes off, socks off—we just went at it. This washing telescopes back in time to the original event, when Jesus shocked the respectable disciples, those who insisted on calling him "Lord," as if he were an aristocrat. But they had another think coming. He got a cloth and a bowl and *he* washed *their* feet. And they knew how smelly their feet were—how the dirt had lodged in the cracks around the big toenail. One can imagine the smell now.

One such Thursday, I was sitting in the front row with Elaine, and I told her I had never had my feet washed. She laughed and said they must be smelly. I huffed and said, "You know what I mean. I'd never had other *people* wash them, although I had been in the choir for so many years. Right in front of me, people were washing away, with the ordinary parishioner, who was now the new "lord," sitting on a chair, and the servant in front with a bowl and a towel—Professor John or whoever he was. The professor did some feet, then another man changed the water and did a spell of washing, and then I noticed a girl of about nine, busily washing someone else's feet and doing a good job.

Then another man got to work. After he washed a lady's feet, she looked for her shoe. The man held up a shoe, but it wasn't hers. I can see the dangling shoe now. I hope it found its home, and the lady, her shoe.

Meanwhile, high up on the right, the choir was singing repeatedly, "You should wash each other's feet, as I have done to you."

Then: "Love one another...," with the refrain of *feet* and *love* over and over.

This washing was a communitas event, encapsulating the grand inversion: don't get the other person to do it. Wash the feet of the other person.

Bar Yohai Day, the Zohar

Another curious time of intense spirituality and great social satisfaction comes into flower every year at Meron in Israel, on the feast of Lag B'Omer, at the beginning of May. Victor Turner and I and a party of fourteen Israeli scholars, anthropologists, folklorists, psychologists, and historians gathered there in 1983 to attend the celebration. Around a sacred spot, the tomb of Rabbi Shimon bar Yohai, the people's second-century Jewish visionary, a tent city developed, full of Sephardic blue-collar workers from Tel Aviv and the new hill cities, accompanied by their longing wives. The wives had been dreaming of the saint, and had heard his promise: "If you come to the tomb your child will be healed," or, "You will have a son."

Each wife vowed to the saint she would come and, as a result—such was the power of the saint—the husband's will was overborne. He got the tents together and took the family to Meron, whether he liked it or not. These men were people who never at any time had much say in affairs, and their wives had less. Now the women had been hearing the word of God through the saintly Rabbi and were in command.

Vic, the experts, and I toiled up the hill of Meron to the shrine, where a kindly student set out a folding chair for the Scottish visitor, who had arthritis. Victor, with a wicked gleam in his eyes, stuck out his hand to the passing crowds and said, "Pity the poor anthropologist." He drew it back when he realized he was getting real shekels.

Meanwhile, I gathered with the women, who crowded around the tomb, already piled up with unlit candles that had been offered to the good rabbi. There was a heady atmosphere of wonder and excitement. That night, the Ashkenazi men were on the roof of the tomb, all in black garb, hats, and side locks—even the boys. Up on the roof, beside the dome, stood a tall concrete furnace ready for the ritual fire. With great care, an old bearded Rabbi lit the fire, and then they all linked arms and slowly rotated, singing "Bar Yohoi" in voices hoarse with emotion. The fire rose, fed by candles and sacrificed valuables. The young boys, dressed in black and yarmulkes, climbed on the dome and gazed in happy wonder at everything, longing to play with the fire. The old men were waiting for the dawn, when they would *see* her the Shekhinah, the bride, the queen, the presence of God, see—come walking up out of the eastern horizon and down the hills to greet them.[2] The linked arms were communitas, as were the deep vibrato voices, shaking with emotion. Communitas was everywhere, out of our control, and if this was a picture of God, then the old bearded firelighter on the roof was God, and so were many of the others. These scenes, foot washing and fire, show to the people a yearly revelation of themselves, and they realize that they are more than just a large number of individuals. At these times, they are a united visionary organism, and the vision rises before them, magnified; we can see every cell.

A much simpler and more immediate version of festivals is laughter. It should be noted how the stories in this book deliberately skip from one major culture area to another. This is partly to show how communitas foxes the reader, and partly to show the commonalities.

Laughter, a Category of the Festive

One has a sense that laughter itself is a welcoming-in, a recognition of the ineffability of communitas—communitas is too absurd to exist. For instance, laughter is the regular condition of daily living among the Piaroa people of Amazonia. Laughter often does more than words for them—and conveys what cannot be put into words in the quick relations of everyday life or ceremonial get-togethers. There are inversions here—communitas for structure, conversation, and suggestion rather than speaker and listener. There is, consciously, no ranking. Laughter overcomes a person freely. The genuine article cannot be ordered or directed—neither can communitas.

Healing by Laughter: An Amazonian Experience

The following story comes from the experience of a young undergraduate student in anthropology, Laura Scherberger,[3] who, in 2001, was visiting an Amazonian village.

Among the Makushi forest people of Guyana, collective laughter is frequent and is interpreted as benevolent. In a Makushi village collective, living in a noncoercive way, laughter is a matter of course. Leaders manage to perform their roles in such a way that power is redirected away from themselves and returned to society. Thus, the village leader uses indirect speech and a passive, humble approach when organizing people to work, which creates an active and intentional undoing of structures and relations of rigid centralization. Throughout the day and sometimes late into the night, the crisp sound of laughter rises from various parts of the village. Laughter often brings people close as they work side by side, and in doing so emphasizes the pleasure and desirability of any shared experience. As laughter buds out of public speeches, festivities, farms, and households, it accomplishes something that words cannot; it tells everyone "we're friends" without saying anything. Even better, collective laughter does not require a differentiation between speaker and listener/audience, in which one "actively" speaks and the others must "passively" listen in order to understand. Through the blurring and blending of voices in collective laughter, the sound of equity is achieved. Laughter uses the voice just as the breathing comes, freely. In this way the gift of collective laughter can actually heal or remove pain from the body.

One morning, Laura discovered that her leg was injured. It could not stand any pressure, much less be walked on. She and her Makushi friend Lorice went to the house of Magnus, their good shaman, where there was a crowd of people. To treat Laura's leg, he took a bunch of hyawa leaves and beat the fine tips of the leaves against her leg. She began to sense a movement of the pain. Like a small, frightened animal, a ball of pain in the center of her knee began to run about in a tight circle.

"The sickness is fighting," Lorice explained. "He doesn't want to go because he's married to your knee and says he's happy there."

Everyone burst out laughing. The shaman's old granny rose from her hammock. She began throwing insults at the pain, cursing it out and commanding it to leave Laura alone. She yelled, "Go! No one wants you here! No one! Go, you fool!" Then everyone else started to join in, and it became an all-out verbal chastisement of the "man married to her knee." Both adults and children were having a riot of a time, yelling and cursing at the thing, their fury and laughter cascading over Laura's knee.

She was quite taken aback. So here was a collective will that actually existed among the Makushi, rather than one observed from a distance or read in a text. Her body was absorbing the energy of this collective will. As she sat, overwhelmed and unable to comprehend anything that was taking place, the pain began to withdraw from her knee like hundreds of long, thin needles. Intense heat and a stinging sensation spread throughout her leg as one by one the needlelike strands of pain were drawn out and cast into the dirt with the hyawa leaves. The leaves worked like the hands of a surgeon, delicately but with great deliberation. Laura could sense that Magnus was exhausted but nonetheless intent on finishing the ritual. He continued furiously to slap the leaves on the ground.

"They've pulled it out!" said Lorice. "The man in your knee was very stubborn. He must have been happy there in your knee! Ha ha!"

Everyone began to ask Laura if it had worked, and she could only respond with a simple, stupefied, "Yes." Uproarious laughter and satisfaction greeted her response. She thanked Magnus, after which he promised to show her his herb garden.

Laughter is also the key to the famous article of Clifford Geertz, "The Balinese Cockfight." This article contained not only Geertz's scholarly analysis of the social context of the cockfight game in Bali but also, dramatically, the scene in which the two anthropologists, Clifford and his wife, Hillie, were caught attending the illegal game and ran away from the Indonesian police along with the Balinese cock fighters. Everyone laughed their heads off, people and anthropologists. Geertz said, "It was the turning point so far as our relationship to the community was concerned, and we were quite literally 'in.'"[4]

Another good example, taken this time from a workshop building in Jerusalem, concerns the sheltering and employment of the indigent elderly.

Tricks and Styles of Humorous Conversation, with Communitas Taken for Granted: Encounters between Friends around the Donkey Tree[5]

Don Handelman, the Israeli anthropologist, is a highly sophisticated, brilliant analyst of the concept of "clown" as a subcategory of certain symbolic figures appearing at rites of passage. Handelman's eye roved greedily over the strange world into which he found himself born, first doing research among Pomo shamans, then Siena's impossibly ancient Italian horse race, and then, what is relevant here, a communitas of old Jewish pensioners busy in their jewelry workshop in Israel. Handelman saw what was going on among these folks; I give his story, not in his own words, but in mine.

Zackaria, one of the old jewelry makers in the workshop that employed the indigent elderly, had left the front room to fetch some more kerosene to refill the heaters of the front and back rooms. He returned some minutes later and stood stock-still in the middle of the room. He had been thinking, and he wanted to tell the others something he'd thought up.

"You know, I visited the old-age home in Givat Shaul. That's a very pleasant place. They live in old Arab houses; they're all Ashkenazim. The food is great and they get to see movies."

"Haw, haw, haw. Hark at 'im," cut in his old friend Shlomo. "Who do you think you are, the new teacher?" His quip elicited general laughter among the front room members.

Old Yihye joined in the fun: "He's not the teacher. He's the famous Tunis donkey. You know what? In Tunis they have this tree; it's a donkey tree! S'fact. In the middle of the night in Tunis it's totally quiet. The animals are quiet outside. All good people are fast asleep indoors with their wives. Then the moon throws light on the donkey tree. Boom! Out of the tree comes a donkey, a baby donkey. It pops out. That's how Zackaria was born, out of the donkey tree! I'm telling you, god's truth." Yihye's eyes popped evilly.

Shlomo can't bear it. "Huh, and in Yemen they've got this woman tree. Every night at midnight, boom! Out of the tree comes a woman. I'm telling you, that's how Mashiah found his wife. Listen, Mashiah. I'm telling everybody about your wife. This happened just after Yom Kippur, the Day of Atonement, and Mashiah was walking about in the desert, drunk as usual. And he fell asleep under the woman tree. In the morning he woke up, and there was this woman. No dowry, nothing. They're very primitive in Yemen."

Mashiah had been listening closely, glaring. "Hey, you!" He grabbed his pliers from the counter and went for Shlomo's face, dabbing at him with the pliers.

"Hee, hee"—Shlomo fended him off and ducked, and at that Mashiah aimed lower, awfully near Shlomo's crotch.

"Get off of there!" yelled Shlomo.

Meanwhile, old Yihye was maundering on. Tunis? Yemen? Nothing! He'd give them Iraq.

"In Iraq you'll find healing water," he maintained. "If a man's sick to the stomach in Iraq, he drinks the water and then he can walk and eat. They say it's like *English* water."

Everyone collapsed.

"Ah," said Shlomo, carried away with eloquence: "Ah, Iraq is a beautiful country. Water everywhere—both sides of the house."

"Huh? *Both* sides?"

"Not like Tunis. Everywhere you look, birds are singing in the trees. And no donkey trees. Only crazy Iraqis."

This conversation appears to consist of nothing but hostility, aggression, and insult. The fact is, they were keeping this up like a game of ball, in a succession of reverse fantasies, each more ridiculous than the last. Everyone around listened carefully to the words in order to shape the topic into something even worse. Handelman carefully explains that between them, Yihye and Shlomo managed to pour doubt on both Zackaria's paternity and Mashiah's conjugal tie. They played with high and low roles, secure in the knowledge that the ridiculous was what mattered, not any high and low roles. It was all open and reciprocal. It was the devil.

Holidays, Fun, and Laughter: An Early Experience of the Frustrating, Endless, and Irresistible Game of "Kickapeg," One Hundred Percent Communitas

We had communitas, all eight brothers and sisters, when we got together on the holidays. In winter, in the big eleven-room house, we'd play a hilarious game called kickapeg. One of us would be the "He." The He would grasp the banister knob at the bottom of the front stairs while all the others hid. After a count of a hundred, the He would rove abroad to find some victims. The He only had to *see* players for them to be caught and sent to the banister knob to hold on. Quite a number of prisoners would accumulate and had to hold hands in a string, with the first victim still holding the knob.

But, the prisoners could be saved by a free player who might dash toward the knob while the He was elsewhere hunting. One touch at the end of the string of tugging children was enough to set the whole string free. (Thus we learned the ubiquity of electricity in a wire, and only now I realize that this was the way I learned the collective nature of consciousness.) The He would return in horror to find that all his prisoners had fled, and the He would have to start again. Or the He might return to "see" the heroic rescuer on the point of freeing the victims, and victimize them all over again.

"Seen George, Jim, Anna, Edie!" And we would return to the string and start cunningly to deceive the He about where the rescuers were likely to come from by leading our string yearningly in the opposite direction. The laughs and excitement of kickapeg were intense. In this way, love and admiration and the glorious process of the game welded us into a communitas of pure happiness through the process of saving each other.

What indeed is this communitas? It keeps appearing as a togetherness that seeks the whole universe as its boundary. Communitas, when in action, is precisely in all the places where unconditional love can be; that is, everywhere—not in the style of *us* apart from *them* or *against* them. Wherever communitas appears, it appears as everywhere.

We can also enter the world of play, British pantomime, which is dreadfully common entertainment, with dancing girls and naughtiness—and it is for *children!* Then there is all the Italian *commedia dell'arte* fun, Punchinello, and back in London, the horrifying *Demon Barber of Fleet Street*, who cooked people in meat pies; then the Sri Lankan Demon, Wicked Ravana, in the Wayang shows, the Wicked (but beloved) Thief in Kutiyattam Indian temple plays, the Grave Digger in *Hamlet*—these are all irresistibly entertaining and likely to be X-rated, but peculiarly refreshing.

Then, the devil appears in Mexican fiesta shows, funny and scary, wearing a mask decorated with "neutrons." Thinkers are exercised about whether demon-clowns are good or bad. Molière is full of such naughty people, and so is Rabelais. Motorbikers are among them. This "bad" communitas was what made Jesus prefer to play with the little children or go to the pub with sinners rather than talk to the grown-ups and do the pretence wisdom-sharing with the respectables. It has been very puzzling to moralists. "What has naughtiness got to do with heaven and our honored circles of cardinals?"

Somehow we have read the geography of the spiritual wrong. It might be that we are trying to get to the wrong place. What is hard to understand is that the same thing fountained out in mid-Russia under Stalin—from Bakhtin.

Mikhail Bakhtin: Festivals and the People's Second Life

Mikhail Bakhtin deeply understood the nature of festivals, and his love for them abounds in his *Rabelais and his World*.[6] He reveled in the imaginary world of Rabelais and his giants, Gargantua and Pantagruel, who raged around a mythical France, and who, when they pissed, raised such floods that the French fields were fertilized for generations to come. Bakhtin wrote in Russia during the Communist period, and with such enormous sympathy for the common people that Stalin was afraid for his own place on top, so he silenced Bakhtin's dissertation on Rabelais in 1941. Still, the work leaked out to the West twenty years later in translation, and became *Rabelais and his World*, 1965. This book enlightened Victor Turner and me during our 1979 fieldwork in Brazil and set us on the track of Bakhtin's new pattern of thinking:

> Carnival is the people's second life.... Every feast is an important primary form of human culture.... People live in it, and everyone participates because its very idea embraces all of the people. While the

feast lasts, there is no other life outside it. During carnival time life is subject only to its laws, that is, the laws of its own freedom. It has a universal spirit; it is a special condition of the entire world, of the world's revival and renewal, in which all take part. Such is the essence of carnival, vividly felt by all its participants. It is a return of the golden age upon earth. It represented a certain form of life, which was real and ideal at the same time....

These forms of ritual based on laughter were sharply distinct from the serious, official, ecclesiastical, and political cults, forms, and ceremonials. They offered a completely different, nonofficial, extra-ecclesiastical, and extra-political aspect of the world of humanity and of human relations; they built a second world in which all the people participated more or less, in which they lived during a given time.

The feast is always essentially related to time...to historic timelines. Moreover, through all the stages of historic development, feasts were linked to moments of crisis, of breaking points in the life of society and man. Moments of death and revival, of change and renewal always led to a festive perception of the world. These moments, expressed in concrete form, created the peculiar character of the feasts.

In the framework of class and feudal political structure...they were the second life of the people, who for a time entered the utopian realm of community, freedom, equality, and abundance....

All were considered equal during carnival. Here, in the town square, a special form of free and familiar contact reigned among people who were usually divided by the barriers of caste, property, profession, and age. Such free, familiar contacts were deeply felt and formed an essential element of the carnival spirit. People were, so to speak, reborn for new, purely human relations. These truly human relations were not only a fruit of imagination or abstract thought; they were experienced. The utopian ideal and the realistic merged in this carnival experience, unique of its kind.

This temporary suspension, both ideal and real, of hierarchical rank created during carnival time a special type of communication impossible in everyday life. This led to the creation of special forms of speech and gesture, frank and free, permitting no distance between those who came in contact with each other and liberating from norms of etiquette imposed at other times.

We have here a characteristic logic, the peculiar logic of the "inside out," of the "turnabout," of a continual shifting from top to bottom, from front to rear, to a second life, a second world of folk culture.

Thus carnival is the people's second life, organized on the basis of laughter. It is a festive life. Folk humor denies, but it revives and renews at the same time. Bare negation is completely alien to folk culture. This laughter is ambivalent: it is gay, triumphant, and at the same time mocking, deriding. It asserts and denies, it buries and revives.... Laughing truth is a liberator. It makes a fool of power.

The communitas phrases come in aplenty. "During carnival, life is subject only to the laws of freedom.... It embraces all the people." It even has a universal spirit, seen in the wildness and fun of the stories here. Bakhtin saw his festivals through a historic telescope. There at the other end of the telescope were many sister carnivals, and he noticed that it was change, renewal in history, and life crises that led to the festive spirit. This accords with Victor Turner's sense that liminality releases communitas. Bakhtin was writing communitas already, with its downing of the "barriers of caste, property, profession, and age," with frank and free speech, and with many of the elements of the phenomenon, including laughter—"gay, triumphant, and at the same time mocking, deriding."

So here we broaden out to show this other major characteristic of festivals and celebrations. It is the *power inversion* in celebrations, where the rich and powerful are lampooned, hazed, or subjected to mocking songs or satirical verses, forbidden by custom to reply in self-defense. This feature makes for the most passionate and hilarious of communitas. The normally poor and powerless dress in the clothes and insignia of upper-class power and often control the course of the ritual or carnivalesque events. Here is the slum-dwelling leadership of Rio de Janeiro's world-famous "Samba Schools," while the habitually wealthy and powerful play the roles of bystanders or subordinates. Carnivals generate their own energies. They often begin, literally, "with a bang," using fireworks and drums. People wear extravagantly beautiful costumes, masks, and cosmetics, overdoing the symbols that demonstrate joy. They overextend themselves, often literally in gross overeating and excessive drinking. Everyday ways of doing things are skewed and overstated, often to the point of caricature.[7]

Thus we glimpse this other element of communitas in carnivals: cheek and rebellion, represented by odd and scary naughty fellows, rascals, and clowns, such as the king's "fool," beloved by Shakespeare (representing an example from the past). The presence of these types seems to be the fault of humanity's soft spot for tricksters, forever importing them into celebrations. I hold that they are gifts from communitas, elements that enter the historical, political, and spiritual equation that no rational or theological analysis can deal with. They seem unpredictable. We need to take note of them.

For example, in Brazil the whole country lives for what they call the *Carnaval* at Mardi Gras—the biggest party on earth.

Brazil's Carnaval

In the season of Mardi Gras, or Shrove Tuesday, in Rio de Janeiro, the slum dwellers reign over the city for four days of communitas. They are desperately poor, yet they work all year to produce a fantastic show, a costume parade throughout the city. Victor Turner and I attended in February 1979, the season of beach swimming and seminude fantasy costumes on parade. The revelers have beautiful bodies and emotional voices that they display as they dance, swaying seductively in serpent formation from side to distant side of the principal avenue in town, the batteries of drums agog, while, high on the central float, the mighty male singer with the nostalgic voice is at full blast over the city—it is the sound of *saudade* itself, nostalgia. Thousands take part in the performance, and many thousands turn out to participate and dance the samba on top of the shaky bleachers.

Communitas glows. Everyone is wearing her fantasy, the costume expressing whoever she would dearly love to be. Is the event all a scam, as the Marxists in Rio say? They argue that the people are exploited and that Carnaval is a useless self-delusion. However, the people have the energy for this and, true, it is an anomaly. Carnaval has these characteristics of communitas: its very existence is an anomaly; it is not an ordinary and necessary fact of life; and, though brief and quickly passing, it is remembered vividly. Severe notes of criticism are heard about the respectability of the parade—for there is nakedness. It is a performance by the people themselves. It is not concocted from without.

Therefore, the next story is a case that bridges the distinction between pure humor and actual naughtiness—which has yet another meaning.

Naughtiness: The Secrets of Cambridge University's "1958 Car on Roof Prank" Revealed

—Patrick Sawer[8]

It is a mystery that has long baffled undergraduates and university historians alike—how did students get an Austin 7 car onto the roof of Cambridge University's Senate House in June 1958? Fifty years later, an explanation for one of the most ingenious student pranks of all time has finally been provided.

The group of engineering students who carried out the stunt have reunited to reveal their identities and explain how they winched the Austin 7 to the top of the university's seventy-foot-high Senate House.

At an anniversary dinner...ringleader Peter Davey revealed he had dreamt up the plan while staying in rooms at Gonville and Caius College overlooking the Senate House roof. He felt the roof "cried out" to be made more interesting and recruited eleven others to help him adorn it with a car. The group chose the May Bumps week, when any passersby were likely to be drunken rowers celebrating after their boat races.

The group towed a broken-down Austin 7 through Cambridge to a parking space near the Senate House, explaining its presence by sticking signs on it advertising a May ball. Mr. Davey, now seventy-two, said a ground party moved the car into position while a lifting party on the Senate House roof hoisted it up using an A-shaped crane made from scaffolding poles and steel rope.

A third group passed a plank across the right-foot gap between the roof and a turret window at Caius—a gap known as the Senate House leap—-and helped the lifting party ferry across rope, hooks, and pulleys.

Policemen who heard noises as the equipment passed above them questioned some of the ground party but were distracted by careless drivers nearby and soon left. Three drunken rowers who spotted the car swinging about forty feet up were fobbed off with the explanation that it was a tethered balloon. But it was the efforts of two student girls who showed the greatest ingenuity in trying to save the pranksters from discovery—they had been deployed to hitch up their skirts a few inches to distract passersby.

However, the stunt almost went disastrously wrong when the team tried to swing the car through the apex of the A-frame scaffold, over the Senate House balustrade, and on to the roof...It crashed on to the roof from five feet above it and, fearing they would be discovered, the lifting team hastily pushed it to the apex before dismantling their equipment and fleeing over the plank bridge.

The following day, crowds of onlookers gathered in wonder to look at the car and watch as the authorities tried and failed to construct a crane to hoist it down. Police, firefighters, and civil defense units fought for nearly a week to hoist the vehicle back down before giving up and taking it to pieces with blowtorches.

The then dean of Caius, the late Rev. Hugh Montefiore, had an idea of who was responsible and sent a congratulatory case of champagne to their staircase, while never revealing his suspicions in public. Many of the group responsible went on to enjoy distinguished careers. Mr. Davey, from Mousehole, Cornwall, was awarded a CBE and an honorary doctorate after setting up automation and robotics companies, while another, Cyril Pritchett, was a lieutenant colonel in the army. Two of the team of twelve live abroad and could not make the reunion dinner at Caius. One, David Fowler, had died and was represented by his widow, Denise. The group said their only regret was that the car was not left in place forever.

Caius officials said the "renegades" had since become generous benefactors of the college.

So, we find that the masters of the structure, the dean, and others, turned a blind eye on the prank. Compare *Stalky and Co.*, by Rudyard Kipling, where the rascally boys got away with their illegal doings, thereby altering the structure of the school.

Fun arises not only in calendrical rituals but also in sacred rites of passage, as in the case that follows, a Pakistani wedding, where the jokes touch on obscenity. There is no way the solemnities were going to be kept solemn here, as we see in the account that Don Handelman set out for us. Handelman shows us a "symbolic type," a figure of dubious reality who intrudes upon serious doings. The presence of this figure says what cannot be said on the occasion when a human being is to begin an entirely new life. The very entrance of the fool informs the company that this wedding is serious. The figure is loathed and abhorred, but elicits helpless laughter.

The Pakistani Migrant's Wedding

The following is derived from Handelman's account with Pnina Werbner.[9]

The Pakistani migrants' wedding consists of distinct phases through which the bride is separated from her family of procreation and her age mates; is changed internally from a state of "weakness" to one of "strength," and from sexual innocence to sexuality; and is united magically with her groom. The proceedings are intended to transform the bride into a strong sexual woman.[10]

During the phase called *mhendi*, a bizarre, clown-like figure appears and communicates what is to happen to the bride. Previously, the bride has been tied to her family. She has been passive and tearful. Wedding songs described the match as loveless and the groom as ugly. The company raises laughs by enacting the grudging reluctance of the bride's family to surrender her. She is dressed in old clothes and sits crying on the floor, surrounded by her girl friends. The songs of the older women mourn the loss of their daughter.

In the *mhendi* phase the bride's hands and feet are decorated with a warm red henna mixture. Now she is no longer an innocent child— nor yet a wife and sexual partner. The young girls start singing songs of love and romance. They perform wedding dances and give sexy gifts to the bride.[11]

Then a girl or young woman enters, dressed as an old man. In one wedding, this "man" dressed in old clothes with a long beard danced an exaggeratedly romantic tango with one of the girls dressed as an older woman. In another...the "old man," his face wrinkled by wet chapatti flour, wearing an old hat and carrying a cane, attacked the mother of the bride with his walking stick and tried to embrace her.[12] In these instances the "old man" is mocked about the virility he projects.

Now the bride is worked up to be at her hottest. She is faced with this clownish figure of the old man, who is neither man nor woman, neither young nor old, but a grotesque combination of all these qualities in one. Despite its disheveled appearance, it is not an arbitrary figure, but a well-defined one, and as an "old man," this figure also is authoritative, and this attribute permits the girls to break taboos on the expression of sexual desire. The wedding brings into existence this in-between figure that is analogous to the changing, in-between condition of the bride. The "old-man" is actually a nubile female, sexually aggressive, but of uncertain virility. The figure is a peculiar composite, one that is moving in the right direction in terms of the progression of the occasion, but one that is not completed. The figure is "half-baked," an ill-designed, playful composite. Yet the bride is headed towards intimate union with a male. Also, the figure combines several paradoxical and ever-changing images, all fantastic and impossible, a figure of play, absurdity, and fun. Everyone is suddenly confronted with the temporary condition of their lives.

Such clown-like figures are well-suited to perform as reflexive agents, showing the people what they are, for they are sited often at the boundary of occasions, that is, at the vital moment of change for a person—an ideal vantage from which to comment on the ongoing event.[13] Within the *mhendi* phase, the clown-like figure also embodies something that is related especially to liminal contexts. Liminality is the milieu of the interstices of mundane order and common sense. It is fluidly unexpected. The existence of a steady future order depends on temporal discontinuity: "If there were no intervals, there would be no structure," said Turner.[14]

Here are the inversions again. Such events exist within periods of change, when matters are "in process." The unknown is ahead.

Clowns

There are thousands of clowns in human culture. Like communitas, the clown, a symbolic type, melts and dissolves hardened structures. In Pueblo and Apache rituals and among many other Native American celebrations, in medieval England, all through the East, and at African funerals, a clown figure may enter some scene of tribal solemnity and push itself between the people and the sacred figure. The clown manages to disentangle people from their proper, respectful attitude to the religious figures. The god-figures themselves, such as the kachinas of the Hopi, would never become banal. They are always mysterious. One loves and respects them in much the same way as one respects a mountain. The is-ness of the god is there. However, these tribes, in their celebrations, need a certain illogical clown figure to enter the picture, act rudely, and tell us in one sense that the celebration is all silly, and at the same time, that the god is indubitably here. You know it, because a clown has arrived. You do not have to understand. Here is the clown. That you see. All things are incongruous. Just be careful you do not try rationalizing what is not rational, what cannot be pinned down. The result is one can laugh and laugh at the rude clown. We're home free. And when you *see* the clown, he is irresistible, just as the god is—not a figure of threat that you would do anything to avoid. The clown dissolves the structure.

In Tucson, the Yaqui performed the dance of the deer god. I saw the jackals, *chapayekas*, little nosey pig figures smelling around the bier of God, right there on Good Friday in 1984, in the Yaquis' barn-like church. The bier stood in the aisle, looking like a man-sized, beautifully decorated cradle, empty. I was there with the Yaqui church women in their black shawls, who were adding yet more carved crosses to the church altar and praying to them—which I did, too. The clown pigs were active and interfering, nosing around, wiping stuff from their bottoms onto the bier. The deer figure that came to dance—young, wearing antlers—was pulled down by those *chapayeka* jackals and killed. But almost at once, he, the holy deer, was up and dancing, and he blessed the ancient Yaqui drum and flutes, and was risen and off and away.

What did I know about these *chapayekas*, these horrid dressed-up figures? At that same Semana Sagrada holy week festival, row after row of marching Yaqui "pharisees" dressed like Darth Vader advanced dangerously upon the church. They were stopped by little boys dressed like angels, with sacred wands. This was all sacred; I could not take photographs. And during these old rites, the entry of the clown-beings brought the people's consciousness of the strange divine into 3D, into the sharpness of full awareness, by reason of the clowns' very freedom to cheek and belittle.

Next, Claire Farrer describes both the Apache gods and the *Libayé* clown who appear on the first evening of the Apache girl's initiation ceremony.

The Apache Gods and their Clown[15]

The Mountain God dancers appear in sets of four, each set with one or more *Libayé* clowns. The Mountain Gods are beautifully and richly garbed: ocher colored buckskin kilts encrusted with jingling tin cones;

tricolor waist sashes decorated with powerful symbols; red arm streamers to which are attached powerful eagle feathers; elegant headdresses extending up to four feet above their heads and piercing the night darkness; finely wrought and decorated moccasins often with family or tribal designs; waists encircled by thick belts and sashes to which large, sonorous bells are attached so that cones and bells produce a lovely rhythmic sound in accompaniment to the singing and drumming that provide their dancing music. Their upper bodies are painted nightly with symbols evoking Creation, a different symbol for each of the four nights they dance....

And then there is *Libayé*, dressed in shreds of Levi's cut off thigh-high or perhaps merely diapered with old flannel. There are no soft moccasins for his feet; rather, he wears worn-out tennis shoes or clumsy, heavy, high-topped work shoes. His headdress is a paper sack or a mask with the long ears of a donkey. The Mountain Gods' dancing produces music—his dancing makes only cacophony. His body has no beautiful painting; either he looks as if he were rolled in ashes and dust or he has English words painted on his torso.

Think of him as contrary, '*ich'ayua'te* [contrariness], the singer Bernard said. But it is difficult to think of *Libayé* at all, for the mind wanders far from clowns and humor to the very edges of the organized and ordered world. Ashes, for ghosts, are conjured by his name and coloring. The orders of existence are challenged by his dancing presence. While the Mountain Gods dance in difficult, exaggerated poses, he stumbles along, more often than not out of step and out of line. Where they are order and properness, he is un-order and inappropriateness. Yet his inversions are the reverse, giving meaning and depth to the obverse—he is essential to the full understanding of the Mountain Gods themselves....

Since he is pure Power personified, *Libayé* can touch other powerful objects—such as dropped costume items containing a portion of the medicine power of the maker—without having to invoke rituals to de-fuse the power in the objects before he touches them. He attends to the most basic of human needs, as it is he who carries water to the thirsty Mountain God dancers....

On another occasion a *Libayé* clown had blatantly contradictory messages painted on his body. His chest read, "LTD FOR SALE," while his back stated, "LTD NOT FOR SALE." Here the conflict was more pointedly represented and the talk concerning the messages more straightforward. What does it mean to enter the Anglo world of economic transactions rather than remain in the Apachean one of reciprocity?

The peculiar power of the Libayé is the power of the inversion itself. It can touch the gods; it never changes; it anchors the transcendent to the very roots of the earth. It relaxes and is funny. It opens a door where nothing else can open a door. It is communitas personified. The Libayé reminds me of the pig clowns at Tucson, who were the only beings that could touch the bier of Christ, defiling it with stuff from their bottoms. I could not have touched the bier, even in reverence. What a picture to have in one's mind. The people—and I—felt secured by the fulfillment of the tradition. Again, I can only feel lucky, more secure, because of it. This is very curious. This oddity is reinforced by other clown traditions.

Heyoka, the Lakota Clown

Black Elk mentions that during a *heyoka* impersonation, the new heyoka is backwards-forwards, upside down, or contrary in nature. He does seemingly foolish things, such as riding backwards on his horse with his boots on backwards so that he's coming when he's really going; if the weather is hot, he covers himself with blankets and shivers as with the cold, and he always says "yes" when he means "no."[16]

A unique example is the famous Heyoka sacred clown called "the Straighten-Outer": "He was always running around with a hammer trying to flatten round and curvy things (soup bowls, eggs, wagon wheels, etc.), thus making them straight."[17]

This is but a scrap of the mystery. Here it seems gauche to talk objectively about communitas. We would have to move right back from this wide picture of clowns to get all the figures in before we could glimpse a flash of what it is all about. These inversions are performances beyond price or wonder—the very beloved union of living communitas and living sacred structure. Who has recognized this as communitas? It's just laughter, ricocheting and hurtling upwards.

More Clowns, More Inversions[18]

We may list as well the disruptive Hobby Horse, cheekily intruding on the formation of Morris Dancers; the whiteface respectable clown and the fool, as in Fellini, with their many variants—Stan Laurel and Ollie Hardy, and the Smothers Brothers; Shakespeare's fools; and Chaucer's dreadful Wife of Bath. Also consider Mr. Punch or Punchinello; Rabelais' giants, Gargantua and Pantagruel; Red

Loki of the Norsemen; the hare-and-lion stories and those of the catlike genet and other small impudent heroes among the African Ndembu and others; Brer Rabbit; the trickster Esu, alias Exu, and the Yoruba trickster, Elegba; and Monkey, in China. There is also the Hindu monkey god, Hanuman; Tanuki the mischievous raccoon and Katsina the fox in Japan; Coyote, Raven, and the disgusting laughable gods of Amazonia; and a huge list of others. Then in our world we find Bozo the Clown, the Discworld fantasy stories, and numerous figures in the Sunday comics, such as Snoopy and Zero. Meanwhile, the children produce their own at Halloween.

The next chapter runs from festivals and clowns to another apparently nonutilitarian social phenomenon, music. We have heard of being in the zone. This applies to music and also to sport, another great nonutilitarian engagement of humankind. In sport's very striving for excellence is reveals a zone like that of music.

Chapter 3

Music and Sport: Being in the Zone

Music has the power of making heaven descend upon earth.
—Charles Darwin, quoting the Chinese annals[1]

The Power of Music to Create Communitas

We can find a key to the nature of communitas through the flow of music, one of the greatest endowments that gives joy. Linked to the phenomenon of the flow of music and its power to draw people together is the flow inherent in other collective arts and in skilled abilities such as the sporting genres. The phenomenon of flow is also termed, "being in the zone." In both music and sport, the sense of an inner helping entity is sometimes strong.

Music is a fail-safe bearer of communitas, significantly because it is the genre that is by its very nature the most ephemeral. Music will always die. It exists only as long as the vibrations continue. Music is not found in structures or abstracts; it does not depend on words or on obeying the rules or, strictly speaking, on capitalism, although capitalism is of the essence in the entertainment industry, as elsewhere. But music in itself is like our blood flow, there and gone, fresh, used, and restored. Even the idea of it is emotional. It has its living existence in its performance, and its life is synonymous with communitas, which will spread to all participants and audiences when they get caught up in it.

Some regard music as nonfunctional. In a practical sense, it does not seem necessary for human existence. However, we accept the implications of recent research on music and the brain that has concluded that musical sounds were the forerunners of speech in humans.[2] In other words, song came before language. We do not know what beauty and emotion it carried then, nor do we know how speech later took the course it did and came to be so practical and precise, and ultimately of great use in technology. What we have today is music and sound, mantras, signs of the deep soul conveying levels of consciousness not directly technological—indeed, recognizably different, producing independent effects on existence.

Music brings heaven, says Darwin, frankly enough. Mantras, repetitive and hypnotic, occur in Ihamba, which is an Ndembu African ritual performed to draw out a harmful spirit from the patient. The sung repetition of "*wuyanga-wuyanga-wuyanga-wuyanga*" as a mantra draws together all those assembled into the one intention, healing. They say, "Unless you sing, the Ihamba sickness will not come out."[3] In such rituals, song simply happens, it transpires—it breaks in when the time is ripe. For the Iñupiat Eskimos "power songs" are shamanic songs that have the power to bring the caribou. Songs carry a great flow of pleasure that floods from singing person to singing person. The eyes regard each other brightly, knowing this is *it*. Thus we know singing has actual effects, though it appears to be nonfunctional.

The question arises, is music inherent in human beings? Below is an excerpt from the work of Colwyn Trevarthen of the University of Edinburgh, describing the musicality of a baby.

The "Communicative Musicality" of Childhood: Seeking Harmony in Companionship[4]

The first expressions of a mother to her newborn are a kind of singing, a praise song. Even a premature baby can respond with musicianly skill emitting simple calls in improvised conversation, and musical sounds can calm distress of a newborn, giving rhythm to delicate life. In early weeks babies are alert to the pulse and subtle harmonies of a mother's speech, turning to tones of sympathy, or withdrawing from their absence. From the start the child is an active performer, listening and moving in time with the whole body, in intimate song and dance.

By exploring the mysterious time before speech, we find the purpose of this early musicality. In games and verses that tease anticipations, babies and their companions make up narratives of expression that draw meaning from the experience of acting together. They learn routines of song and gesture, and show them off with pride to people they trust. They enjoy musical jokes. At the same time they fear misunderstanding in presence of strangers, and show shame when communication fails. The toddler is a creative musician and dancer, loving theatrical play with peers. Dramatic acts of meaning seize hold of human inventions with a special pride, then wickedly transform them in nonsensical ways, for fun. A baby who speaks no sentences is already experimenting with expressive conventions of a culture....

Our nature is to be active individuals engaged in social experiences, seeking others' approval, and avoiding their criticism and dislike. In this way, the history of human life is part of the dynamic harmony of all evolved nature—and it is a part that must make music to be understood.

Trevarthen has observed in babies the flowering of a natural skill, that of music. This skill can become a conscious technique for entering communitas; that is, a vocation, sometimes destined to occupy a person's whole life as pop singer, bard, griot (West African), medicine person using music, carrier-of-the-torch, gospel singer, or a Beethoven. There are many types.

Does the communitas of music come as a visionary experience? One is surprised at the numbers of examples of music or drumming that reach the point of breakthrough or the spillover effect—that is, the peak effect when music opens into the *unio mystica*, the experience of revelation. David Stang has gathered the statements of professional musicians who describe their high spots in this way. William Benzon, a scientist who also adores music, constantly refers to the well-known effect in his book, *Beethoven's Anvil* (2001). Through this experience at its height, the musicians' eyes may be open but are unseeing because they have *become* the music. This occurs among the Grateful Dead in full form, and is described by Colin Turnbull on hearing Mbuti Pygmy singing.[5] We include "Amazing Grace" and the Hallelujah Chorus. All are prime communitas experiences.

How does musical exaltation come about? In fact it is easy, whether in a great ritual or in an everyday modern engagement with music. We go back to the obvious. It is achieved through the common phenomena of sound waves. It consists of a physical effect, created in a human-biological way, by voice, or hands on an instrument. Thus, its effect is direct, so direct that the physical effect bypasses the mind and goes straight to the soul—and this can happen even unconsciously. Music, as the anthropologist Robert Desjarlais says, wakes a person, alters the sensory grounds of the body, and changes how a body feels.[6] Desjarlais says that in British social anthropology it is thought that the shaman's concern for healing is an intellectual one, to instill belief. He says that the French and American symbolist schools of anthropology focus on symbols that alter and portray meaning, but again, this is for the mind. In Desjarlais's study of Yolmo Nepali healing, he shows the process as an actual activation of the body's senses, with the multigenre process affected by use of music, taste, sight, touch, and kinesthesia. In this research, the anthropology of the senses has made a step forward, in a movement started in 1989 by Paul Stoller in his book, *The Sense of Ethnographic Things,* a movement now joined by many others. It can be seen in the present book which shows scenes where communitas exists without help from the intellect, where the intellect often does not know how to deal with it. Desjarlais, with remarkable insight into communitas, tells how:

> ...the divine forms part of a cultural circuit of knowledge. This circuit transcends individual bodies. It encompasses interactions between bodies, households, and the environment. It draws from and contributes to collective experience. It courses through the laughter of a teashop, the dreams of a shaman, and the "rivers" of the body. Its value lies in its collective aspects...This collective system of spiritual knowledge communicates what it knows through tacit sensibilities and divine musings.[7]

This power, then, derives from real sound waves, human made; but they are spiritual sounds that are super-subtle. There occurs a germination by means of that very subtlety. Music is almost infinitely flexible. Because of this, the subtle spirit can develop in the flexible form of music, and the spirit can give itself a shape, recognizable in the music. Roy Wagner[8] says of classical music (especially Mozart) that it starts with a "germ" containing the whole of the piece. Music has been there from time immemorial, before language, before belief, before sentience, says Wagner.[9] Music does not so much "change consciousness" as it is simply "there," and a different kind of consciousness applies to it. Then the "germ" or "seed" flowers into the bloom. The New Guineans speak of the soul as the "seed of singing."[10] Thus, when the phenomenon of singing breaks out, you hear something for which the soul has a built in potency. You hear the soul, that awakened seed: this process goes back many eons.

Mickey Hart and Jamming

Mickey Hart was known especially for his habit of suddenly opening up a curious quietness around him. I remembered how at the Grateful Dead performance at the Hampton Coliseum in 1984, the audience and performers became one. We, in the immense crowd, were with Mickey all the way, as if we all knew just what new sounds were going to come forth.

"C'mon, c'mon," I yelled with the others. How can I describe it? We were beside ourselves, in the state called ecstasy. I can see Mickey now, bewildered, wielding the drumstick like a pickaxe, finding the gold in surprise.[11] Then the roar—my heart was completely satisfied.

There are further strange characteristics of music. Music performers sometimes seem to talk as if they have proof of God or a god. They have become aware that the music is playing itself. They sense a mysterious control from outside. David Stang,[12] a scholar of religious experience and music's power, quotes from Ashleigh Ellis, a young harpist: "Well, it's like you don't even know you're playing. In your mind, you're not thinking about anything. It's as if the music is coming through you. Then you're really doing your best, and you know you won't make a mistake or anything like that. So it's really good. Time just seems to stand still. It just doesn't go anywhere."

Thus, when Ashleigh is playing the harp, "something else" takes control of her hands and whole body. As a player, she knows that she has to continue and that she will always be willing for this—she bows her head to it, submits to it, hears how it plays through her. It is communication in progress. The person who plays is hardly there, yet is there.

A composer said, "You are in an ecstatic state to such a point that you feel as though you almost don't exist. I have experienced this time and time again. My hand seems devoid of myself, and I have nothing to do with what is happening. And the music just flows out by itself."

When the musician Eckhart Krupp describes being in the zone, he says, "I get out of my body and experience timelessness, just like a medium who leaves the body.... I feel a deep thankfulness for the experience, for being allowed to go to such a height."[13] Musicians have to let go, and take risks. They are knowing, but not knowing. One wonders why some of the churches have missed this curious principle. If it is God, it is not a god of judgment for sin or a god of authority or of any particular culture.

These statements are about being fully alive on two levels that curiously become one, this merging, is also an example of the communitas feature of "alignment," a distinct and recognizable act described in Chapter 10. This brings us to the heart of the communitas of music, well illuminated by my student and helper, Matt Bierce, who describes jam sessions in Victor Turner's terms of liminality and communitas. He says of his band,

> We have been writing songs together for six years now and our cooperative powers have grown immensely. We are intimately aware of each other and our abilities, tendencies, favoritisms, styles, moods,

and emotions. This intimacy allows us a form of jamming or improvisation that I think is a rare and cultivated closeness bordering on telepathic intuition. Above all else, we are friends. In the context of a jam, we communicate in a way that supercedes speech and cognitive logic, in a language of suggestions, weavings, liminal stances, pattern formations and dissolutions, patience, intensity and calm, and private exploration. You have to give yourself totally, without reservations. It's not enough that you believe this or that is going to happen.[14] By beholding behind the closed eyes of your co-musicians and in sensing the nerve impulses and the movements of the muscles in their bodies, you will attain a security in relation to what is going to happen. We are also working together to keep the song whole or coherent. It often happens that, as one new pattern is woven into the mix, other players pick up on its inherent beauty and find ways to integrate what they are doing into this new structure. Strummings and pluckings are added by these instruments until a new structure is implicitly agreed to. Once this new structure is found and woven in, the improvisation can really commence. The conscious mind is put on the back burner and the unconscious is given more control. One has to become like a child.[15]

And he adds, "It almost becomes like a trance, a religious experience, and it is the most fun thing I do." This delicate "agreeing to help one another" is a prime component of communitas, found in creative collective activities such as music. Other musicians say the same thing. It is communitas, becoming more and more recognizable.

Music is no ordinary aspect of human experience. Our bodies have boundaries—skins—so we cannot merge all of our body with all of the others. But by intimately sharing precise *time*, owing to the transformative power of rhythm, we *can* merge, and we find we are not separate. In music, you join your voices completely, you are joined, you are in the same place, because you have gone altogether into the sound, and the sound is one sound with all the other people in it: one, in the same space.[16]

Another form of this happened to me during Ihamba, the Ndembu African ritual to draw out an offensive spirit from a patient: "I had just found out how to clap. You simply clap along with the beat of the drum, and clap hard. All the rest falls into place. Your own body becomes deeply involved in the rhythm, and everyone reaches a unity. Clap! Clap! Clap! All of us were on our feet. This was it."[17] The percussion effect can be reached very simply. Even spontaneous group harmonizing in a choir can bring up the same bliss when we look into each other's faces while creaming out a delicious chord, and we smile. We have given ourselves to a tune, totally, for a time.

Another characteristic of sound in the form of music is that it does not make a detour through language, and will not translate into words. The emotional sense we have of it is more akin to "energy" and "power," and such good anthropologically recognized words as "*weya*," "*wakan*," "*mana*," "*winu*," "*/num*," "*shakti*," and so forth (words for energy/power in Pomo, Oglala, Polynesian, Ndembu African, !Kung bushman, and Hindi). Music, like these powers, can give us goose bumps. The power of music is a feature of religious experience; it is ubiquitous, compelling, and preferably analyzed in its own terms, in whatever way it might choose, and not statistically, sociologically, nor in old science terms.

When everything comes together musically, moments of thrill reward the participants. This spiritual event conveyed through the biology of human beings is the fruit of communitas, which begins as the linking of intent among the people concerned. In those great moments in the zone and flow of music, no one form may be ranked as greater than another, even when it is a religious form. Each moment is "grace" or "the anointing," a bit of the beatific vision: it cannot be claimed exclusively in the holy words of any one language or religion.

It is as if music by its very limitation—sound—provides a clean path to spirituality, and allows the spirit language to enter it easily. Sometimes music is not merely the vehicle of the spirit, a means or channel. At certain moments music *is* the spirit; it incorporates all one's consciousness at these times, and spirit is right there. In those moments, one hears the spirit playing in the music like a fountain, as in Sibelius's *Finlandia*. Again, this kind of religious experience, music, may change one's life. We ask, what is this "focusing and deep attention" that sometimes brings about a shining moment?

Flow and Zone

Many activities go with a flow, sometimes in work and sometimes in sport—not just the genre of music. There are moments when ability has become second nature, and one's very actions are blissful, locked in a kind of inevitability of perfection—the sense the great soccer and basketball players experience when they are in flow.

We can best understand the communitas in flow through living accounts—that is, stories. They are to be found when conversing in company with others. If we follow inward from the workings of musical improvisation, we arrive at a spotlight that is flow, the enjoyment of true work that is "off and running." Much of music enters this realm. The term flow was first used by the anthropologist John MacAloon and the psychologist Mihaly Csikszentmihalyi, students in Turner's seminar in 1972. Flow in many walks of life—music, sports, the arts, and much of work—is a state of the psyche in which our acts appear to follow each other in a united, organic way without our conscious participation.[18] Csikszentmihalyi explains that in flow we feel we are in control of the situation and yet at the same time we are fully absorbed, so that it seems to be in control of us. We forget to make a distinction between ourselves and our surroundings, between stimulus and response, between the present and the past. Consciousness and behavior becomes one, life is expanded and full of meaning.

Csikszentmihalyi, in his publications on flow, explains more.[19] It is an interior state of the alignment of action with awareness, so close that the two click together in one, achieving a single overwhelming sensation of joy with the work. It is present when we act with total involvement, when action follows action with no apparent need for conscious intervention on our part. We recognize it in play and particularly in sport. There is a loss of ego—that "self" that looks around and compares, watching our real self. Often we are in some sport where everyone in the field is taking the same immediate delight in the game.

When in flow, we are without the expectation of some future benefit but act simply because the doing itself is the reward (in philosophy the term *autotelic* is used, but that is not an exact description). When in the flow and zone, people say the self is surpassed; we are in a different dimension of human experience, one that is recognized the world over, regardless of culture, gender, race, or nationality. It is also Zen, a way that concentrates on direct experience rather than on required creeds or revealed scriptures. Wisdom is passed, not through words, but through a lineage of one-on-one direct transmissions of thought from teacher to student."[20]

The Shadowy Divinity in Sports: What Exactly is the Zone?

> Being in the Zone is one of the great secrets of sport. There is a certain point of unity within the self, and between the self and its world, a certain complicity and magnetic mating, a certain harmony, that conscious mind and will cannot direct.... The discovery takes one's breath away.
>
> —Michael Novak

> Mystics and poets aren't the only people who experience the transcendent.
>
> —Andrew Cooper on sports beyond conventional mind

Communitas and flow can come at any time. Scott Osborne describes his times of communitas while playing soccer with a group of migrant workers. This version of communitas is deeply satisfying to him in his liminal stage of life as a student. He knows it is communitas that has been inhabiting his soccer field.

The communitas elements are clear. Scott says, "I get into a state of *unio mystica*." We know in general, not just from these examples, that practitioners of both genres, sport and music, say the same kind of thing about the zone. The various uses of zone—although the word is markedly non-theological and seemingly more to do with city planning or maps, even smacking of science fiction—have in no way taken away the mystical meaning of the experience.

Again the communitas element shows. Osborne says, "I am always with my team, who are my friends and partners in communitas," and, "This energy ebbed and flowed throughout the game bringing us triumph and loss, but more importantly it *entwined* us together as a single unit." And markedly, he says, "It is always an impromptu game."

Turner, who loved soccer, admired the dexterous placing of the ball among the players that produced the "chess-player" positions that made a goal inevitable. For him, it was the merging of soccer with chess and communitas that he loved—a "multiple zone." The zone, the time in the game where nothing goes wrong—when team, opponents, and spectators are at one in a great play—is considered rare. But many people do understand what it is. The stories multiply, and merely a reminder of one will set people off with more stories. One asks, how rare is that? When zone happens in a public arena it is immediately on the media. Millions of people know about it; but what is rare is a place for the zone in anthropology. Anthropologists simply "don't know what to do with it"—just as they "don't know what to do with shamanism." Is zone out of their depth?

Yet, it does elicit this common recognition; it does produce this marveling. There is one defining characteristic of the zone: it is unpredictable; it comes when it wills.

In this section, I quote from a book that best grapples with the mysterious nature of the zone. It is *Playing in the Zone*, by Andrew Cooper. He says that, yes, zone is rare, a "diamond in its setting," but that our culture does not yet have the concepts that can hold and give adequate meaning to these experiences.[21]

He says, "Peak experience and flow refer not to material objects but to qualitative states of experience. Different individuals will perceive and name that experience in different ways. Words carry an overlapping surplus of meanings, and these meanings are unfixed and dynamic."[22] Here he could be talking about the wildness of communitas, how it cannot be pinned down. Cooper goes on, "The Zone happens when it happens. Self-transcendence cannot be produced by force of will. It is a kind of state of grace."[23] With this astonishingly spiritual term that millions of Protestants and Catholics will recognize, we have touched religion.

Then he deals with the aspect of zone that is communal connectedness: "One's opponent becomes one's partner in lifting the level of play."[24] This is the weird and spontaneous aspect of communitas itself. Then: "The game seems to have a life of its own. The individual player is an expression of the game's intrinsic patterns. The game plays the player."[25] Here you have the music insight again. "You can feel the natural religion in sport, the interpenetration of nature and spirit. You can sense a spiritual presence in the physical acts of an athlete."[26] And, "It is the life energy that flows through and animates all things. One participates in life's creativity."[27] Cooper has indeed touched on the religion that certain anthropologists, using good indigenous material gleaned from the Amazonians and Maya and Zulu and many others, have themselves been learning to accept. We are a spiritual species.

A mystical participation exists. We do not form it. It is there all the time, everywhere.

Thus this concept of spirit is somewhat different from the church's idea. It is nearer to that of Native Americans, nearer to what happens in music, nearer to communitas with its obstinate refusal to be pinned down. It looks as if one might suggest that sport is a gift that has been deliberately implanted and nourished by personal spiritual entities, such as ancestor spirits, supplying a much needed venue for truly great spiritual moments not permitted by our dulled philosophies.

Cooper claims that the word zone, with its rich ambiguity and layers of meaning, says it best. It is indeed a place, but a map won't get you there. You cannot get into the zone through an act of will; you can only prepare the ground for it to happen. To quote a Zen master, "Enlightenment is an accident, but some activities make you accident prone."[28] Like a "second wind," it takes a person further along than before. The zone event *glows*—a kind of sudden dramatic state of *satori* arrives. The anthropologist Max Gluckman, the old mentor of Turner and myself, was interested in this phenomenon in 1956. I can see him now telling us how the psychologists were trying to train athletes to reach this curious state of being, for which they had few words. Max and Vic saw and experienced flow and zone in their time when they watched the "reds," the Manchester United soccer team.

You could see in their eyes when something marvelous happened in soccer. They knew. Among many good moments, the following was the strangest. Immediately after most of their beloved Manchester team had been killed at Munich in the fatal air crash of 1958, Turner went to Wrigley Field to support the decimated team in their next game. On the field was the substitute player for the dead hero Tommie Taylor. Toward the end of the game, the substitute tried a shot at an impossible goal, an utterly impossible one, yards out. Halfway through its flight, the ball took a bend in the air, all by itself, and flew straight into the goal. The crowd went crazy. Everyone knew that it was Taylor who had put that ball in the goal. It was a magic moment, and it brought everyone to their feet, singing.

At once we recognize the kinship between zone and communitas. At first it looks as if the zone performer is some kind of individualistic hero; then we see that he or she is not that at all but is in the hands of some other entity, who gives to the recipient and the spectators great pleasure as well as success. We note zone's unexpectedness. It often has a short life span, being vulnerable to a return of ordinary consciousness that breaks the link and ends it. Nevertheless the moment of zone is forever remembered. There is quirkiness here, an elusiveness, that cannot be controlled, yet a warmth and person-to-person sense, also felt by the players on the opposite side and by the spectators, who no longer seem to be taking sides but are fascinated. Furthermore, achieving zone by act of will does not gain any traction here and, like communitas, a map will not get one there. It is always best to follow the road it wants one to go by. Like communitas, it is a law unto itself.

There is some reticence about speaking of the zone. Nevertheless the world often praises its manifestation without even naming it. Similarly, communitas is often anonymous. It derives from nature, as we have been discerning it, and in some societies is associated with spirits, often with the sense of a creator. There are skills—rituals—in various cultures, taught by the spirits, aimed to "catch" the spirit and be friends with it, align with it, as the Ndembu of Africa know. Similarly, the Iñupiat catch a whale by aligning with its spirit, touching its spirit with mutual love, so that the animal agrees to feed them, and they agree to return its head to the water to reincarnate in a new youthful life.

Zone and flow are given to us, and they are part of communitas in this respect. Approaches such as meditation or prayer manifest themselves as the skill of alignment (with prayer's humility). There is a willingness to be permeated by the power, to let it enter. It will discipline a person who, by means of it, will suddenly find the way in. One simply loves it, not fears it. We often see the concepts of zone and alignment overlapping, and it also appears that people initially need to do some alignment to break into the zone (see Chapter 10). It has become obvious that we are encountering something spiritual. None of these happenings, either in music or sport, occur on our command. For the communitas in music, flow, and zone, its coming is greeted with joy, and we often attribute the benefit and wonder to something "out there," outside of ourselves. It looks strangely like the gift of religious power that was given to the Apostles at Pentecost. But communitas does not have the flavor of institutional Christianity. It is not necessarily something that is an answer to prayer. It is not a technique for reaching God; it is a plain and outright gift, and unpredictable. One begins to suspect that it coincides with the mystical side of Christianity almost fully, except for Christianity's ranking system; that it is a Christianity or Judaism or some other religion that has healed from its own ailments or side-stepped around them. Its coincidence with something at the heart of religions also becomes clearer.

So we cannot congratulate ourselves on our own genius for music or sport. Those gifted find themselves having to press on. We are still unaccommodated human beings. Curiously, following the trail of these beings in their ascription to "something else," the next chapter appears to go considerably downhill to the most boring realm—that of everyday work. And what do we find there but communitas, along with much pleasure.

Chapter 4

The Communitas of Work: Surprising Conclusions

Communitas comes easily when the hands are working.
—Kara Skora, at her knitting circle

The Pleasure of Work?

What is this "work"? In fact, it is not work at all. Work with communitas gives the workers pleasure—it is an activity that also pleases those who need it done. People find communitas in the comradeship and fellowship of work, and also wherever they find a chance for their ordinary humanness to flourish amid the pressures of life. Communitas is something anthropologists experience in the field, as Bronislaw Malinowski did when he saw it manifesting itself in others. It can also be seen as unconditional love, as in the Maori term *aroha*, a friendly hand-touch laid on knowingly as an immediate cure for depression and fear. A real love of work reigns when the workplace is free from involvement with social structures and moral status. This is the concern of the employers. The communitas of work flourishes when stress about status flakes off and nobody bothers about rank.

Victor Turner was a private soldier in the British Army—a nobody—when I first met him. He had hardly a penny to his name. His standing was of no great importance. He was not "accommodated," and, apart from his army barracks, did not even have a home. But he had his body, his head, his sense of humor, his reaction to being bullied around. He was fond of his mates and identified with them, those ordinary fellow human beings. Vic used to feel this in everyday work during the war. Later still, as a researcher, he saw that there was camaraderie in the field, a sense that was not yet discussed in the social sciences. Vic, in his research, looked out for this phenomenon and, like many others whose accounts appear in this book, wondered what engendered it. It seemed to have been ignored in the anthropological training he received, or reduced to the ordinary, or explained by the need for friendly organization to make life function better. This explanation, known as functionalism, was espoused in 1915 by Emile Durkheim, the leading sociologist of the twentieth century.[1] For Durkheim, the roots of any human activity could ultimately be found by looking at the activity's function and determining if it had survival value. The implication of this was that religion was a system the people unconsciously invented as an ideal, "the wonder that is society"—that it gave them a sense of awe, and that it was good for them. People would feel the excitement once they had fabricated it and erected it into place, and they would worship it. Durkheim called this excitement "effervescence."

In this book, people's pleasure and excitement is respected and not reduced to something lesser—it has been seen in the babies' reactions to real communitas and false communitas, during the bank rush hour, and in festivals, music, and sport. It is easily recognized by those who work in restaurants during the rush hour, where there is a distinct pleasure in completing the brunt of the rush hour successfully. What is it that is innate, so joyful, and recognizable? This ordinary yet mysterious thing is jealous on behalf of its own genuineness; it refuses to work any other way. It has a way of "doing it right" that is unmistakable. It cannot be bowdlerized or imitated. What *is* this? What has come through the evolution line that is like this? We shall see more. First, consider Victor Turner's experience with the British Army Bond Gang in 1942.

The Bond Gang[2]

Victor Turner was a conscientious objector in England of World War II. He had had his status vetted as genuine by the army board. Once this was established, the army posted him to a large new railroad marshalling yard in the English midlands. There he was drilled with other "conchies" and put to work loading military consignments by rail. He and his fellow pacifists—Quakers, artists, and writers, mainly—worked out an arrangement with officialdom whereby the materials they loaded were not weapons, but food and housing materials. His own group numbered the artist Keith Vaughan, Cosmo Lang, a writer, Fred Taylor, a poor man, and a visionary, as well as

Phil Sargent—a blond, good-looking Quaker, recently married—and John Bate, a poet who had leanings toward publishing. These were like the characters in Aleksandr Isaevich Solzhenitskin's later book, *One Day in the Life of Ivan Denisovitch*,[3] who were articulate Russians exiled to a concentration work camp in Siberia for their repudiation of state structures and for wild dreams that were not enamored of Marxism but sometimes radiant with unfettered love.

In this English marshalling yard, Vic and his friends talked continuously between and during jobs. They also became infected with the enjoyment of work—this bug—laboring together at the loading, for the mere rhythm of the thing: fetching the heavy boxes of canned food standing in tall piles on loading pads, dragging them out with forklifts, having men ready at the railroad wagon doors, ready and willing to stack the boxes neatly inside; on and on. The wagon was filling, the piles of boxes rapidly becoming closed in toward the entrance—then full! Immediately the men shifted to another wagon. They were "box-bashing" all day long: box, heave, box, heave. The men, Vic, Cosmo, Phil, Fred, and the others—more and more merrily—found that they were breaking labor records and experiencing communitas—just like Solzhenitskin's as-yet-unwritten friends, and as the British prisoners of war in Burma did under the Japanese when rebuilding the famous bridge over the river Kwai to help the Japanese—and with equal irony.

The men in England, like the prisoners in Burma, had gotten themselves into the zone. They hit their target of twenty wagons a day, a feat unheard-of in the British Army.

Vic told me the story of the loading of the twenty wagons and its irony: his group was exceptionally good at helping a system they knew was doing wrong—to them, the mutual killing of English and Germans made no sense and was no answer to the problems of the unaccommodated man. As we know, the next deeds of militarism were the bombing of Coventry and also of Cologne. Even so, the men who did those jobs were in fact, themselves, nothing but unaccommodated men.

Among Vic's group, two of the simplest conditions for communitas were present: hard physical effort and a group that could become friends. The result: they wanted to go on working as long as they could. Furthermore, Vic never forgot the scene and often talked about it.

Given the right conditions, people will always be able to find communitas in their regular work. The young Marx was right about the alienation of the worker from his product,[4] in the sense that if the worker *is* in touch with his product, no one is alien. Communitas, differing from communism, is the reverse of anger; it reverses suffering rather than producing anger. However, the togetherness and empathy that people felt in suffering was not considered politically correct. Unfortunately, Marx wanted rage.

Aleksandr Isaevich Solzhenitsyn's Gift: Communitas Springs up among Prisoners Building a Wall

In Solzhenitsyn's story *One Day in the Life of Ivan Denisovich*, we see men getting in the zone and not wanting it to stop; we see this resulting in stronger communitas. In the book, the highly detailed circumstances are focused down on the smallest and humblest of human scale. All is ordinary and real.

The Gulag prison camp system in Soviet Russia lasted from 1929 to 1953 and later. Solzhenitsyn was a prisoner in one of the camps in Siberia from 1945 to 1956, for associating with dissidents. He and a group of political prisoners were put to work to complete the derelict half of a new power station in the camp area. In 1961, Solzhenitsyn wrote *One Day in the Life of Ivan Denisovich*, based on that experience. This was after Stalin had died, but even so its serialization in *Novy Mir* was soon confiscated and forbidden. Western reviews of the book mainly focused on the extreme cruelty of camp conditions and the courage of the prisoners, but few mentioned the extraordinary pleasure the men experienced in their labor, building the wall for the power station. As in Vic's army dump, the actions of the men did not elicit sentimentality; they were ironic. Like foot soldiers or prisoners anywhere, they scrounged anything they could get, and endured privations. The men always had their own way of doing things. In Solzhenitsyn's camp, the prison gang members kept their own members up to the mark. The system was this: either everyone got a bonus or they would all die together.

Here I shorten Solzhenitsyn's story and include some of his passages that show the working class phrases that instinctively poured out of the man and that went toward earning him a Nobel Prize.

The Wall

The men themselves arranged what they basically needed to do the work of building the wall. First off, the mortar could not be used frozen, so they had to find a stove that was working to warm it up—but

COMMUNITAS OF WORK

to use the stove, they had to mend the stovepipe. The temperature was twenty-seven degrees below zero. Solzhenitsyn (Ivan Denisovitch Shukhov) saw that to mend the stovepipe, they had to find the tools:

> Pavlo had brought the tools and Shukhov could help himself. There was a metalworker's hammer and a hatchet. He'd manage somehow.[5]

Once they had got working:

> Every other thought went clean out of Shukhov's head. He had no memory, no concern for anything except how he was going to join the lengths of pipe to fix them so that the stove would not smoke. He sent Gopchik to look for wire, so that he could support the chimney where it stuck out through the window.[6]

And so the fire was lit and the thawing began; Shukhov gave a look at the wall and the bricklaying they had to do:

> Whoever had been laying there before was either a bungler or a slacker. Shukhov would get to know each inch of that wall as if he owned it. That dent there—it would take three courses to make the wall flush, with a thicker layer of mortar every time. He sized up how many blocks he should have ready, and where.

Shukhov scrubbed off the snow. He was getting deeply involved in the work:

> Pavlo shouted from below: "Still alive up there? Mortar coming up!"

Shukhov was now working with Senka, the deaf man. He was making it easier for him.

> The deaf man understood. Biting his lip and rolling his eyes, he nodded at the foreman's corner as much as to say, "Let's give them hell! Let's beat them to it!" He laughed.

Shukhov spotted faulty blocks right away and placed them in good spots. No one was feeling cold any more. The men were even over the chilling sweat.

> The frost wasn't getting at their feet, that was the main thing, not even that thin, nagging wind could take their minds off their work. Shukhov wasn't going to fall behind the other two: to hurry the mortar up that ramp, he'd have run the legs off his own brother.[7]

The men decided how to reorganize the work.

> Alyoshka the Baptist would work with the captain. Anybody who felt like it could order Alyoshka about, he was so meek and mild. Alyoshka smiled humbly. "We can go faster if you like. Whatever you say."
>
> Everyone was glad he was in the gang; he could take just about anything.
>
> It was going like a house on fire. Nothing to it, anyway.
> "Gang 82 are hanging their tools in," Gopchik reported.
> The foreman flashed a look at him. "Mind your own business, small fry, and get some blocks over here."
> Shukhov looked over his shoulder. Yes, the sun was going down.

Shukhov was thinking about how Alyoshka never refused anybody. Shukhov thought he would be like that himself if he could. Help anybody. There was something in that.

> Now that the others were out to break records, Shukhov stopped forcing the pace and took a good look at the wall. To leave a bulge in the wall or make a mess of the corner would be a disaster. Take half of tomorrow to put it right.

The sun had actually set. They had to hurry. The foreman was pleased.

> "Good bit of bricklaying, eh? For half a day's work. Without a hoist, or any other effing thing." He laughed. "They'd be crazy to let you out! Any jail would be lost without you!"

Shukhov laughed, too. He didn't stop a minute—he was working with the deaf Senka, who was better than any of them.

> Slap on the mortar! Slap on the block! Press it down a bit. Make sure it's straight. Mortar. Block. Mortar. Block.
> "Time to be off!"[8]

Later that night, Shukhov talked to Alyoshka. He agreed with his religion, only he didn't believe in heaven and hell. Alyoshka, astonishingly, was quite happy to be in prison. He had time to think about his soul.

> Alyoshka had no sense at all. Alyoshka never earned a thing, but did favors for everybody.

"Here you are, Alyoshka!" Shukhov handed him one biscuit. Alyoshka was all smiles. "Thank you! You won't have any for yourself!"
"Eat it!"

Shukhov ate his own sausage. He'd almost had a happy day. In this Russian story, the mute experience of communitas made Shukhov/Solzhenitsyn realize—*made him experience*—what was happening in that camp more vividly than reason can explain. "Everybody gets a bonus or they all die together." The bricklaying workers in the camp had an "equality of suffering" rule, which gave a kind of peace to their communitas. Because of the ad hoc type of work in the prison camp, the place had become more of a natural community than an assembly-line factory ever could be.

There is a regularity in this process. When some of the people in a new group exhibit communitas, and if there has passed around a drift or sense of it, then the whole group gradually rearranges itself, just as a person tries to solve a Rubik's Cube, by turning it and turning it until it makes sense, adds up. The community jigs itself into position for a full-scale, perhaps year-long term communitas. This is clearly illustrated in the Solzhenitsyn story, and the process gives great satisfaction.[9] Therefore, just as with the box-bashing in England, the men developed a physical work rhythm that gave pleasure, especially between comrades. Nobody could get Shukhov down from the bricklaying on the wall—he and the deaf man were so geared to finish it. There existed a winged communitas, even at twenty-seven-degrees below.

Mowing the Meadow

Another great Russian novelist is useful here because by means of his story the reader will easily catch the central phenomenon, which is the plunge through the barrier of ordinary socialization (beyond that which can be induced and measured). I quote Leon Tolstoy writing as Levin at the end of *Anna Karenina*. Levin—Tolstoy himself—is out in the early morning with forty-two workers, mowing the meadow. In these passages, Tolstoy, master of the detail of actual experience, gives us his own experience, hidden in the medium of a novel. From his own end of the line of mowers, he could see the steady movement of the men across the meadow, not quite in time, swinging their scythes.[10]

> Levin thought of nothing and desired nothing, except not to lag behind and to do his work as well as possible. He heard only the swishing of the scythes.

His work was undergoing a change which gave him intense pleasure. While working he sometimes forgot for some minutes what he was about, and felt quite at ease; then his mowing was nearly as even as that of Titus.

But whenever he began looking at himself working it felt like a hard task, and he mowed badly.

Those unconscious intervals when it became possible not to think of what he was doing recurred more and more often. The scythe seemed to mow of itself. Those were happy moments.

He really began to forget that it was him working. It was the scythe itself that was mowing. He felt blessed.

The sense grew and, with it, the pleasure in the friends around him, who just kept on scything. One showed him a sorrel stalk he could eat; another pointed out a quail's nest.

[After a meal of bread soaked in water, they came across mushrooms] grown plump amid the juicy grass. The old man stooped each time he came upon one, picked it up, and put it inside his jacket, saying, "Another treat for my old woman."

The old man, even at the end of the day when the light began to fade, was still at it, joking around with the others and much satisfied. Tolstoy/Levin felt himself under the control of this great valley, at one with the men. He heard the call:

"We've finished the whole of the meadow!"

In further passages, Tolstoy/Levin is reflecting on the life of hard work, using a metaphor. He himself used a plowshare and, with its curved blade, he couldn't help making a difference to the soil as he moved, turning it right over. Therefore, he had a place on the earth; he needed to be there for his family, to do bee-keeping, to work with all those friends whom the upper classes called peasants. Here, Tolstoy was not looking at those upper classes. He knew how the people worked, incessantly, of necessity, to bring the crops in and plow the fields to make them ready for the next year. There was no stopping the work. When I myself read Tolstoy's book in 1980, I knew from my two years of farm work in the 1940s what the peasants' work was really like. Tolstoy's words rang true.[11]

[It was necessary] to work unceasingly those three or four weeks, three times as hard as usual, living on kvass, onions, and black bread, threshing and carting the sheaves by night and sleeping not more than two or three hours out of the twenty-four. And this is done every year, all over Russia.

Levin had a friend, old Plato, a character deeply satisfied with his relationships in his little world. Plato valued these links and knew that they were often sacred. This consciousness, at some mysterious level, seemed to give Plato the greatest of pleasure. The clue was that Plato was an upright old man. Levin had heard that he wouldn't cheat anyone. He lived for his soul and remembered God.

"'How does he remember God? How does he live for the soul?' Levin almost cried out."

Thinking about this, Levin became very excited. It was important, because Plato's goodness was beyond cause and effect, beyond the struggle for existence—as Tolstoy himself put it—beyond scientific reason, beyond all questions of class and rank, bursting out from some place that dazzled Levin with its light. The old man, Plato, was simply *given* it. Levin was also given it.

Here are our staples of communitas—the pleasure of working together, the rhythm; this mysterious matter of goodness; the zone, which one could slip in and out of; Levin's consciousness of being full of life; his blessedness; his description of the work accomplishing itself of its own accord—which arises repeatedly—prompting the idea that there is something out there manipulating all this. He preferred the peasants' food and company, and the joking; he came to a final admission that this love was simply unreasonable. Just as Trevarthen indicated in his studies of mothers and babies (Chapter 1), this love was already in his soul as a child.

Another matter of everyday work comes up in a modern-day piece written by Van Griffiths, a Habitat for Humanity volunteer. Griffiths has been able to put into words what is hard to find, a close-up account of the ordinary process of building a house—a workaday job that tends to give a lot of happiness, whether in the Habitat movement or not.

It will be noted that for a work on a theme like communitas, not widely known as a part of the public's vocabulary, descriptions of work are recorded by people who are existing scholars. There will indeed be a paucity of consciously written examples by the *subjects* of this strange phenomenon, that is, of anything written by the unscholarly public. Sentimental or religious stories and novels abound, as well as plenty about branches of skills and work milieus that we are fascinated to hear about. They comprise a generous look into our culture. The tellers may be unaware that they are fulfilling a rather mysterious function in everyday life, that of communitas—seen in the figure whom Kierkegaard identified as "the Knight of Faith," an ordinary guy who had "been there" in the vision and had come back peaceably, just to live. Many of these accounts are religion specific. The writers are not often aware of the significance of the commonalities linking people's lives all over the planet. (Luckily, the Olympic Games are one platform for the linking.) Therefore, this book is deliberately unspecific about any resulting hard and fast conclusions and philosophical thoughts on the structures of society. These dwell inside the stories.

Building a House with the Helping Hands of Doctors, Businessmen, and Professors: An Open Frame

The follow is a condensed version of the story told by Habitat for Humanity volunteer Griffiths.[12]

> Six months ago, I helped on the framing day of a new building being sponsored by a small law office. On a chilly morning in rural North Carolina, we gathered around the construction manager to hear our instructions.... A regular volunteer in New Orleans named Andrew, himself a former carpenter, described the gathering from his point of view. "There's a lot of ego involved—doctors, businessmen, professors—they come out and think they know what they're doing and move everyone out of the way, tell people what to do. But they don't know what they're doing.... I don't get involved in it. If there's a shovel with some sand nearby, I'll just leave it to them and go shovel sand...." The real excitement belonged to the vast majority of the group who, regardless of their experience, were doing the same job of grabbing wall pieces, hauling them onto the floor deck, and nailing them together. The two managers moved around the floor deck, stepping over and around volunteers to take care of technical tasks, give instructions, and answer questions.
>
> Once things were moving, even that small group of men seemed to lose their concern about rank.... You would fall in with two or three people, nail a wall together, hoist it up, nail it in place, and jump in with another group. Every so often, the clapping of hammers would stop as everyone lined up to lean, push, and pull on an exterior wall while a manager brought it into plumb and locked it with a brace. These ad hoc efforts succeeded with surprisingly little instruction from the leadership—the manager's intentions would often travel, without

much discussion, from person to person, down the wall. For all the noise and rapid shifting from job to job, people appeared more or less attuned to what was happening around them. Over the course of a few hours, the house sprang up around our group of mostly office workers. It happened under seemingly sparse management with a general absence of conversation, except the occasional joke or quick introduction. Things had gone well, and by lunch we were walking around in what felt like the interior of a house....

The framing period is the high point of that circle. Framing day is the point in the building of a Habitat house when people's excitement appears to explode outward. It's the easiest phase in which to feel linked with others on a common task and for the hesitations of alienation to dissipate. At other points in the building process, a good day can still be created; a great site manager with enthused volunteers can turn almost any task into a wonderful experience. But the powerful phenomenon of that unspoken connection between strangers is most consistently found in the first few days of framing.

What happens on a good framing day is not very familiar to academia, but the words of Martin Buber give a clarifying testament to its reality: "No factory and no office is so abandoned by creation that a creative glance could not fly up from one working place to another, from desk to desk, a sober and brotherly glance which guarantees the reality of creation that is happening—*quantum satis* (for the amount that is needed). And nothing is so valuable a service of dialogue between God and man as such an unsentimental and unreserved exchange of glances between two men in an alien place."[13]

Griffiths tells of the feeling that can occur on framing day, when the house rises around them, and it is *their* work. In this story one sees the communitas that keeps coming into people, the irrational anti-ego pleasure in getting out and doing something to help. Groups of people who are actually proud to be human in a world we are not very proud of, and who understand what being human means spring up.

Now for some action that might be mistaken for banal.

Amongst Diesel Engines and Radio Transmissions: An Exploration of Moments of Communitas Shared by Bus Drivers

The following stories are told by bus driver Ashleigh Elizabeth Shepherd.[14]

"Good morning, ma'am," his smiling face says to me. His arm goes out to open the office door to allow me to enter first.

"Good morning, sir," I say. "How are you today?"

It is 5:15 A.M. and the bus drivers are arriving at the office. The earliest fleet of buses soon has to leave the central bus lot, bound for the various start-up points where they will begin to carry passengers to their destinations at work and school.... The smiling face of the man who so thoughtfully held the door for me belongs to the gentle sir by the name of John DePuma, one of the most genuinely kind individuals I know. From the manner in which he reaches out to people with such enthusiasm, one would never guess that he is on dialysis three days a week because he is still waiting his turn for a new kidney.

"Good morning," we all say to one another as we sip our coffee and listen to the symphony of diesel engines waking up just outside the door. We coffee-sipping folks who wake before dawn and put on our blue-collared uniforms are the bus drivers for the University Transit System (UTS) of the University of Virginia (UVa). It is our job to drive thirty-five-foot transit buses, weighing in at 13.5 tons, along the most highly frequented areas of the UVa grounds in the hopes of safely and efficiently transporting people where they need to go. Perhaps some would think it strange to find genuine human connection amongst gigantic pieces of machinery and their noisy diesel engines, especially since the drivers who sit behind the wheel of these gargantuan vehicles sit there alone. But UVa bus drivers share in genuine moments of communitas.

"Courtesy"

Dave, a full-time driver, gives Erin, another driver, a smile as they prepare to board their buses.

"How many courtesies do you think I'll get to give you this morning?" he asks. "Do you think we'll be lucky enough to get three or four?"

"It's hard to say," Erin replies. "We'll just have to see what the morning brings."

To a non-bus driver, Dave's use of the word courtesy in this context would not make much sense. To any UTS bus driver, however, the word courtesy is not only a crucial part of bus vocabulary but a word, when spoken, that naturally induces a smile. Courtesy is literally the act of one bus giving another bus the right-of-way at an opportune moment, allowing another bus to merge into a busy line of traffic or to make a difficult left-hand turn at a stoplight that does not operate a leading green. The bus giving the courtesy stops and puts on its emergency flashers, generally referred to as "four-ways" among drivers, which allows the bus receiving the courtesy to proceed first. The exchange is basic, but the joy generated by the simple act of deference on the part of one bus in the service of another is something quite palpable. This courtesy exchange is the source of a mutual feeling of gladness among drivers. It is communitas.

The courtesy exchange also comes with an exchange of human voices over the radio waves to round out the courtesy conversation.

"Unit eleven, you're terrific," says John DePuma to the kind driver who gives him courtesy in a highly trafficked area. "I hope you're having a great day and a great block."

"You're welcome, sir," responds unit eleven's radio voice. "I hope you're having a great day as well. Thirteen clear." Though I cannot see the driver of unit eleven, as I am on a completely different part of the bus route, I can sense her surge of joy over the radio simply by the way she speaks. The pleasant radio transmission, even though it does not directly involve me, leaves me with a feeling of warmth, and I know I am not the only other driver who catches the contagious smile over the sound waves. Even when a driver other than you receives courtesy somewhere else on route, all drivers become aware of the generosity over the radio and allow a smile to fill their faces. Like a stone thrown into a pond that creates a series of ripples that flow out from its center, the good feelings of communitas radiate outward, generated through the gift of courtesy.

"Thank you for your patience and kindness, twenty-three," says another appreciative driver over the sound waves of the radio system. "I hope you're having a great morning."

"It was my pleasure, sir. You have a great morning as well. Twenty-three clear."

"Block six to twenty-nine," yet another unit calls. "Thank you so much. I hope you're having fun on this beautiful morning! Unit sixty-two clear." A cascade of good thoughts travels joyfully over the sound waves that flow between the drivers, wrapping them comfortably in a symphony of positively charged energy.

Courtesies do not grow stale, but work constantly to create a sense of connection among drivers. Courtesy exchange among drivers points us to the observation of Buber that "community is where community happens."[15] Each occurrence grows out of the present moment and is therefore unique. The visionary William Blake knows what it means to "do good" in the world. "He who would do good to another," Blake says, "must do it in Minute Particulars. General Good is the plea of the scoundrel, hypocrite, and flatterer...."[16]

The courtesy, then, has its place as an element of the highly structured system and time schedule. Indeed, people continue to work for UTS in large part because of the sense of community that brings the drivers together.

The peculiar features noted in Shepherd's account rarely occur in the other examples of communitas in this book, but they are revealing. The courtesy phenomenon is like that of an usher actually being glad to seat a person, or a salesperson being glad at each transaction, glad she is able to do it. But it is more than that. These courtesies are a kind of extra treat, counted up and valued. They constitute real and oft-repeated occasions of communitas in the world of work.

The joy of communitas is out of all proportion to the banality of the event. These drivers mutually love the circle of giving, as the Trobrianders of the Kula Ring did in Melanesia[17] and the Iñupiat certainly do in their potlatch-of-giving called the Kivgiq, at Barrow on the north slope of Alaska.[18] The other outstanding feature of the example of the bus drivers is the attention given to being in the moment; in particular, to "luck." Although driving under a highly structured routine, the bus drivers were dependent on luck for their meeting and helping each other. They often got the chance of a lively experience of communitas, and they regarded themselves as lucky each time.

The Communitas of Food

> Shared food, and all shared substances, carry elements of the spiritual substance of the universe.
>
> —Knowledge of the Amazonian Waiwai[19]

Here I will portray perhaps the most pleasurable communitas: the communitas of food.[20] The example given here could well have been painted as a landscape scene on the broadest of canvases: the Combine Harvesters' Banquet set in Kansas in the 1930s.

Feeding the Harvesters

John Bunch gave me this word picture, one of the largest food communitas scenes known, set in the Kansas he remembers from the thirties when he was eight, before his mother died. This was in August. The eat-fest occurred every August during the cutting of the wheat. To begin with, before the farmers started harvesting, they had to cut off the entire irrigation system in the region because they were going to use combine harvesters, enormously heavy machines that needed bone-dry land on which to work. Once the irrigation was stopped, the wheat would dry up and had to be cut in three days. If a storm came up and blew the wheat flat, the farmers would be ruined.

The farmers formed one huge gathering, and many combine harvester machines were brought to the spot. Often, farmers would get free use of the machines—such was the working farmers' communitas in those days. John recalls the enormous meals that were provided for all the gathered farmers and workers, cooked by the women and served on huge trestle tables. They had potato salad, cabbage, turnips, pies, strudel, and fried chicken. Meanwhile the kids, got to play in the neighboring pond, catching "water dogs."

"What are water dogs?"

"Salamanders," said John with enthusiasm. "Black and blotchy—and we caught kangaroo rats, with big back legs, trying to jump out of the furrows. And we sent for alligators by mail order. They grew to two or three feet long." This was the communitas of the children when the adults were busy.

All John's cousins came to the gathering from several counties around. The scene was a clan gathering many times glorified.[21]

The Communitas of Powdered Sugar Cookies

The following is told by Naomi Shihab Nye.[22]

> After learning my flight was detained for four hours, I heard the announcement: "If anyone in the vicinity of Gate 4-A understands Arabic, please come to the gate immediately."
>
> Well, one pauses these days. Gate 4-A was my own gate, so I approached the desk. An older woman in full traditional Palestinian dress, just like the one my grandma wears, was crumpled on the floor, wailing loudly.
>
> "We need help," said the flight service person. "Talk to her. What's her problem? We told her the flight was going to be four hours late, and she did this."
>
> I got down, put my arm around the woman, and spoke to her haltingly. "*Shu dow-a, shu-biduck habibti, stani stani schway, min fadlick. Sho bit se-wee?*"
>
> The minute she heard words, she knew; however poorly they were used, she stopped crying. She thought our flight had been canceled entirely. She needed to be in El Paso for major medical treatment the following day.
>
> I said, "No, no, it's not cancelled, we're fine. You'll get there, you'll just be late. Who's picking you up? Let's call him and tell him."
>
> It was her son, so we called him, and I spoke to him in English. "Look, I'm going to stay with your mother till we get on the plane and I'll ride next to her.... We go by Southwest."
>
> The woman talked to her son herself. Then we called her other sons just for the fun of it. Then we called my dad, and he and the woman

spoke for a while in Arabic and found out, of course, they had ten shared friends.

Then I thought, "Just for the heck of it, why not call some Palestinian poets I know and let them chat with her?"

All this took up about two hours. She was laughing a lot by then—telling us about her life, answering questions...She pulled out of her bag a sack of homemade *mamool* cookies, little powdered sugar crumbly mounds stuffed with dates and nuts—and she was offering them to all the women at the gate. To my amazement, not a single woman declined one. It was like a sacrament. The traveler from Argentina, the traveler from California, the lovely woman from Laredo—we were all covered with the same powdered sugar. And smiling. There is no better cookie.

And then the airline broke out free beverages from huge coolers, non-alcoholic, and the two little girl flight attendants for our flight, one African American, one Mexican American, ran around serving us all apple juice and lemonade, and they were covered with powdered sugar, too. And I noticed my new best friend—by now we were holding hands—had a potted plant poking out of her bag, some medicinal thing, with green furry leaves. Such an old country traveling tradition: Always carry a plant. Always stay rooted somewhere.

And I looked around that gate full of late and weary ones and thought, "This is the world I want to live in, the shared world. Not a single person in this gate—once the crying and confusion stopped—has seemed apprehensive about any other person. They took the cookies." I wanted to hug all those other women, too. "This can still happen anywhere. Not everything is lost."

I offer another example to test the spirituality of shared food—no one would believe that the humble and grease-loaded pizza could have anything to do with communitas. Again, the setting is an airport—a place classically betwixt and between other places, a gateway, a limen, always different, peopled with strangers who are at the same time fascinating and strikingly human—us.

The Communitas of Pizza

I had come from yet another vast impersonal urban airport. We now boarded a small plane with about ten or twelve passengers. Once we were well in the air, the news came through that storms were breaking out in Washington, and we would have to be rerouted to the east. We landed in Salisbury, Maryland, a familiar-sounding name, but not home. It was getting on to seven. Our luggage stood about us in the empty ticketing section. Through the window you could see a pleasant evening, a lawn, and little else. We waited. A white-haired official turned up.

"The café's closed," he said when we asked. "It closes at six P.M." We looked, and indeed there was no sign of life in the café. My stomach twinged despairingly.

The old guy went behind the ticket desk, and we crowded around it. There was a tall retiring young man, two ordinary middle-aged business guys, and a party of about four modern types in good clothes, who finally rented a car to take them to their original destination, Washington, D.C. "We'll get there much quicker than you!" they told us triumphantly, and they left. I also saw a quiet friendly man while we were wandering about waiting our turns at the desk. He gave a smile to my wondering eyes; we started talking and found we both loved the same religion. We sighed. The tall young man, strange and aloof, spoke with a foreign accent when he did speak.

The next plane would be at 10 P.M. I took the new ticket from the white haired man and stood back a step. I said the words they were all thinking.

"I'm hungry."

There was a stir in the little crowd. The white-haired man drew back, face thoughtful. Another small official appeared beside him. White hair bent to him and muttered instructions.

"Tell them to..."—and we lost the rest of it.

We all waited, the six of us, gazing out the window at the fading lawn. We'd forgotten to watch when we heard a sound—a car arriving. The back door of the waiting room opened and two men appeared, balancing about six big boxes. Pizza! There was a large round table in the waiting room where pizza after pizza was now being laid out—pepperoni, all star, sausage and broccoli, artichoke and eggplant, Hawaiian—you name it. Piles of napkins appeared; hands went out; the floppy triangles were raised—and, yum!

I sat next to one of the business men, who was dealing in ladies underwear (so he *said*). The conversation ripened. Giggling began. Oh my. I had the other business man on the other side. They were both into sport. After a bit they got together and told each other scary sports stories. The little quiet guy and I grinned at each other. The tall young man drew up to the table. We asked friendly questions. I was surprised; he was going to the University of Virginia on a scientific mission from the University of Aachen. He was a metallurgist.

"A metallurgist?" I said. "What do you do? Work with metal?"

"It's for computers," he said. "We've found a new metal that has a very important use in computers."

"Hm. Marvelous," I said, looking him up and down. A quiet shy young man, with that German accent, pleased with what he was saying. Everyone was talking like mad. I realized that I was in the middle of a full-blown communitas—the communitas of pizza. The two sporting/business guys were practically hugging each other. The white-haired man beamed. The old lady over there was happy and I was, too.

Our plane came. We traveled to D.C., and I went on to Charlottesville. I finally disembarked, unwillingly. The communitas of pizza had ended.

Here we may trace many of the conditions that favor communitas. This episode was a break in our ordinary travel arrangements—and often these breaks liberate communitas. The small crowd at the ticket office was a random group of people, undifferentiated and equal. Randomness ruled since our whole predicament owed its existence to an unpredicted storm. The encounters with each other came just as needed, with understanding glances, as among the Habitat group. Our words were appropriate, as if we were all inventing our own story. Strange. The food surprise, along with its benison of communitas, was a matter of bodily hunger and we were thankful. Through that food, the people grew to a spontaneous communitas.

Our identities were far from being merged; on the contrary, each person was alive in his or her own particular way. This glimpse of communitas stimulated the various small habits of social behavior, pulling up chairs, parceling out the pieces, enacting our roles with gentle awareness. Anything anybody said went easily; the talk came into being as a spring of pure possibility with no putting on of airs, no structural claiming of rank. What we experienced was openness—a time of enjoyment. It had something magical about it, in the way of communitas.

The next chapter takes another step down, to the communitas of disaster, where people undergoing disaster can find joy in their struggle for survival.

Chapter 5

The Communitas of Disaster

Storm

In 1970, Claudette Bethune was on a boat with her family; her uncle was the captain and there were ranked jobs on board for everybody, even the children. A terrible storm developed and grew worse, until at last they realized it was going to go down. At that moment, the whole group became as one, they all hugged each other with great love, young and old. Now each performed their duties with joy, and all idea of rank was gone. This was what Claudette emphasized: the great unity and love aboard the boat, each person distinct and absolutely valuable, even the smallest. The storm lessened a little and came on again, but finally they made it home. The feeling lasted for many months, and Claudette never forgot it.[1]

The communitas of disaster exists, in a sense, underground, sometimes simply as the tender sympathetic moments between sufferer and comforter. It also develops in full strength in an environment sheltered by the hope and love between the members of a badly shaken community. This chapter consists of two main parts: one is centered on the Dakota floods of 1997, a natural disaster valiantly overcome, along with the truncated tale of Katrina in 2005, a sorry answer at the mouth of the same river system, the Mississippi. The other part is about the communitas that finds its way to the heart of cancer patients—in spite of the cancer, which is caused by the monstrous disturbance of our natural, healthily evolved physical and chemical balance on the planet, due to industrialization and greed.

The Great Floods of Dakota in 1997

The account of the floods of Dakota in 1997, originally recorded and published by the anthropologist Linda Jencson,[2] describes a region that already exhibited a strong on-the-ground sense of community. The story of the disaster showed the guts and humor of the people in their 1997 crisis and the love humans can have for each other. Jencson noted the surprise the people felt at their own sense of pleasure and happiness during the days of stress and cooperation. All of them were aware that something was going on that was different from normal.

The land affected was the North Dakota/Minnesota Red River valley, under the waters of the Red River. The people battled the river for a month and not one person was lost—it was, for them their "finest hour," as they called it, even "a positive experience," although many lost their homes.

As one woman put it: "The flood itself was not a negative, bad experience. It was something I don't want to go through again, but we made lemonade out of the lemons. And so that aspect of it was a very positive, good thing that happened to us down here."

All kinds of people from the region helped. "I think the camaraderie was just amazing," they said. Although many of the neighborhoods were destroyed, the flood event had a carnival atmosphere.

One woman hesitated, "—it was kind of a social thing, actually.... We were preparing, but, ah, it was fun, and it was a lot of people bringing food. I'm not saying that it was a gay time, but it was; people had all their friends here, and it was people helping one another. It was a very—it was just a wonderful time in that sense of coming together."

Jencson gives the conditions.

The Red River Valley Flood of 1997 was no flash flood. It was the result of a record snow year in a climate so cold that snow did not melt between snowfalls. At the end of March, nearly ten feet of the white stuff all began to melt at once. Although this meant that people had weeks to prepare, diking and sandbag operations were interrupted by "the Mother of All Blizzards," a killer storm with raging winds that began as rain on Friday, April 4th and turned to ice overnight. The ice and wind pulled down most of the power grid in the region, and did not stop until late Sunday when people emerged from frigid, darkened homes to find everything but the deepest, fastest moving floodwaters turned to ice. But what looked like solid ice often had several feet of floodwater beneath it. Prefilled sandbags had turned into "frozen turkeys" that would neither stack nor settle to fill holes. Without power, sump pumps and small town sewage stations failed and the rest of the week saw the evacuation of farmsteads and several small towns. Tens of thousands of citizens mobilized to build dikes, rescue neighbors, and staff shelters. By mid-April the Red River crested at a remarkable 23 feet above flood stage in besieged Fargo, North Dakota. On April 18th, the next largest urban area in the region, Grand Forks/East Grand Forks, began the rapid evacuation of some 40,000 people. On the 19th, when water breached the 18 foot high dikes defending "The Forks," and hit the recently restored electricity, much of Grand Forks went up in flames above the icy water. The Grand Forks Air Base and the cities of Fargo, ND and Moorhead, MN huddled behind their own leaky dikes, and then became the center of increasingly urgent relief operations.

Most roads, including interstates, were under water. Cities, urban neighborhoods within them, small towns and farms that survived, did so as diked islands in a lake of fresh ice water some 8,000 miles square. Access was often only by boat and helicopter. With the power grid down for the eastern half of North Dakota, many had the sense of being "cut off from the twentieth century."

People compared it to the London blitzkrieg—this time, though, it was the battle of the Red River. The people were by now living with others, in firm community. The newly forged groups sandbagged with heroic perseverance: sandbagging was life.

"My own wife came home and she had two wrist braces on. I said, 'Well what's goin' on,' and she said, 'Well, I was up sand baggin', up at the Solid Waste.' And I said, 'well, we're tryin'ta set that up for two hour shifts, you know, cuz it's demanding work.' She was there six hours!"

People simply talked about practical things—how to build tall stable heaps of sandbags; injuries; food. Salvation Army trucks of food arrived, and here the game was to catch one before it disappeared down the street. One family described Grandfather yelling, "Wait for me, wait for me!" like a kid after the ice cream van. Sports were canceled, colleges went part time. Everybody, high and low, was out sandbagging, rich kids were working in affordable-housing areas, and rank was forgotten. Women and men toiled together in the long lines, passing sandbags from hand to hand. The rhythm of common work itself created communitas.

The Fargo Director of Public Works, Dennis Walaker, was right in the center of it all, in his tall rubber boots. By the simple means of wading through the worst hit areas, always there, fixing problems, hurrying on to the next, this man became a hero to the people—to such an extent that rubber boots like his became known as "Walakers." People heard his voice on the radio and they listened with excitement and hope. It was Walaker who noted the strength of the women sandbaggers, "women that were unbelievably wiry!"

Sharing became a beautiful passion with the people.[3] Those with electric generators gave them away to those with young children.

Citizens awarded Walaker thousands of dollars for his good works, but he gave it to charity. The man was humble about the gift, stumbling in his words. The good Dakotans joked about their flooded farms, and they painted funny graffiti on them. Slogans expressed a variety of puns, thank yous, threats to idle tourists, prayers, and, especially, silly sayings: "Yah shure you betcha! I'm ready for federal help V. P. Gore, Clay County did not!" They contrived to go to parties, even at night. And over the frozen land they saw the comet Hale-Bopp passing near the horizon, and the northern lights. These strange signs felt like a natural salute to their courage.

Linda Jencson asked, "What is there about the active process of coping with stress that is the real creator of communitas in disaster?" Again, we note it was the use of the body, the hands, the active process itself, that engendered it. It is innate in us, as Trevarthen showed with the babies in Chapter 1, and it does come out if given a chance. We are made that way. It is the way everything is and, simply, humans have become aware of it.

The distinguishing marks of communitas were fully present at the Red River flood: the great and famous mixing with the humble; the simplification of life; the sharing of necessities; and the long hours and backbreaking work that counted as pleasure. The communitas was unexpected, as it usually is. Yet, when it came into play, it was unforgettable. People grew open to the wonders of nature and to curious lucky events, and they could tell you about miracles.

People in the grip of these great events became fired with the challenge. They found that folks had been through this before, and they warmed to the idea of these connections to the past. The people were both proud of this and humble, too—each individual vivid with personality, dwelling in a community as firm as a rock.

So a question arises: How important was the official management in this crisis? Walaker was needed everywhere and was found, not in his office but up to his knees in water, doing his job. The sandbagging women were out doing theirs. Everyone focused in on the problem and found their place in the organization. People found a style that worked, and it turned out to be a style like that of Martin Buber: practical. What we witnessed was the *communitas* of disaster, a powerful force. And it was equal in this case to the power of the raging flood.

The Disaster of the Hurricane Katrina

During Hurricane Katrina, August 23 to 30, 2005, America, as well as the city of New Orleans itself, was in a state of shock. This disaster found the weakest spot in the nation's body; the old slave world in decay, our healthy humanism leached out of it, and its remains left in the doldrums. Guilt and anger emerged as it became apparent that the disaster was largely the result of long-term neglect of the poor. Here, many of the real-life stories are already lost and generalizations are rampant. But the cases of communitas exist. While researching them, I was looking at something so pathetic I was ashamed.

During the first days of the disaster, as thousands died and hundreds of thousands struggled in survival mode,[4] many people found ways to help one another. One group called "the Robin Hood Looters"[5] found boats and took food from abandoned grocery stores to the starving crowds, with the connivance of the police. Communitas was present here. The helpers were "antistructural," breaking the law. They were unarmed, and proud of the name of the ancient rebel leader, Robin Hood.

Another group of Katrina stories would never have been told if the record collector himself, Carl Lindahl, had not been flooded out of New Orleans. The survivors, as many as 100,000, had been taken in countless buses to the Astrodome at Houston, leaving New Orleans with only a few thousand inhabitants. At the Houston facility, Lindahl worked on a project to listen to and collect stories from the displaced New Orleans residents. To help with the project, many people who were survivors themselves were quickly trained how to record the stories of victims. Actual collector-survivors found it easier than did academics to obtain true personal accounts. The great strength of the project lay in the common bond that was established when one survivor listened respectfully to the story of another. In the Astrodome, one of them remarked, "When you're sitting across the table from another survivor, there's something therapeutic about sharing even the losses. I feel closer to the people who are telling me their stories, and I believe they feel closer to me."[6]

A man among that mass at Houston told Lindahl what had happened to him. He had been trapped with seven elders for four days, upstairs in his house, which was surrounded by water. Being the only one strong enough, he got out of the window and swam through the littered water to find a store. He broke into a drug store where he got rope, food, and many cases of water. He tied them all together and swam back, towing the goods painstakingly behind him. The swimming water-carrier looked after his seven companions for four days. "We all got out fine, thank God." This gaunt man was as humbled by his own superhuman acts as we are. He just would not let those seven old people die.

The listeners respected the rights of the storytellers to take control of the narrative and tell it however they wanted. Ordinary rules were inverted as well: the antistructural lawbreakers, such as the man who swam with groceries and the Robin Hoods, were considered "good looters." This oxymoron was well understood by the survivors.

From a world-shaking event to the most individually focused, we go to cancer. It is around us all the time, and it has some remarkable features.

The Communitas of Life and Death: Inversions and the Liminal State of Cancer

People in liminal states tend to be humble. They usually do what they are told to do—often without complaint. They accept regimens of pain. They are reduced to a common denominator so that they might be reconstructed. These processes create an intense camaraderie, which washes away previously recognized differences in age, social status, and ethnicity. Turner called this camaraderie "communitas"[7]

Communitas and the Liminal State of Cancer

The following is based on Diana Collins's account of events in.[8]

The mother of Diana Collins was diagnosed in 2004 with adenomacarcinoma, a rare form of stomach cancer. Diana learned during her visits to the cancer ward just how suddenly the change in her mother's life occurred, how she was cut off by society's own dread of cancer. Her mother was both marginal and also suspended between life and death. This was one type of Victor Turner's "state of liminality," and it was to be a permanent betwixt-and-between condition for the rest of Diana's mother's life, whatever the outcome.[9]

Once an individual is diagnosed with cancer, she ceases to be a busy person who is active in society, ordinary like everyone else; she is a patient, then eventually either a survivor or a victim. The doctor has made his dreaded statement during the initial check-up and after that, the knowledge never ceases for the patient. The patient's new condition alienates her from others in society who do not know many of the details about this generalized thing, cancer. Nor did Diana's mother. Her poor mom was overwhelmed, trembling with the news. How was she now to be a mom to her family? No way. Here was her potential death uncontrollably growing inside her. Nothing was normal any more. What happened to her was sending her into a state of chaos—but it was one that eventually subsided. During Diana's visits to her mother, Diana began to see in her a desire to recreate or find order. Marcy, another afflicted woman at the cancer center, told Diana, "After I was diagnosed, I stayed in my bedroom for three hours crying, howling, and cursing. After my breakdown of self-pity, I realized I had to be strong to survive. So, I got up and started to try to figure out what I could do about the situation."

Similarly, for Diana's mother, a different world was developing, all on its own. Straight away, the doctor's prognosis established an order, a protocol of steps: chemotherapy and radiation treatment, which loosely provided a social network for the patient as well as a framework to help mediate the new liminal existence between health and death. Such a stage of living on the margins of society is full of inversions, and afflicted individuals will adapt to them in order to establish a worldview of their new reality. For instance, anonymity is a classic inversion relating to the ritual character of the space. A patient is more likely to know the cancers and major concerns of each of the patients in the room than their names. A person is treated like a thing by the doctors, and yet as something sacred. The patients are useless, yet they are the material for highly advanced research, as seen in the doctors' eyes. They have poor health, yet they are going to be rich in a final experience of which we are all in awe. This inversion is hard to contemplate, but it is there. Such a place, the cancer room, inverts all rank among the patients and even among the staff and doctors, because of the total helplessness of the seriously sick. The inversion of rank can be seen in war hospitals after a battle. Here among the seriously sick we see the lineaments of the basic person which is the kingpin of the human rights idea.

What may happen when the ward is left to itself is that the occupants form a kind of merry band of outlaws from society, often joking. The process toward grasping some kind of cheerful companionable world, whoever it is among, can be the very stuff of communitas. The structure of the chemotherapy ward leaves space for this communitas but cannot create it. The lives of the newly diagnosed patients are betwixt and between ordinary life and death. They have been put by society in a special category, knowing they are different, and society does not know what is going to happen to them. Even so, they are all the more human. They are liminal, on one side. Being assigned thus creates many an inversion in the group, with new patterns, topics, and approaches to conversation, conversation that would be considered unacceptable in the noncancer world. Conversation with patients is a curious business within the secured ritual space of healing, and relies heavily upon trust. "Bonded by the cancer experience, strangers feel comfortable enough to express their fears—of pain and death—to one another in ways that would make an outsider uncomfortable."[10]

In the infusion room, patients are safe, and tend to don athletic wear or other loose-fitting clothing to receive hours of treatment while seated in the room's plush La-Z-Boy recliners. Comfort in the infusion room is of primary concern. Here the free flow of speech marks another inversion of cultural norms, conventions that entirely silence the dialogue about cancer amongst the general populace. Beatrice, one of the patients, said, "There is something about talking to people. I love to hear people talk. It soothes me. When you talk with someone, you get to know a background that you didn't have and wouldn't know otherwise. You learn something about the other person and sometimes about yourself. It's amazing how alike we can be with such different backgrounds".

Turner said of liminal people that they "seek a transformative experience that goes to the root of each person's being and finds in that root something profoundly communal and shared."[11] Diana, who saw communitas in action, said that the strongest example of communitas in the world might arguably be found in the existential relations and pursuit of mutuality sought out by two strangers receiving infusions in a cancer clinic that is purposefully arranged to give comfort and inspire open discourse.

Dark humor, the greatest tool of communitas in frightening conditions, came into its own in the infusion room. Diana and her mother, by now taking part in the "say anything" mood, were quite a pair for raising a laugh. Her mother, balding from the treatments, told everyone, "Hey, I've got so few hairs left that when I brush one out, I pick it up and stick it back in." Raucous laughter.

The jokes about dying were the best. Diana couldn't resist her own, being known as "the gloomy hopeless daughter." When her mother began to have the treatments, the old lady couldn't sleep a wink (we can imagine her terror). So the doctor prescribed a strong sleeping pill. Diana and her sister had no idea of what that sleeping pill could do. Diana walked into the bathroom and there was her mother on the toilet, head down between her knees—and there was not a trace of movement—no sound of breathing. Diana was stricken. She yelled out to her sister, "Come quick, Mom's dead. Dead on the toilet!" However, the sister thought Diana was making one of those jokes, and yelled back, "No shit?" howling with mirth.

They looked at the old lady.

Fortunately, she was only in a deep sleep, which they came to realize when she suddenly snored. Much to Diana's embarrassment, this story went around and around the infusion room giving a lot of pleasure, and gradually Diana saw the joke that was there in everyone's eyes. Diana found she was really loved for it and knew she would not fret so bitterly when her mother was finally freed from her pain. The cancer room had gained yet another story. Thus, for Diana and her mother, the definition of time changed, and death, with the help of jokes and other means of acceptance, ceased to cast a dark cloud across her family. There was now nothing they could not talk about. The commitment to openness and truth within her family provided growth and improved their relationships.

A diagnosis of cancer will make a patient question her grasp on the world around her. She comes to fear uncertainties, society, medical procedures, strangers, death, pain, suffering, and the return of cancer. In the ward, the fear that most middle-aged women admitted to was the impact upon their families if they were to die or become a burden. Each was imagining her home without herself and her active presence in it. What would happen to the family?

Each one was slowly getting used to this state of unknowing, and now they were assigning different values to time and to life.[12] When the mother was first diagnosed, she was given two months to live. After that time had elapsed and people ceased coming around to their home, Mom said, "Finally, the funeral is over. Now I can live for a bit!" Death and dying are phenomena in the realm of structured society, of formality, and of false sympathy, and if the liminal person realizes this as the mother did, she has a chance to escape structured life and live intensely until the end. And that chance creates a communitas with death.

Paul Stoller

The case of Paul Stoller, who is well known in anthropology as our cancer-surviving professor, describes his own chemotherapy treatment; it's a story that has a different ending. Three things were different. Being a professor, Paul read every word about the grim treatment, about the side effects of the substances used, and about all the details of the scannings and injections. He was utterly stricken by the diagnosis, as everyone is. Second, he was helped by an African medicine man; his fieldwork had been in Niger, West Africa.[13] Third, he finally became a survivor, a healthy remission patient.

Back in the 1970s, Paul was a Peace Corps volunteer in Niger, and then a PhD research candidate working there. As with Victor Turner and me, he was persuaded by his doctoral committee to link his descriptions of Songhay knowledge to social theory, in order to make a contribution to the discipline of anthropology. Like Victor Turner, he did so and received his doctorate.[14] But his anthropological odyssey left a spiritual thirst in his life. He went on and actually learned the people's power. On one of his trips, he suffered a night paralysis and used the power for the cure. This was well within the realm of the supernatural, so similar to my own transformative experience in Africa in 1986. He learned more. He apprenticed himself to Adamu Jenitongo, an old sage, a man like a priest, much sought after for healing, and whom Paul termed, dubiously, a sorcerer. Paul himself was now a practitioner of African power rituals. Adamu Jenitongo and Paul became the dearest friends, constantly working together until the old man died. Paul learned the people's heavenly prayer to N'debbi, God, with words similar to the "Our Father." The people forced him to learn it by heart. One day, his friend Moussa begged him to work his magic, to put an end to the power of a "mean European chief" in the area, a petty tyrant. Paul finally agreed. The result was that the wife of this "chief" was paralyzed, and was only released by the correct medicine. Paul relates that he soon wished he had never used the power.

Fourteen years later, Paul was teaching at West Chester University. A body of thinkers, on reading his publications, jeered at him up and down the halls for reporting these "impossible" powers. Here is where a horror entered the life of Paul—the diagnosis of cancer, the infusion room. It all had to be played out. But in the midst of the much feared preparations for the needle, Paul sensed a familiar tingling, the tingling of African spiritual communication. His senses awoke. He heard the soft voice of Adamu Jenitongo: "You've found your way back to the path. Step onto it and walk forward."

Paul put out his hand to his own brother who was with him, and the other hand to the doctor. "This will help me to cope," he said, and he recited the old prayer he had learned by heart, the prayer to N'debbi, the *genji how*. That night, after his treatment, he dreamed he was helping Adamu Jenitongo circumcise the boys of the village. A lion appeared, and Adamu Jenitongo bade him face it, and it backed off.

Paul was determined to carry on teaching and enjoying life through these hard months. Adamu Jenitongo visited him often, from thousands of miles away and more than a decade in the past. Paul worked and drank champagne with his friends at each good report from the doctor. He joked about his state with the students, and the lectures went well. The treatment was a success.

This was communitas with a spirit, with healing effects.

The Sick

I asked Elaine Bunch, in our church sharing-group, to tell us a communitas story. She was in her fifties, a grandmother, and she had been a nurse.

She looked sideways and up for a bit. "It was—it was when I was nursing." "In Japan?" I asked. She had been in Japan during the Korean War, working in an army hospital. "Yes. They were bringing in the wounded, *lots* of them. We all worked together. Rank and distinction just disappeared; we were all in it together."

She conveyed the scene, the quiet quick movements, everybody's eyes on the problems around them, helping each other. She didn't say this, she didn't say much at all, but somehow we saw the scene without words. She didn't know how to deploy her words on this—it was a matter of, "You can't put it into words." But it came through: the American nurses, young and old—not "American" any more. Not black or white or Asian. Not high nor low, Caucasian or with slant eyes—all simply *people*, doing a desperately hard thing, saving lives. She said that rank and distinction disappeared. She didn't mention "doctors, nurses, and directors." We knew what she meant.

The Bonding Power of Disaster

Facing stress collectively can produce the opposite of stress, a steady cheerfulness and even happiness, sometimes called "the human spirit in adversity"—and that very phrase has echoes of real spirituality. The communitas of the Dakota flood was homegrown, spontaneous, and at the same "twenty-seven-degrees-below" level of comfort as found in the story of Solzhenitsyn and his unseen "winged spirit" of courage and love. Survivors of Katrina reveled—strange to say—in their overnight antistructural paradigm, and cancer patients felt the bonds between each other. Through the exchange of stories, they imparted vitality to each other. This vitality is a miracle, a vision, real and existing all the time, but we do not see it.[15] However, we come to know each other through our sharing, finding the door to the world of another person and to a deeper understanding of ourselves.

One last tale describes how my friend Barbara Myerhoff greeted me long ago when she was dying of cancer.

"How are *you*, Edie?" Barbara wanted to know, with a big question mark.

Why was she taking such an interest in *me*? I was embarrassed. But she was going to be alive, in me, as an ancestor; I just couldn't face it, then. For communitas is a sympathetic and compassionate entanglement with another person. There are times when it can make a hole through space. Communitas can make staggering views open, can sweep all before it—us with it—and right over the edge into an actual spirit realm.

The next chapter in the book, "The Sacredness of the People: The Communitas of Revolution and Liberation," takes an upturn. The center of it is a certain place in history. The people, this multiple of the "naked unaccomodated human being," is being pushed hard to it to maintain its true nature. Wars, impelled onward by powerful autocrats, have ravaged the known nations again and again. The coming of prophets and saviors has given the people the message. The insights, the inversions, the spiritual reassurances are still stamped on humanity—there shall be peace. My sense, my own "historic memory" goes back to the women of Paris in 1789—those women with starving children, ready for revolution, yet under the power of a stupid greedy king. The women's unorganized throng stormed the Bastille and upset the most barbarous and unnatural system humanity had come up with: industrial feudalism in an enlightened era.

So, I follow how that came about—where the power of the people of communitas overflowed in a great innocent wave; how the people took up the knowledge of the power for certain. In the distant past, Abraham and his ten laws had showed them how. In a vast step to their own time, Thomas Jefferson had showed them how, a few years before. The world now knew that the people were going to decide their own fate—democracy was alive—like mammals in an age of dinosaurs.

Chapter 6

The Sacredness of the People: The Communitas of Revolution and Liberation

One's-self I sing—a simple, separate Person;
Yet utter the word Democratic, the word En-masse.
—Walt Whitman, *Leaves of Grass*

We have seen the communitas of disaster as a semi-miraculous non-rational phenomenon. Why did people actually love working together in the Dakota flood? We wonder at communitas that may even be present when death is certain, as in the cancer ward. We seem to be born for just such emergencies. We can see an opening beyond; we make a kind of jump into hope, into the future, such as occurs in the now-generally accepted near death experience. We were born for this hope.

Now I am grappling with revolution, a huge phenomenon—bigger than these occasional experiences with disaster. Revolutions have overcome entire societies from ages past until now. We seem to regard them with horror; we see violent death in many of them, and we have loved them not at all. But this chapter reveals a train of events that has strong connections with our present condition, down to my being able to write peaceably in the middle of the night. Through the flashes of gunfire in the past one can see the flashes of communitas, bringing liberty and a safe home.

Since 1973 I have been identifying the effects of communitas in human history and particularly its presence in revolutions. I have come to the astonishing conclusion that communitas is nested at the very hinge point of people's revolutions down the paths of history—that is, communitas is a kind of cartilage between changes in the social body that allows for movement and change. The political scientist Aristide Zolberg in a seminal article in 1971, "Moments of Madness: Politics as Art,"[1] recounts the series of revolutions that took place in France from 1841 onward until May 1968. Within each revolution—each takeover of the city of Paris by the common people—is nested a little island of heavenly perception closely akin to the *unio mystica* of the saints, the beatific vision of the saints. It should be noted that the experiences are not the solitary visions of the mystics, but are, rather, richly *social*, throughout an entire city—each occasion being the immediate phenomenon of communitas.

To discuss the communitas in revolutions we have to venture into history. History is cool in tone. It aims to present the true, impartial, unemotional facts of the past. It is linear in form. To achieve this impartiality, this concern for truth, history must depend on the remains of civilizations for the proof of its truth—principally, common sense conclusions drawn from ruins, objects, and various long-lasting images and writings. Here we encounter a serious difficulty in tracing communitas, because history is largely recorded from the point of view of literate people, those who have used stone and books—that is, it almost always comes from the point of view of those with power. That power, in the political, religious, and legal systems, often became wielded without the influence of the ordinary people. The principles enunciated by the scholars thus tended toward the manufacture of social structures, law systems that now appear to the modern eye as blind and obstinate bastions of a class, caste, race, age group, and, most often, gender. Nevertheless, the people, if they are not tyrannized, have always been able to frame a good customary life—if not enact laws—out of their natural culture and leave enough life and flexibility in their customs to adapt and respond to circumstances.

Tyranny has indeed held sway throughout too much of the history of civilization. This chapter tells how the people were given visionary moments that embodied their hopes of freedom, and also how the people came to trust the gifts of their own culture and sociality. Literate leaders, who could see what was happening to the human family—the loss of their oneness—also arose. There have been messages, engagement, reaction, points of breakthrough. The chapter tells of the unfolding of knowledge regarding the sacredness of the simple human being and the possibility of the people's liberation from overly adamant structures. This history comes from a different perspective than that of the traditional elite. To help with the problem of evidence of the far past, anthropology has been looking into prehistory, gauging what the social patterns might have been. Today those who are furthering this research conduct fieldwork among nonindustrialized peoples, hunters and gatherers; these anthropologists harvest knowledge of the lifestyles and sacred stories of the people, and also take note of their own in-depth experiences as wholly participating ethnographers, as described in the "Introduction." Through all of this, much communitas has been found, which is only beginning to be included in formal history.

In our ordinary western world, distant history presents us with the herding and ownership of animals, then the ownership of land. According to record, here begins competition, and here ends the general custom of sharing. War, strong leadership, and property consciousness have been the inevitable result. In linear succession, laws began and morals were turned into laws. The law of mystical participation was forgotten or jelled into religious systems. Heaven, hell, and systems of reward and punishment, hardly known before, were likewise erected. Natural communitas was replaced by a system of conditional rewards for goodness: one will be rewarded with joy on condition one obeys the will of God. Behind that lies control for the sake of control. But this overemphasis on control also results in a flip to the opposite, the now-familiar prevalence of inversions.

Communitas and Inversion in the Historical Record

Much of written history begins in the religious record. According to both Judaic and Christian accounts, Abraham was visited by God in Canaan, around 1900 B.C.

God gave Abraham a strange command—he told him to slay his only son, Isaac. Abraham moved to obey but, mercifully, God countermanded the order and rewarded Abraham with a covenant of success. The inversion lesson was that of the willingness of the worshiper to sacrifice everything. Loss is gain. The same God was also one of terror, burning up the cities of evildoers, yet also showing a vision of a lion lying down with a visionary lamb.

The Yajurvedas of India in the eighth or seventh century B.C. spoke of nonviolence, *ahimsa*. They said:

> One should not use their God-given body for killing God's creatures, whether these creatures are human, animal, or whatever.[2]

In northern India around the year 563 B.C., Siddhārtha Gautama's enlightenment also gave us a power inversion. The moment that Gautama left his father's palace and arrived, a poor man, at the foot of the Bo tree was a path-breaking change in the nature of much Asian history. Under that tree, as the Buddha, Siddhārtha experienced the holy sense of "no-mind" with no attachments—which left his being in peace with the universe. It was an inversion that activated communitas with the whole of things.

Other prophets arose, also with curiously inverted messages, such as the Chinese philosopher Confucius, 557–479 B.C., who stated: "Never impose on others what you would not choose for yourself." And from 100 B.C. through 700 A.D., the inversions appeared in the Upanishads of India. For instance, the sage Yajnavalkya Smitri taught the great doctrine represented in Hindi by *neti-neti*, the view that truth can be found only through the negation of all thoughts about it:

> Whoever sees all beings in the soul
> and the soul in all beings
> does not shrink away from this.
> In whom all beings have become one with the knowing soul,
> what delusion or sorrow is there for the one who sees unity?
> It has filled all.
> It is radiant, incorporeal, invulnerable,
> without tendons, pure, untouched by evil.
> Wise, intelligent, encompassing, self-existent,
> it organizes objects throughout eternity.[3]

The appeal of Yajnavalkya Smitri was contrary to the times, for he, like Confucius, spoke of all beings as one.

In Israel, around the year 5 A.D., Mary, the mother of Jesus, sang "The Magnificat."

> He has showed strength with his arm; he has scattered the proud in the imagination of their hearts.
> He has put down the mighty from their seats, and exalted them of low degree.
> He has filled the hungry with good things; and the rich he has sent empty away.[4]

Christians have been repeating the song for centuries, often without realizing how revolutionary it was and is. Somewhere near Galilee in the year 28 A.D., Jesus gave the Sermon on the Mount. It was rich with inversions and contained a radical manifesto:

> You have heard that it was said, "An eye for an eye, and a tooth for a tooth."
> But I tell you, do not resist an evil person.
> If someone strikes you on the right cheek, turn the other to him also.
> And if someone wants to sue you and take your tunic,

COMMUNITAS OF REVOLUTION AND LIBERATION

let him have your cloak as well.
If someone forces you to go one mile,
go with him two miles.
You have heard that it was said, "Love your neighbor and hate your enemy."
But I tell you: Love your enemies and pray for those who persecute you.[5]

After the Romans killed Jesus, Pentecost followed. Jesus's spirit came to his eleven friends in the form of living fire. It was an astonishing experience of communitas, an inversion of the normal reaction to death. Thinkers are still trying to interpret the story in a rational or psychological way, but it remains obstinately what it is.

Afterward came many kingdoms with a simulacrum of Christianity, slave-fed nations. False communitas was everywhere abroad in support of the ruling class. Still, through the centuries, along with the socially preserved written word, laws protecting humanity from violence gradually accumulated, including the traditions around King Arthur whose feats were first documented in written form by the Welsh monk Ninnius in 830 A.D. King Arthur is said to have sent out his knights to help the weak and powerless.

In central Italy, the teachings of Saint Francis of Assisi (1181–1226) were traditionally nonviolent, like the Buddha's. Victor Turner drew attention to the beliefs of St. Francis as an example of the spirit of antistructure.[6] The churches say in Saint Francis's name:

> Lord, make me an instrument of Thy peace;
> where there is hatred, let me sow love;
> where there is injury, pardon....
>   For it is in giving that we receive....

This prayer, very popular in the twentieth and twenty-first centuries, contains the principles of nonviolence and spiritual inversion. Also like the Buddha, Saint Francis began his life in riches. His conversion, which was dramatic, came on the famous day he cast off his grand clothes and walked naked into the church. Religion, through this turn to the unaccommodated human being, was also providing the seeds for revolution.

Francisco Suarez

At the turn of the sixteenth century in Spain, Francisco Suarez, a Jesuit and archbishop, was reckoned in his lifetime to be the greatest church philosopher since St. Thomas Aquinas (1224–1274). Suarez gave a pronouncement on the role of the people in politics that has had far-reaching effects on our planet. He said:

> Human beings have a natural social nature bestowed upon them by God, and this includes the potential to make laws. When a political society is formed, therefore, its nature is chosen by the people involved, and they give their natural legislative power to their ruler. Because they gave this power, they have the right to take it back, to revolt against a ruler—but only if the ruler behaves badly towards them, and they are obliged to act moderately and justly. In particular, the people must refrain from killing the ruler, no matter how tyrannical he may have become. If a government is imposed on people, on the other hand, they not only have the right to defend themselves by revolting against it, they are entitled to kill the tyrannical ruler.[7]

In 1613, at the instigation of Pope Paul V, Suarez wrote a treatise dedicated to the Christian princes of Europe, entitled *Defensio catholicae fidei contra anglicanae sectae errores*. This was directed against the oath of allegiance that James I of England exacted from his subjects. It was a treatise outlawing the divine right of kings. Recognizing the danger to himself, James I had the treatise burned by the common hangman and forbade its reading under the "severest penalties," and at the same time complained angrily to Philip III of Spain that he should not harbor an enemy to the throne and majesty of kings.[8] Thus, it was that Suarez and Pope Paul V urged humankind toward protection of their direct rights under God and pride in those rights.

If we look forward in time to the American Revolution, we see Suarez's treatise reflected in the Declaration of Independence. We may further trace its effects to France, Latin America, and the many countries across the world that existed as colonies in the possession of European nations and whose people later learned from the French Revolution. The treatise of Suarez is the hinge around which this chapter moves and sees history still developing. The Suarez enlightenment seeped through everywhere—revolution was contagious. The utilitarian philosophers in England, Locke and Hobbes, among others, knew that the divine right of kings was dead.

Not many people today are familiar with the name of Francisco Suarez. Victor Turner, with his interest in communitas, the naked unaccommodated man, the ordinary person, found Suarez to be his star, his stronghold. The countervailing effect of Suarez's voice over the power of the Holy Roman Empire in Europe influenced many minds in the seventeenth and eighteenth centuries. This was how the illusion of its holiness ended. Our own perspective today does not include such a struggle, so we have forgotten Suarez, but it was from this perspective that Jefferson in his declaration looked at the past.

Communitas at the Heart of Revolutions

Chapter 6 tells the story of what happened to those under the oppression of the king, aristocracy, and power structures, and how, once the struggle produced an opening, the sufferers in each era knew the marvels of communitas, if only for a brief time. The unsung histories of communitas show the unfolding of the value of the human being as that value grew in the slow rise of democracy. Judging from the research of and conclusions made by anthropologists, communitas had always existed among the people themselves. Later occasions of communitas were associated with love of one's country, with a strong protective sense of justice which, under tyranny, might explode in violence. Violent outbreaks could become pathological, such as during the political regimes of communism later in history, causing as much genocide as warring kingdoms. This chapter distinguishes communitas from its pathological version, showing its original links with the joy of liberation from captivity.

One vital principle runs through the histories and should be noted at every turn:

> there occurred increments of democracy after each episode. Each revolution, stage, and landmark, of however short a duration, left behind it an increment of liberation, justice, and democracy.

I look first at the American Revolution, which was fired by an extraordinary rise of the consciousness of the people up to the climax—the nation-creating act of the signing of the Declaration of Independence, July 4, 1776.

The American Revolution

All the events in this chapter were linked to one another, so it is instructive to remember the ironic connection between the American and French Revolutions. In 1776, King Louis XVI of France gave huge funds to aid the Americans in their struggle for independence against the British, thus emptying the French coffers and starving his people. Thus it was that the French Revolution showed its head, thirteen years after the American one.

The climax came when Thomas Paine arrived in Philadelphia from England and published the pamphlet *Common Sense*, which carried the passion that fired the American Revolution. It set off the communitas that stirred the country into action; it enabled the vacillating European population of the new continent to come to a decision. *Common Sense* helped those who did not know their passion to find it and have words for it. It was the material they needed, and it also fanned the flames for those already involved.

Thomas Paine was born in 1737, a Quaker, in East Anglia, a region that had been affected by the peasants' revolt. East Anglia was the home of Oliver Cromwell, of Lady Huntingdon's Chapel dissenters, and much later, in the 1930s, of the Cambridge socialists. It was my home. Paine lived among the differences and social inversions of the philosophers and radicals of England. He later became a friend of the poet William Blake, who wrote of the "satanic" cotton mills of England and the repressive life-sucking industrial revolution. The two of them could see how a monarch was merely a plunderer, "the principal ruffian of some restless gang who had obtained for himself the title of chief among plunderers."[9] For them, America was already a country seething for its freedom; they could see their hopes there.

The 1760s and early 1770s in America were the years of the British harassments, and in 1774 Paine went over to America to join the resistance. His starting place was in Philadelphia, the center of the action. On arrival he went to stay with a printer—and thus he found himself with a print shop right there in his hands. In November 1775, he began to write *Common Sense*. In January of the next year, when it was printed, it sold 120,000 copies in the first three months, and 500,000 copies by the end of the year. The pamphlet flooded into England and was translated all over the world. Everyone said it was little short of a miracle.

Paine was opening the door for America, showing it to be open, in fact. It was common sense: kings were not divine. The people, as Suarez had written before him, have the duty to expel bad leaders. This principle came to the colonists in the same way it came to Suarez, as if something were pointing them the way ahead with a message. When the words came home to them, the revolution blossomed.

Nature righted itself after an age of feudalism in which falsehood had been imposed upon it. We can see vividly how the words turned the people around, and inspired them to do their real work for the world. Paine said, "The authority of England over America was never the design of Heaven." That authority was a form of government that must have an end, he said. "As parents, we can have no joy" because under the current system, all that people would have to leave their children in posterity would be something rotten.

We ought to do the work of it, otherwise we use them meanly and pitifully. In order to discover the line of duty 120 degrees correctly, we should take our children in our hand, and fix our station a few years farther into life; that eminence will present a prospect, which a few present fears and prejudices conceal from our sight.[10]

Paine's mind leapt a few years ahead, onto an eminence from which he could see the view. His "120 degree leap into the future" has many analogies later in this and the next chapter. He took all his readers up to Mount Moriah, so to speak, so that they could see the promised land for themselves. That was what broke through the barriers of prejudice and fear: the vision of the facts, distinct in the future. The people's response was the communitas that swept into the American Revolution.

The actual pamphlet was an "opening" occasion, like the joy occasions at the heart of many revolutions, similar to the root paradigms of the Exodus and Pentecost. There it was: the leaders of the new America had work to do. The increment of freedom, one that they now knew *could* be theirs, was right in front of them to be *made* theirs. John Adams collected the votes and the day came. The delegates required Thomas Jefferson to write the declaration. For them, this was the point where liminality—change, the people's sense of it—began to *rise above* what went before. That higher point was where the communitas began. It was like a person connecting wires by pressing the plug into the outlet—and suddenly the light goes on.

The declaration under Jefferson's hand told the people what they knew but had not said. It went further, at a higher level—further than anything has ever gone before—*over*, by Tom Paine's 120 degrees. It struck the gold of democracy.

The language of the declaration was music to their ears. All present on July 4, 1776, were very happy with the edited result, and Benjamin Franklin said, "Not a word should be altered, not a word."[11]

From "The Unanimous Declaration of the Thirteen United States of America"

When in the course of human events it becomes necessary for one people to dissolve the political bands which have connected them with another and to assume among the powers of the earth, the separate and equal station to which the laws of nature and of nature's god entitle them, a decent respect to the opinions of mankind requires that they should declare the causes which impel them to the separation.

We hold these truths to be self-evident, that all men are created equal, that they are endowed by their creator with certain unalienable rights, that among these are life, liberty and the pursuit of happiness. That to secure these rights, governments are instituted among men, deriving their just powers from the consent of the governed,—That whenever any form of government becomes destructive of these ends, it is the right of the people to alter or to abolish it, and to institute new government, laying its foundation on such principles and organizing its powers in such form, as to them shall seem most likely to effect their safety and happiness.

Thus begins the Declaration of Independence; I draw attention to the people finding it necessary "to assume the separate and equal station to which the laws of nature and of nature's god entitle them": here are direct resonances with Francisco Suarez. What is this "nature's god"? Nature has her laws and she also has her god with its laws. Suarez, at the turn of the sixteenth century, said:

> Human beings have a natural social nature bestowed upon them by God, and this includes the potential to make laws.

Then, in this phrase of the declaration: "That to secure these rights, governments are instituted among men, deriving their just powers from the consent of the governed." Suarez says:

> When a political society is formed, therefore, its nature is chosen by the people involved, and they give their natural legislative power to their ruler.

And here in the declaration is yet another phrase: "That whenever any form of government becomes destructive of these ends, it is the right of the people to alter or to abolish it, and to institute new government, laying it's foundation on such principles and organizing it's powers in such form, as to them shall seem most likely to effect their safety and happiness." Suarez says:

> Because they gave this power, they have the right to take it back, to revolt against a ruler—but only if the ruler behaves badly towards them.... If a government is imposed on people, they...have the right to defend themselves by revolting against it.

It seems to me that the language of all who were engaged in this great new find—democracy—was luminous and grave, and was handled like something that was sacred. These people, who were not kings or priests but just people, had wagered their all on being *just the people*. And, as Suarez said, they were simply and truly in touch with this awareness, this type of consciousness that was people-minded. Now, therefore, there existed a precedent for the world, a successful revolution.

The Increment. The outcome, when all was completed, was independence itself. The power was taken over by voters responsible to the thirteen states, lands that were no longer colonies.

Meanwhile, in 1795 in Scotland, a laughing voice was heard that cut through all grand state power of Britain. It was a reminder of the ordinary working people, suffering under their own overlords of the aristocracy and owners of factories and mines. The people were voiced by their own poets. The poem says that we may yet live to see the "eternal reconciliation of the classes" of Michelet; we "shall brothers be for a' that." It is by Robert "Rabbie" Burns.

A Man's a Man for All That[12]

> Is there for honest poverty
> That hangs his head, an' a' that
> The coward slave, we pass him by
> We dare be poor for a' that
> For a' that, an' a' that
> Our toil's obscure and a' that
> The rank is but the guinea's stamp
> The man's the gold for a' that
>
> Ye see yon fellow called a lord
> Who struts an' stares an' a' that
> Tho' hundreds worship at his word
> He's but a coof for a' that
> For a' that, an' a' that
> His ribbon, star and a' that

> The man o' independent mind
> He looks an' laughs at a' that
>
> A prince can make a belted knight
> A marquise, duke, an' a' that
> But an honest man's above his might
> Good faith, he minna fault that
> For a' that an' a' that
> Their dignities an' a' that
> The pith o' sense an' pride o' worth
> Are higher rank than a' that
>
> Then let us pray that come it may
> as come it will for a' that
> That Sense and Worth, o'er a' the earth
> Shall bear agree an' a' that
> For a' that an' a' that
> It's coming yet for a' that
> That man to man, the world o'er
> Shall brothers be for a' that.

Rabbie Burns, a poor man, racked with rheumatic fever from his privations, sang out from Edinburgh for all the poor, everywhere. These verses were much beloved by Victor Turner, also a Scotsman. They spoke of communitas, the simple human being; honesty and the inversion of rank; laughter; free agreement; free communication, with the simplicity of brotherhood holding its own "o'er all the earth."

The French Revolution

> Bliss was it in that dawn to be alive
> But to be young was very heaven!
> ...Not favored spots alone, but the whole earth,
> The beauty wore of promise, that which sets....
> The budding rose above the rose full blown.
> ...happiness unthought of....
> Not in Utopia, subterranean fields,
> Or some secreted island, Heaven knows where!
> But in the very world, which is the world
> Of all of us—the place where in the end
> We find our happiness, or not at all![13]

Such was the feeling of William Wordsworth and the upcoming Romantics about the French Revolution. These poets were working in what was then the English counterculture. We see again what Paine said about the future—that the budding United States would grow into the future *above* its first declaration, into its "rose full blown."

In France, during the beginning of the industrial revolution, the divine right of kings was still in force, a perpetual parasitic drain on the country. The dead and stinking feudal system eventually produced what can only be called hell in Paris in 1798.[14] The people of Paris were without money and had been starving for years, while in the fields the peasants were in the hands of the land sharks.[15] Forty-five percent of foundling children died young; women were desperate. The history of the first days of the revolution in Paris is full of little vignettes of obscure people snatching bread and wheat from price-gouging bakeries and hoarders. Nameless women dominated these scenes, often armed and dressed in their best, though poor. They were obviously *not* going to allow their babies die of starvation.[16]

Ironically, as we have seen, Louis XVI had no money because he had donated the country's wealth to the American revolutionaries to help them fight the British. Louis, therefore, ruled a starving population and was forced to call a session of his National Assembly, a body that had not gathered since 1614. This period spanned a time of untold spending and selfishness among the aristocracy, doings that displayed the absolute corruption existing in feudalism, the system of absolute power.

The gathering of the National Assembly took place at Versailles on May 5, 1789. The people were happy because a change was taking place: they had an Assembly; it was a great occasion. The popular minister Jacques Necker stood up for their cause, struggling to find a constitution by which to run the country. The historian Crane Brinton described the scene:

> The ceremony went off with processions, carpeted streets, flowers, banners, choruses, lovely women, and crowds. They seemed to have produced in those who shared them an extraordinary exhilaration, a communion in hope and love, never wholly to be lost in the bitterest days of the Terror. Thus at its outset the French Revolution bore the unmistakable imprint of religious emotion. Ferrieres said of it, "My country, my fellow citizens, the monarch, God himself, all became me. I rested sweetly and peacefully on so many objects; they were alive in me, I was alive in them. The same feelings penetrated everywhere; and, far from weakening as they spread, acquired a strength which could hardly be resisted."[17]

This was communitas right at the beginning of the great change: "my fellow citizens became me.... I was alive in them." Here was a moment of unity, and the feelings were spreading. This explicit documentation of the scene at the assembly was a prototype of the later manifestations of revolutionary festivals through time, and it is a key to the present chapter and to Chapter 7.

The assembly was gathered from the aristocracy, the church, and the third estate, which comprised commoners, men of property. The church and the aristocracy had a vote—the commons did not. On June 20, 1789, the assembled unenfranchised people left the assembly along with Necker, their favorite minister, and set up their own assembly at the indoor tennis courts. There they swore to give France a constitution, with votes for the third estate. This, the cardinal point of the revolution, was exactly what the commons needed in order to constitute themselves as a people.[18]

The king tried to dismiss this Assembly; he did dismiss Necker. He also recruited more troops. A contemporary participant described the state of Paris like this:

> How things have changed over the last three days! Last Sunday, Paris was dismayed at the dismissal of M. Necker. Although I was getting people worked up, no one would take up arms. About three o'clock I went to the Palais-Royal. I met a group of people and complained to them about our lack of courage. Just then three young men came by, holding hands, shouting "To arms!" I joined in, and since my enthusiasm was quite obvious, they surrounded me and persuaded me to climb up on a table. Immediately six thousand people gathered around me....
>
> I was choking from the hundreds of ideas that overwhelmed me and my thoughts were a jumble. I managed to say: "To arms!" Then I yelled it, "To arms! Let's all wear green cockades, the color of hope."...I grabbed a green ribbon and was the first to pin it on my hat. My action spread like wildfire![19]

July 14, 1789—the Storming of the Bastille; Seeing it Happen

Now the king's troops started to approach Paris. From sources and paintings of the scenes, one can see the throng facing the awesome walls of the Bastille, the bastion of power, where arms were stored; the place where those who represented the people had been subjugated and never heard of again. People of all kinds now faced the Bastille, some with good weapons. In fact, anything with a point on it was seen sprouting from the crowd.

"Lib-er-té-Lib-er-té!"

Many courageous women were among the crowd with their smiles, catching the eye. The noise was terrific; the shouts rose to roars, then songs—the farandole with its rude lines—and the crowd behind hustled their fellows forward. They moved up to the high-arched gate and found it locked. They yelled, and then yelled for the prison governor, the Marquis de Launay. The governor, by now a scared man, had his armed men fire on them. Battle raged and eighty of the poor rabble died beneath the firing of the guard. Finally the people swarmed in, captured the governor, and killed him. He was in fact the only person the crowd killed. They searched all the cells and found only seven prisoners, so lax was the king's command.

It was done. The city was in festival. Now the bread could be simply taken from the hoarded supplies of the bakeries: it was their city, a city of the people. Communitas reigned, just for a time. France now had her own Assembly—the commoners—who were busy framing a constitution and the Declaration of the Rights of Man and of the Citizen. The women marched to Versailles and won their demand for bread, and they brought the king back to Paris under their own control—one of the greatest scenes in history. I bow to the women of Paris, my sisters. Jules Michelet,[20] a well-loved commentator in 1845, said these words:

> Versailles, with an organized government, king, ministers, a general, and an army was, without any hesitation, doubt, or uncertainty, in a state of the most complete moral anarchy.
>
> Paris, turned completely upside down, abandoned by all legal authorities, in total disorder, on the 14th of July achieved what is morally the most profound order, that is, the unanimity of spirits.

This is Michelet's picture of Paris inverted and glorious—often the condition of communitas. Crane Brinton described the assembly as a communion of hope and love, and spoke of "an extraordinary exhilaration." From that July 14 onward, the people began to play an increasingly important part in the revolution, both in town and country. As the centuries moved on and many revolutions recurred, we will sense the freedom within Paris a number of times.

There is a cogent link between the revolution and the anthropologist Claude Lévi-Strauss. He wrote the following, using the word "myth" to avoid using "spiritual," a word that was taboo in anthropology. It should be noted that now in 2011 the taboo is fading, and we are finding the language of spirituality easier.

A myth always refers to events alleged have taken place long ago. But what gives the myth an operational value is that the specific pattern described is timeless; it explains the present and the past as well as the future. This can be made clear through a comparison between myth and what appears to have largely replaced it in modern societies, namely, politics.... But to the French politician, as well as to his followers, the French Revolution is both a sequence belonging to the past—to the historian—and a timeless pattern which provides a clue for its interpretation, a lead from which to infer future developments.... In Michelet's words: "*That day...everything was possible....Future became present...that is, no more time, a glimpse of eternity.* It explains how myth can be an absolute entity on a third level which, though it remains linguistic by nature, is nevertheless distinct from the other two....Hence cosmology is true.[21]

Interestingly, Lévi-Strauss says that politics have taken over from myth as regards these events. This is like the signing of the American Declaration of Independence. Both events widen to the surprising nature of the naked unaccommodated human, the basic person who is the carrier of communitas; we seem to be touching on souls. The French Revolution gave us a new path to democracy, and did so with a load of kings and aristocrats on the people's backs, right there in their country, strangling it. The remote consequences of the acts of the French are to be seen here and now—in which we see, too, through Lévi-Strauss's spyglass, a glimpse of eternity.

Communitas in the French Revolution

In the French Revolution we recognize the sense of communitas, and the strengthening and spreading of the phenomenon. There it was, like glorious goose bumps, like a new species hatching in the heart of fundamental change. It is these very occasions that give birth to the acts of liberation that never go away, that leave their increments of self-determination, and whose giant steps of liberation in the later progression of centuries are now seen to be irreversible. France found itself reconstituted with a precious jewel, the commoners' vote, even though this bore a property and gender qualification. But, it was a vote.

The Increments. At this point, the increments included the abolition of feudalism in France, the adoption of the Declaration of the Rights of Man and Citizen (taken from the American Rights of Man), the adoption of the national motto "Liberty, Equality, Fraternity," and male suffrage, limited to the moneyed class.

Paris Fifty-Nine Years Later: the February Revolution; the Second Republic

It is always bitter to survey the appalling genocide of the upper class that followed the French Revolution—the result of a scourge of minds like the scourge that has infected a number of other nations after their turn to democracy. History tells it: the rich showed no signs of submitting to democracy. As a result, they were simply destroyed. The age of gentle Leon Tolstoy had not yet arrived; the sufferings of the poor had bred revenge, a gangrene of society.

Time elapsed. After the eras of Napoleonic rule and war, the monarchy was reinstated. In Paris in 1848, the large masses of industrial workers on the eastern side of the city suffered from serious unemployment and poor conditions. The vast majority, 99 percent, was denied suffrage, not being "men of substance," and King Louis Philippe XVI remained adamant, refusing the people's demands for a vote. The minister François Guizot, known for his obdurate support of the restriction of the suffrage, advised those who wanted the vote to "enrich yourselves" (*enrichissez-vous*) through hard work and thrift.[22]

At this insult, crowds of workers streamed into the center of Paris and were welcomed by their own working men's national guard. As the king's army reacted, the people built barricades against it, quickly taking possession of the whole of Paris. The old government had no course but to resign.

Immediately a Second Republic was proclaimed. This government instituted national workshops on a wide scale, employing 100,000 workers. In the heart of Paris there ensued for a short period one of the deepest experiences of communitas—the working people's sense of freedom within Paris. The political scientist Ari Zolberg tells how: "In spite of all frictions, the day after the proclamation of the Republic there was an extraordinary impression of freedom, of happiness, of fulfillment."[23] Zolberg noted that Gustav Flaubert, the novelist, was present at the time:

> Flaubert records the joy, the playfulness, and the harmony of the crowd. In the palace, after the crowd throws the throne out the window, "joy burst out, as if, instead of the throne, a future and unlimited happiness had appeared.... The city is as peaceful as if on a Sunday morning...[they] walk without care, stepping lightly.... It is a time for games.... Ah! What happiness, my poor old buddies! The People triumphant! Workers and bourgeois are embracing! Ah! If you knew what I've seen! What wonderful people! How beautiful!"[24]

In these revolutions there existed a religion suitable to be learned and followed by all the people. That was the really new part of the old scene. For the first time, we learn what the ordinary people of Paris were experiencing. In the February Revolution, the people could breathe freely and enjoy their city.

However, by June 1848, the taxpayers could not be persuaded to pay the necessary funds for the wide-scale workshop system, so the scheme had to be abandoned. Instead, an old style Party of Order was instituted. At this the people, once more unemployed, rose up in anger. The ending was tragic: the revolution was crushed, 1,500 people were killed, and 15,000 were deported.

Nevertheless, the people had gained their universal male suffrage and, later, help for the unemployed. These were the increments for this short uprising. After 1848, humankind was going to hear from the people of nonviolence: Henry David Thoreau and Tolstoy, Gandhi and Martin Luther King Jr., Martin Buber and Nelson Mandela.

What was never forgotten was that 1848 Paris, a city of two million, had experienced a wide-spread change. Within the freedom provided by the barricades, a person was glad to exist without the aid of a calculating consciousness—they just *were*. They did not have to calculate to reach the truth; they experienced it.

Inversions abounded at these festivals, both in 1789 and 1848. The inversions themselves became realized in the many transformations. The poor became powerful; the governed became the governing. Spendthrift luxury was replaced by activity, by the creation of a constitution and the spectacle of the people taking history into their own hands. In the February Revolution, the king's throne was tossed out of the window: things of awe were literally inverted. Moreover, the reconciliation of opposites was the order of the day. Workers and bourgeois embraced. In the work of renewing Paris that followed the 1789 revolution, the mayor, in his sash, was down digging with the laborers; the simple laborer embraced the colonel. Michelet said, "That day...everything was possible...the future became present...that is, there was no more time, a glimpse of eternity." It happened as a double reconciliation of history and a vision of communitas, one that became an actualization. It created more than history; it had its imprint on eternity.

What did it matter that the happiness was short-lived? It quickly spread, and no one wanted it to stop. Although the movement was soon crushed, it fathered new revolutions for the future, each with a solid increment. The whole era of revolutions represented a way of suffering with much pain, coming before the present era of nonviolent protest. The sure advance of the people was not halted. Our current generation owes gratitude for those struggles, those votes that were won, for social security for the unemployed, and for the gradual adoption of the necessary benefit schemes by the world's populations in country after country.

The Increments. When completed, the increments of the February Revolution were universal male suffrage and, later, help for the unemployed.

The Paris Commune, 1871

The next advance in France was perhaps the greatest and the best understood. In 1871, the city of Paris suffered food shortages due to the war with Germany. The citizens formed their own sizable National Guard, comprised of men whose memories harked back to the February Revolution. But Napoleon III, then emperor, fled from his war with the Germans and simply left his cannons behind in Paris. To save the cannons from the Germans—lacking any other assistance—the women tugged the huge weapons up to the heights of Montmartre, where they would be out of the Germans' sight.

When the government saw the radicals taking control of Paris, they sent in soldiers to fetch the cannons and arrest the people's leaders. Instead, the troops fraternized with the Parisians, and there were immediate scenes of communitas. At this point, the Central Committee of the National Guard took over the government in the capital and formed an elected Commune, or House of Commons. Those in the Central Committee considered taking huge sums from the national bank, for the city's expenses, but they were hesitant about displeasing the outside world. The old government out at Versailles, on the other hand, took the money and brought together a powerful army against the Parisians. In response, the people threw up barricades, 160 of them. Within the defenses, they were happy, successfully depending on their own communal organization, which they ran with great joy. Under their hands it became a highly democratic social democracy.[25]

By then it was springtime in Paris. The feeling of release and communitas existed everywhere inside the barricades. People were in the mood for festival, with sunshine, flowers, flags, and brass bands. Everyone was alight with happiness, for a proud hope had appeared on the scene, the sense of a great unselfish achievement.

> Give us a hug, old pal, you're grey-haired too. And I can see you there, sonny, playing marbles behind the barricade. You're saved too,

kid! You're lucky, you don't have to grow up in the fog and mud and then die, completely forgotten. You're free! I tell you, it's the soul of the crowd that's inside me—I could die with happiness—and then resurrect.[26]

Can one send a hug back in time? If time is circular and not linear, then maybe we can. In her book *Eat, Pray, Love*, Elizabeth Gilbert writes:

> ...the Zen Buddhists...say that an oak tree is brought into creation by two forces at the same time. Obviously, there is the acorn from which it all began, the seed which holds all the promise and potential, which grows into the tree.... But...there is another force operating here as well...the future tree itself, which wants so badly to exist that it pulls the acorn into being...The already existent oak...[is] saying the whole time: "Yes—grow! Change! Evolve! Come and meet me here, where I already exist in wholeness and maturity. I need you to grow into me!"[27]

We feel the future movements for justice, liberation, and nonviolence calling through time to the movements that were their predecessors.

Here was the moment of communitas. The defenders at the Paris Commune were in generous mood, laughing. They actually burnt the guillotine. This was not how Versailles described the revolution. Bureaucracy and the old institutional structures were gone. The working people had risen up, reinvented themselves at one leap, and set themselves free. Work, joy, pleasure, and achievement of needs—and communitas—would never have to be separated. In the commune, for just a few weeks, this utopia was actualized.[28] The workers of every nation loved to hear what was happening because the commune was made by the people themselves, and aimed for true equality for all humankind.[29]

The commune lasted just over two months. At the end, a traitor let in the outside army, which immediately committed a terrible massacre. Seventeen thousand were killed in the commune in only one week, far worse than the destruction in the French Revolution and the Reign of Terror.

The elements of communitas had been there: spontaneity, an unexpected happiness even in troubles, and being happy for their children and the legacy they were leaving them. It was the same awareness as in the American independence movement, as Paine had foreseen. One even heard the word resurrection, which is apt when people are carried along in a progression of repeated events through centuries.

The Increments. The increments now realized include laws enacted later as the Jules Ferry laws, which established, first, free education (1881), then mandatory and laic education (1882). Also, in 1905 came the separation of church and state. This included the rule that the churches should keep their doors open for public political meetings during the evenings.

1936: The Popular Front

Much went on throughout Europe in the twentieth century: World War I, the Russian Revolution, the Great Depression. In France, there was another mini-revolution between 1936 and 1938, named the Popular Front. A Mafia-like crook and embezzler called Alexandre Staviski had mounted the most toxic corruption of almost the entire French upper class, possibly worse than America's era of toxic assets and derivatives in the decade following 2000. The country was full of riots, its financial base leached and rotten. The middle class and the working class became sudden allies and won the parliamentary vote on May 24, 1936, taking 376 seats out of 608. Leon Blum became prime minister, supported by Edouard Daladier and others. Many factories were occupied, involving millions of people in a peaceful struggle. An observer reported:

> A few million workers were affected by the most spectacular movement in French social history. For three days I went from factory to factory.... I didn't see a single case of brutality...of damage to a single machine. The sit-down strike is a protracted picnic...a whole ritual of rallies and parades, of slogans and songs, of gestures and flags. Amid this camp life, a sort of warmth arises...not limited to the workers...a human contact which is never useless between the one who commands and those who carry out his orders.
>
> The spirit of 1936 was not limited to the workers. Brotherhood, solidarity, hopes of happiness and of peace—all these feelings were experienced with confused intensity by the hundreds of thousands men and women of the Popular Front. These sentiments are to be found in the literature and films of 1936.[30]

This would have been hard for us to imagine in our own day if it had not been for the comradeship in 2011 in Egypt, in Tahrir Square. Observers from different sides agree on its spirit. Simone Weil, the martyr mystic of French labor, found joy in the factories where she herself had worked a few months earlier. She noted:

> The workers were not merely concerned with grievances: after having always bowed, suffered everything, taken it all in silence for months and years, it is a matter of finally having the guts to stand up. To stand upright. To take one's turn to speak. To feel like men, for a few days.[31]

The new government failed in 1938, owing to lack of money. Daladier took over the government, and later, in World War II, he was the one who ceded France to Hitler.

What were the signs of communitas in the accounts? First, becoming a whole person, a complete and simple human, with a soul, is a major sign. Second, the feeling was hard to put into words—the movement was "of another order." Looking back in memory it was "difficult to bring it back to life." Third, it spread suddenly and widely. Fourth, there was a sense of festival. The alliance of the political parties was a sign, and the hint of the coming spirit of nonviolence. Moreover, there was the disappearance of ranking between workers and those who command. This was not class war. For France itself, a community of people, the movement held a touch of prophecy, a warmth spreading over decades—perhaps the notion that from a "1936" would come a "1944" (the liberation of Paris in which women won the vote), and even a "1968," an *événement de Mai,* perhaps the biggest Paris scene of all.

The Increments. The incremental progress now included the forty hour week, the nationalizing of the Bank of France and the armaments industry, abolition of the death penalty, a raise in the minimum wage, a law mandating two weeks of paid vacations each year for the workers, and a law legalizing collective bargaining.[32]

May 1968: Événements de Mai *in Paris*

An amazing two weeks of student power took place in Europe in 1968, the year when news of Vietnam, hippies, civil rights, and the death of Martin Luther King Jr. were occupying America. Over in France, a huge students' movement, fired with hopes of liberation and justice on one side and with the politics of the working people on the other, produced in Paris what came to be called the Événements de Mai. Twelve million working people came out on strike. As usual, the French put up the barricades.

The primary cause lay with the University of Nanterre. It was new and inadequate: built for 20,000, it housed 50,000. On March 22, 1968, eight students occupied the dean's office at Nanterre to protest the arrest of six members of the National Vietnam Committee. They included in their protest their parlous conditions and the hegemony of the academy. The young group's courage became known and the movement escalated. Factory workers, a quarter of whom were only receiving about $20 per month, joined the students in strikes that were "turned into joyous bivouacs in the name of participation." Owing to the use of barricades, the protesters came to control the city of Nantes, and they ran it very well.[33]

The news spread and the movement exploded in enormous numbers.[34] Older men of the resistance movement were amazed at the possibilities ahead. Now raising children of their own, they realized what it meant to have hope after twenty years. Everyone started talking. Groups of people took over lecture halls and held forth on any and every issue, challenging and replying. When they talked sense, the hearers were rapt. If they talked nonsense, they were booed off. The lid of silence had suddenly disappeared, as in all communitas moments. The people knew they actually could make a change. Apathy disappeared and shyness was gone. Graffiti read: *Déjà dix jours de bonheur* (ten days of happiness already).

The communitas effect of an opening was in progress. People were no longer controlled from without, the victims of circumstances. Each one mattered. On May 13, 1968, a million people marched down the streets of Paris. There were all kinds of groups from factories and workplaces—hospital personnel in white coats, railway men, postmen, printers, Metro personnel, metal workers, airport workers, market men, electricians, lawyers, bank employees, building workers, glass and chemical workers, waiters, municipal employees, painters and decorators, gas workers, shop girls, insurance clerks, road sweepers, film-studio operators, busmen, teachers, and workers from the new plastic industries.[35] The million were silent when they passed a hospital, for the sake of the patients, while the nurses waved from the windows. There was respect.

The Sorbonne was suddenly full of free talk, often to do with self management and, particularly, nonselection. Fees and exams were questioned. The people saw the communitas of education in progress—and wherever that is seen, it breeds marvelous scholars. In the yard, a grand piano appeared and all kinds of people came and played on it. They played Chopin and the old cheeky farandole of the French Revolution. The amphitheatre was crowded when they had a business meeting, where anyone could speak: the crowd listened and judged. What they wanted was to restore their little communities to their own ways of democracy and self-management,[36] not to be swamped by bureaucracy. A man of about forty-five, an "old" revolutionary, told of the tremendous possibilities now opening up. He suddenly came out with a memorable phrase: "To think one had to have kids and wait 20 years to see all this...." Old issues of journals, yellowed by the years, were unearthed and often sold, as well as more recent material. Everywhere there were groups of ten or twenty people in heated discussion—people talking about the barricades, about their own experiences, and also about the commune of 1871, and about France in 1936.

Although the events of Paris simply evaporated after two weeks, up through the imposed structures of religion, patriotism, and respect for authority had grown an interest in equality, gender justice, and human rights. The people recognized the difference between sincerity and deceit, genuine communitas and false communitas. They did not like the universities' hold on the principle of selectivity. In communitas there is no ranking.

In the Événements de Mai celebrations there was music and beauty and total freedom of speech, so like the recognizing glances of person to person that Buber described. And what is most interesting is that Buber's picture of true and living democratic organization was fulfilled in the good sense of the assembly scene in the amphitheater.

The Increments. The result of the Événements was better labor laws, a 35 percent raise in minimum wage, a reaffirmation of the forty hour week, a lower retirement age, independent and not government-controlled television, and lower food prices.

The Connecting Thread between Revolutions: Aristide Zolberg's Sense of the Hundred and Twenty Years' Struggle

The political scientist Aristide Zolberg made a remarkable connection between several great revolutionary moments: the February Revolution, the Commune, the Popular Front, the Liberation of Paris, and Les Événements de Mai. He noticed the tradition of revolution that simply would not cease in France—those flashes that he called "moments of madness," living scenes of communitas. He said:

> We know with assurance that they occur, if only because those who experience them are acutely conscious of their unusual state. Speaking

with tongues, they urgently record their most intimate feelings. Furthermore, they are often aware of affinities across time and space with others in similar circumstances. In the Paris of May 1968...for all the commentators, the sensibility of May 1968 triggered off a remembrance of things past. By way of Raymond Aron, in touch with Tocqueville, readers of Le Figaro remembered February 1848; by way of Henry Lefèbvre, French students remembered the Proclamation of the Commune in March 1871. French workers listened to elder militants who spoke of the occupation of factories in June 1936; and most adults relived August 1944, the Liberation of Paris. These connections across one hundred and twenty years establish a tangible set available for analysis.[37]

The evidence contained in this purposely heterogeneous body of testimony is remarkably consistent. Whatever the attitudes of the writers at the time of writing, whatever role they played in the events, whatever their mode of writing, they record intense moments of festive joy, when great outpouring of speech, sometimes verging on violence, coexists with an extraordinary peaceful disposition. Minds and bodies are liberated; human beings feel that they are in direct touch with one another as well as with their inner selves. The streets of the city, its objects, and even the weather take on harmonious qualities. Falsehood, ugliness, and evil give way to beauty, goodness, and truth. Factions and parties appear unreal while personal networks appear strong as steel. The private merges into the public; government becomes a family matter, a familiar affair. Simultaneously...through the medium of collective memories recorded in sophisticated or demotic culture, in historical works or in folklore, human beings connect the moment with others. Liberated from the constraints of time, place, and circumstances, from history, people choose their parts from the available repertory to forge new ones in an act of creation. Dreams become possibilities.[38]

Those who experience these historic moments of communitas, as Zolberg said, are "acutely conscious of their unusual state. Speaking with tongues, they urgently record their most intimate feelings. Furthermore, they are often aware of affinities across time and space with others in similar circumstances."[39] At the beginning, Paine prophetically envisaged American children, thankful in a free world that their parents had created. Not long after, the French revolutionaries had their vision of the oneness of all their people. Later still, the Commune people were proud that their children would no longer live in degradation, and the factory workers discovered they did not have to lie down in the muck of the satanic mills. They were awake and living deeply in the past and in the future. There appears a unity all along the line, from before the liberation of Paris when women first had the vote, on into the Événements and into an age of nonviolent protest and a planetary consciousness. Now, there is hope that this book will engage the reader with what we never realized—the kinship of our present events to what has gone before—and it may suggest that the reader extrapolates onward, to follow where the graph goes off the paper into this developing twenty-first century. We are beginning to see the world as one living network, feeling and hearing its own mutual parts across time and space, recognizing its kinship and its particularized humanity.

In the next chapter, Chapter 7, the history of communitas goes back in time and brings into focus the precursors to the nonviolent movements of modern times. In 1848, the solitary American hero Henry David Thoreau started off a progression of linked social movements around the world, first taken up by the powerful prophet Tolstoy, then Gandhi the liberator, and subsequently Martin Luther King Jr., the creator of social justice. These leaders vowed nonviolence, thereby consciously distinguishing themselves from philosophies that promoted violence, such as Communism, while finding ways to control the merciless stranglehold of empire, corporate business, and capitalism.

Chapter 7

The Communitas of Nonviolence

There is a growing awareness among the people of the world that the power of armed force is of negative value. Large numbers of people hold to the lore of humanism, what it means to be human. What people respect is a kind of compassionate Buddhism, like that of the Dalai Lama—perhaps the most religious person in the world. Love and care for nature is right, a concern for the oppressed is right, and sometimes a willingness to die for these causes without returning a blow in the struggle is right.[1]

What the world discovered, back in the mid-nineteenth century, was a way to attain what is right by means of passive resistance. During the same era as the February Revolution in France, the first seeds of civil disobedience and passive resistance were hatching in America. In order to continue the story of liberation, the tale of communitas in this book goes back in time to Henry David Thoreau's civil disobedience in 1849 and from there continues into the present.

1849: Thoreau and "The Duty of Civil Disobedience"

Thoreau, greatly respected in his own small cabin at Walden Pond, was disengaged from structured life. He would not pay taxes to a government that waged a territorial war and that supported slavery. So he quietly went to jail. His insight was that there is a moral emptiness in government unless it is filled by the actions of citizens on behalf of justice. This corresponds to the democratic philosophy of the Declaration of Independence. In Thoreau's essay "The Duty of Civil Disobedience," he urged the people to drop any respect for a bad government:

> The mass of men serve the state...not as men mainly, but as machines, with their bodies. They are the standing army, and the militia, jailers,

constables, posse comitatus, etc....wooden men...that will serve the purpose as well. Yet such as these even are commonly esteemed good citizens.... They are as likely to serve the devil, without intending it, as God.[2]

Leon Tolstoy (1828–1910) took up Thoreau's essay with its indignant message and published it in Russia. Tolstoy said of the essay that its great merit lay in its clear statement of a person's right to repudiate and refuse in any way to support a government that acts immorally. Tolstoy's own book, written later, *The Kingdom of God is Within You* (1893), was in many respects the Thoreau's essay extended, with instructions to the soldiers in the Russian army to disobey the command to kill.

We can see the strong leading rope of democracy from ancient ages coming unbroken from the past, from Jesus's refusal to change his allegiance from his "Kingdom of Heaven" of the poor and his refusal to accept "all the kingdoms of this world"; through Francisco Suarez's proclamations; down to the Declaration of Independence and the Rights of Man; and so to Thoreau, who taught the duty of civil disobedience. This connection, this rope of democracy, is the strength of the people, and it held fast when Tolstoy read Thoreau's essay. Then from Tolstoy, it reached Gandhi, then Martin Luther King Jr., Martin Buber, Nelson Mandela, and, in time, Aung San Suu Kyi of Burma.

Tolstoy and Nonviolence

I propose we take Tolstoy's call very seriously. He was well aware that in his era he was in a "different place"—he was defending the delicate existence of people's souls. Before this, in 1845, Marx had written alluringly about the possibilities of leisure in a well-ordered industrialized communist system. Tolstoy, on the other hand, in 1902, sixteen years before the Communist revolution, wrote an urgent message about the humanism that had become lost in the capitalist age. It showed the obvious catch in communism:

> Railroads, printing presses, tunnels, phonographs, X-rays and so forth, are very good.... But what is also good—beyond comparison with anything else—are human lives, such as those of which millions are now mercilessly ruined for the acquisition of railways and tunnels, which instead of beautifying life disfigure it.... As long as we do not consider human lives the most sacred of all things—on no account to

be sacrificed...we will always find...means to exploit human lives for the sake of profit.³

This was political—even environmental—and the message is now quite familiar to us. Nevertheless, in 1917, Lenin, the self-drilled positivist, beat the humanists and the nonviolent in the game of politics, and entered Petrograd at the famous Finland Station, where he spoke with stentorian and iron authority and took control of the country.

Nonviolence Versus Intransigence

The spirit of Tolstoy and those who followed him is alive in our own culture. Many of us adhere to nonviolence in our political activities. The principles of Marx and Lenin are wrong. Those principles produced pockets of extreme left-wing militarism and genocide all over the world. The worst result was Hitler's most fearsome state, his "Germany for the *volk*, the people": Nationalsozialismus, National Socialism—that is, Nazism. His prey were the Jews, prosperous and able people. For him, the holocaust was correct. The whole balance of power veered over into governmental military power and became right-wing.

The same murderous attack on the middle class, and with the same ostensible purpose, occurred in Cambodia; in Uganda under Idi Amin, who favored Ugandans over incoming Indian business men; in Kosovo, with Milosevic's pro-Serb ("slave, peasant") policy of "ethnic cleansing"; in the Rwanda massacres, carried out by the lower sub-tribe of Hutus against their enriched Tutsi overlords, in a crazed defense of their democracy.

Contemporary episodes of murder and starvation continue; for instance, suppression of democracy in Burma is still perpetrated by a military junta with a socialist origin. All of these situations basically derive from the Marx/Lenin/Stalin method. This philosophy repudiates the ordinary people's idea of humanism, *ubuntu*, the human heart, with its grand inversions and the consciousness of the sacredness of the people.

The pattern becomes clear. Past inequalities have been the trouble, and there has been little attempt to rectify these, to heal the split populaces, rich and poor; there's no chance for the two sides to sit down together and see the other side as human. Now, the ominous results stare us in the face. All nations need constantly to watch and adjust the economic discrepancies before it is too late.

The new call to nonviolence has been coming from below; it is not a matter of armed enforcement or the controls of government, law and order. It has the quality of a big swing in values, a different way of looking at religion and at the presence of the soul, and a consciousness of what is real happiness.

Gandhi

In Mohandas Gandhi one sees the heroic life of absolute nonviolence. Gandhi's life began in Gujarat, India, in 1869, in a family that could afford to give him an education. In 1888, he went to England to train as a lawyer, and he also studied Christianity, Buddhism, Islam, and with Jains. By 1893, he was working in South Africa. While he was experiencing the bitter taste of racism there, the hinge event of the era occurred.

On a train journey in 1894, Gandhi read Tolstoy's newly published book, *The Kingdom of God Is Within You*, which incited the Russian army, in the name of God, to lay down its arms and become nonviolent. Reading it, his life was changed. He understood the full implications of what his own people called in Hindi *ahimsa*, nonviolence, and saw its enormous power. He was overwhelmed.

He began to practice nonviolence in South Africa. On a trip to Pretoria, he was physically assaulted and refused to press charges. He gathered Indians in South Africa to protest, using the method of nonviolence and love to dissolve the power of the state. He was learning how to alter history.

By January 1908, he came to an understanding of *satyagraha*, the power of truth. Nonviolence combined with the power of truth was unbeatable because of the very nature of things. He spent time in South African jails. He was now launched on the radical protest to which Tolstoy had called him. The two men were friends and correspondents: the one taught the other.[4]

Eventually Gandhi realized that he owed his gift, his conviction, and his energy to the country of his birth, and he returned to India.

1919–1946: Gandhi Leads the Struggle for India's Liberation by Nonviolent Means

In 1915, when Gandhi returned to India, it was a country suffering under British power. But he now carried with him the nonviolent method for achieving independence. This method, differing from those of the American, French, and Russian Revolutions, was directly inspired by Tolstoy's "return evil with good," and also by Gandhi's own religion of Hinduism. On April 13, 1919, in Amritsar, the British fired on 5,000 unarmed people who were demanding independence, killing 1,000. In response, Gandhi organized a countrywide boycott of British cloth, goods, and all institutions, and also a strike, in passive resistance against British injustice toward Indians—always in nonviolence and strengthened by civil disobedience. In 1922, he was arrested and sentenced to six years imprisonment.[5]

For decades, Gandhi added to the power of India's people, practicing long solitary hunger strikes when he needed to reproach his own people for their internal conflicts. He promoted shaming, both of the British and of his own people, reacting with nonviolence whenever he was attacked. For a whole year, he and the people fought the British-imposed Salt Laws, marching to the sea with an enormous peaceful singing throng to harvest the salt in deliberate disobedience of the law. A great scene of communitas. One hundred thousand Indians were jailed. In the 1940s, the British government, after feeling the brunt of many acts of resistance, found itself failing to keep hold of India—the "jewel in the crown" of the British empire—and it began to let go. At this point, the British insisted that Hindus and Moslems must have separate territories, India and Pakistan. Despite his reservations, Gandhi agreed and tried to make the partition easier. All in all, the tyrants were gone in 1947. But on January 30, 1948, Gandhi was assassinated, to the sorrow of most of the world, except Britain.

The Increment. India's Independence

Remembering this event as from England, and as a young woman, I took little notice of the all-India waves of communitas that surrounded Gandhi, nor of the appalling ruthlessness of the British. This was to be expected. I was a Marxist, and there was supposed to be a kind of dialectical inevitability about the India events. Now, seeing an old picture of Gandhi marching to the sea amid the enormous crowd, and seeing the tender love in the eyes of those surrounding him, that old communitas is transmitted to me. Some fond goddess, Shakti, with her loving miracles, was succoring her people. On a later anniversary of Gandhi's death, an Indian follower, Sri Sridharan, gave a memorial speech that tells of the love of the people of India for their liberator. It conveys what kind of man Gandhi was. Furthermore, it shows the next strange step in the path of communitas as it reached other countries—to the black people of America.

Garland of Stories[6]

I am here to talk about a man—to talk about a man, no ordinary man. Toward the end of his life he was honored with the title of Mahatma, Great Soul. A person who identified with the poorest of the poor was a rousing inspiration as a leader to millions—one who loved the very people from whom he was demanding justice and freedom. Great soul, but he would say, "I am just an average man." He studied Christianity in London and very much loved the saying, "Love your enemies"....

You remember how young Gandhi—a young barrister from London—traveled in a train in Africa. He was dapper, all decked out in a suit, holding a first class ticket. But the train inspector threw him out. He said "First class; whites only." After he was roughed up and dumped on the platform, he slowly got up. It was night time. Out of the shadows a man comes out—a white man. "I am a lawyer," he says, "I saw everything—I want to sue that inspector and want to see to it that he is punished." Dusting off his knees and elbows, straightening himself, Gandhi says, "Revenge will do no good.... An eye for an eye makes the whole world blind. Truth is not just speaking the truth. It is that you have aligned your life with it....

For my final story, I am going to speak of Martin Luther King, a great civil rights leader from the South. He never met Gandhi, although he did travel to India after Gandhi had died, and he met with all the great disciples of Gandhi. What is the story of how he came to follow the principles of nonviolence? The connection is through a fellow we hear very little about: Bayard Rustin.[7]

Bayard was a Quaker, an African American activist.... In 1955 he was invited to Montgomery, Alabama, where the historic bus boycott was under way—you may remember Rosa Parks. Bayard provided crucial training and organizational expertise for Dr. King and his colleagues in Montgomery. For seven years he was special assistant to Dr. King. He was later the chief organizer of the March on Washington where Dr. King gave the "I Have a Dream" speech.

On the night Bayard Rustin arrived in Montgomery he passed armed guards at the door of Dr. King's home. Once inside, his first order of business was to ask Dr. King to let go of the guards. Racial tensions were severely high then in Montgomery.

Both sides were armed to the teeth. Violence was likely to erupt at the slightest provocation, sometimes even without provocation. Dr. King argued that the guards were necessary to hold off those who sought to harm them. Bayard spoke of the nonviolence of intent and the nonviolence of the spirit. He quoted Gandhi saying, "There are a hundred causes for which I am prepared to die, but not a single cause for which I am prepared to kill." By daybreak, the two men were still talking nonviolence and strategy of action. That morning Dr. King relieved the armed guards. Later he spoke to everyone in the boycott about unarmed resistance.

As I think about this story, I pray that we all have indomitable courage and unwavering goodwill.

In history and in the stories one can trace a number of communitas features. The processions during the Indian independence movement were full of happiness and song. The people saw their way through their troubles. One notices Gandhi's inversions in the story—giving up fine clothes, becoming poor, forgiving his enemies. Communitas shows the power of the ordinary uncluttered human; Gandhi called it *satyagraha*, which is much the same thing. Thomas Paine called it common sense. Here, Gandhi called himself "just an average man." The principle of nonviolence, "whose property is always to have mercy," is of no use in a rigidly structured life. Nonviolence, mercy, loopholes—they're inversions of the principles of the state and efficient institutions. What is more, Gandhi did not have any barriers between him and the people. This same principle was passed on to Dr. King.

Again, communitas is beyond one's own words. Gandhi said that the words just flowed through him. They were not his but were voiced by another. Gandhi did not "come to" nonviolence—nonviolence came to him, unheralded, without warning, all of a sudden. These are the very lineaments of communitas—similar to the way musicians see their music, and the way people may strive and unexpectedly find themselves in the zone. Gandhi's skill was to align himself with truth, in simplicity, despite all danger. Furthermore, he said, "No one has to look expectantly at another...all are leaders and all are followers."[8] There was no ranking in this communitas.

We see how national barriers are so easily and frequently bypassed—from Thoreau's writings in America, to Tolstoy in Russia, to Gandhi in South Africa and then Gandhi's liberation of India, and back to America and Martin Luther King's nonviolent revolution. However much one nation may be preoccupied with its own affairs, still we have been one world for a long time, and the ethos of nonviolence has impregnated the awareness of many cultures and countries around the planet. What was done from 1955 to 1965 during the civil rights movement in America created its own American-style tradition of nonviolence, one that those of us who are concerned about peace and social justice are striving to develop further.

The Civil Rights Movement in America

In the American civil rights movement, communitas arose among people working for a common cause. Most of us know this story, but let us bring into focus its elements of communitas.

Rosa Parks worked for the National Association for the Advancement of Colored People (NAACP) and the Voters League and was trained by them. She was also tired, she said, tired of being denied the right to vote because of her race.

On the evening of December 1, 1955, she was coming home from work in the bus. She sat down on the bus in the first row of seats in the "colored section," but the bus began to fill and more whites boarded the bus. The driver, J.P. Blake, ordered her to move to the rear. But she would not move. Blake said he would have to call the police. She said, "Go ahead."

When she was arrested she asked the officer, "Why do you push us around?" "I don't know," he replied, "but the law is the law and you're under arrest."

Rosa Parks had no idea she was making history. She relates, "I did not think about the consequences. I chose not to move. When I made that decision, I knew I had the strength of my ancestors with me. When one's mind is made up, this diminishes fear. Love, not fear, must be our guide."[9]

On December 2, Joe Ann Robinson, a professor of English at Alabama State College, created some leaflets announcing a one-day bus boycott on Parks's December 5 court date. Along with the help of two students working overnight, she printed tens of thousands of copies. Many helpers distributed them in the Montgomery area. The result was an overwhelming African American boycott of the bus system. On the day Parks's case was heard, most buses were almost empty.

That night, the religious and political leaders met at the Holt Avenue Baptist Church and formed the Montgomery Improvement Association (later the Southern Christian Leadership Conference). At the church there was a new pastor, a Rev. Martin Luther King Jr.; the assembly appointed him to lead the association. Reverend King was twenty-six years old, about the age of a graduate student. The church was overflowing with thousands of boycotters whose will previously had been paralyzed and dominated by the whites. A new history started to unfold when the young preacher stood up to speak.

> "My friends, we are certainly very happy to see each of you out this evening. We are here this evening for serious business. [Audience:] (*Yes.*) We are here in a general sense because first and foremost we are American citizens. (*That's right.*) We are here also because of our love for democracy (*Yes*), because of our deep-seated belief that democracy transformed from thin paper to thick action (*Yes*) is the greatest form of government on earth. (*That's right.*)
>
> "But we are here in a specific sense because of the bus situation in Montgomery. Just the other day, just last Thursday to be exact, one of

the finest citizens in Montgomery was taken from a bus (*Yes*) and carried to jail and arrested (*Yes*) because she refused to get up to give her seat to a white person. (*Yes, that's right.*) I want you to know this evening that there is no reserved section. (*All right.*) The law, the ordinance, the city ordinance has never been totally clarified. (*That's right.*)

"Mrs. Rosa Parks is a fine person. (*Well—*) Mrs. Parks is a fine Christian person, unassuming, and yet there is integrity and character there. And just because she refused to get up, she was arrested.[10]

[His voice rose] And you know, my friends, there comes a time when people get tired of being trampled over by the iron feet of oppression."

A flock of "Yeses" was coming back at him when suddenly the individual responses dissolved into a rising cheer, and applause exploded beneath the cheer—all within the space of a second. The startling noise rolled on and on, like a wave that refused to break, and just when it seemed that the roar must finally weaken, a wall of sound came in from the enormous crowd outdoors to push the volume still higher. Thunder seemed to be added to the lower register—the sound of feet stomping on the wooden floor—until the loudness became something that was not so much heard as it was sensed by vibrations in the lungs. The giant cloud of noise shook the building and refused to go away. One sentence had set it loose somehow, pushing the call-and-response of the Negro church service past the din of a political rally and on to something that King had never known before.[11]

"There comes a time, my friends," he went on, "when people get tired of being plunged across the abyss of humiliation, where they experience the bleakness of nagging despair. (*Keep talking.*) There comes a time when people get tired of being pushed out of the glittering sunlight of life's July and left standing amid the piercing chill of an alpine November. (*That's right.*) [Applause] There comes a time. (*Yes sir, teach.*) [Applause continues]

I want to say that we are not here advocating violence. (*No.*) The only weapon that we have in our hands this evening is the weapon of protest. (*Yes.*) [Applause] That's all.

"My friends, I want it to be known that we're going to work with grim and bold determination to gain justice on the buses in this city. [Applause]

"And we are not wrong; we are not wrong in what we are doing. (*Well—*) If we are wrong, the Supreme Court of this nation is wrong. (*Yes, sir.*) [Applause] If we are wrong, the Constitution of the United States is wrong. (*Yes.*) [Applause] If we are wrong, God Almighty is wrong. (*That's right.*) [Applause] If we are wrong, Jesus of Nazareth was merely a utopian dreamer that never came down to Earth. (*Yes.*) [Applause] If we are wrong, justice is a lie (*Yes*), love has no meaning. [Applause] And we are determined here in Montgomery to work and fight until justice runs down like water (*Yes*), [Applause] and righteousness like a mighty stream. (*Keep talking.*) [Applause]

"There is never a time in our American democracy that we must ever think we are wrong when we protest. (*Yes, sir.*) We reserve that right. And now we are reaching out for the daybreak of freedom and justice and equality. [Applause]

"And as we stand and sit here this evening and as we prepare ourselves for what lies ahead, let us go out with the grim and bold determination that we are going to stick together. [Applause] We are going to work together. [Applause] Right here in Montgomery, when the history books are written in the future (*Yes*), somebody will have to say, 'There lived a race of people (*Well*—), a *black* people (*Yes, sir*), "fleecy locks and black complexion," (*Yes*) a people who had the moral courage to stand up for their rights. [Applause] And thereby they injected a new meaning into the veins of history and of civilization.' And we're going to do that. God grant that we will do it before it is too late. (*Oh, yeah.*) Let us think of these things." (*Yes.*) [*Applause*][12]

The people flowed out in their thousands to spread the message.

During the next year, the Montgomery Improvement Association coordinated the bus boycott, and the young preacher with his pride and his marvelous voice inspired those who refused to ride the buses.[13] It was during King's work on the boycott that there occurred his meeting with Bayard Rustin referred to earlier. Rustin had studied nonviolence techniques from Gandhi's leaders in India.[14] After meeting Rustin, King read Mahatma Gandhi and it reinforced his insistence that protesters retain the moral high ground. "We must use the weapon of love."[15]

In this manner, the racist arrest of Parks led to the 1956 Supreme Court decision banning segregation on public transportation. The boycott ended over a year after it began. Ms Parks said later: "I found out for the first time in my adult life that this could be a unified society...I gained the strength to persevere in my work for freedom not just for blacks, but for all oppressed people."[16]

The March on Washington

The movement grew. In 1963 at the Lincoln Memorial in Washington in his path-breaking speech to a crowd of over 250,000 on the cause of jobs and freedom for black people, Dr. King said:

> Let us not seek to satisfy our thirst for freedom by drinking from the cup of bitterness and hatred. We must forever conduct our struggle on the high plane of dignity and discipline. We must not allow our creative

protest to degenerate into physical violence. Again and again, we must rise to the majestic heights of meeting physical force with soul force.[17]

In 1965, a fresh movement, for voters' rights, came to the fore. This protest movement also practiced nonviolence. John Lewis—who would later be elected to Congress—and other leaders asked the demonstrators not to fight back against anyone who committed violence against them on the day of their peaceful protest. This was to be a Sunday, a date that is now known as "Bloody Sunday."

The First March from Selma, March 7, 1965

Instigated by the killing of Jimmie Jackson, a black army veteran in Selma, Alabama, organizers decided to arrange a protest in the form of a fifty-four-mile march to the capitol in Montgomery.[18] When the mass of black people started their march, they were singing, "We shall overcome." The long file of people proceeded from Selma along the sidewalk to the Edmund Pettus Bridge, which is still today named for a proslavery Confederate general. There on the bridge, with no outlets on either side, they encountered a barrier of police and state troopers, armed with clubs and tear gas. Some were on horseback and all had orders from Alabama Governor George Wallace to stop the march. The marchers paused for a moment, and then kept walking. The police attacked, firing tear gas into the crowd and severely beating protesters.

> A shrill cry of terror, unlike any that had passed through a TV set, rose up as the troopers lumbered forward, stumbling sometimes on the fallen bodies.... Periodically the top of a helmeted head emerged from the cloud of gas, followed by a club on the upswing. The club and the head would disappear into the cloud and another club would bob up and down.
> *Inhumane.* No other word can describe the motions... My wife sobbing, turned and walked away saying, "I can't look anymore...."[19]

The demonstrators were tear gassed, clubbed, spat on, whipped, trampled by horses, and jeered at. The police "...literally whipped folk all the way back to the church," and Lewis was wounded.[20]

Within forty-eight hours, demonstrations in support of the marchers were held in eighty cities. King and many of the nation's religious and lay leaders flew to Selma. Congress responded to these events, and by the end of the year, in 1965, the Voting Rights Act was signed by President Lyndon Johnson. It was antidiscriminatory and also prohibited literacy tests for voters.

Three years later, on April 3, 1968, Dr. King gave an address at the Church of God in Christ at Memphis and said:

> I just want to do God's will. And He's allowed me to go up to the mountain. And I've looked over. And I've seen the promised land. I may not get there with you. But I want you to know tonight, that we, as a people, will get to the promised land. And I'm happy, tonight. I'm not worried about anything. I'm not fearing any man. Mine eyes have seen the glory of the coming of the Lord.[21]

The next day he was assassinated.

Exactly forty-five years after King's "I Have a Dream" speech in Washington, on August 28, 2008, John Lewis spoke in support of the soon-to-be President Barack Obama at the Democratic National Convention, recalling Dr. King's speech. He too was aware of the importance of what he was saying, and it slowed his words.

The powerful United States of America had become enmeshed with lies and the doctrine of greed. The folks who had been hurt by this doctrine clung to their God and responded with nonviolent acts—and they ultimately rendered racism illegal. Their acts, along with the movements inspired by Tolstoy and Gandhi, were the crowning acts of communitas on behalf of us all. Moreover, Dr. King in his speech at the Holt Avenue Church had brought the *future* into view, just as Paine, in 1776, had put before the new Americans the 120 degrees of change that they had never contemplated before. Communitas jumps the gap into the future. It doesn't know "limit."

The Increments. The changes: in 1956, the Supreme Court banned segregation on public transportation. The Civil Rights Act, passed in 1964, banned racial discrimination in public places, and legislated equal employment opportunities. The Voting Rights Act, signed by Lyndon Johnson in 1965, eliminated literacy tests for voters and prohibited all discrimination in registration and voting.

The Unfolding of the Petals

The gradual swing toward humanism crept into visibility in the words of the folk singers. It is significant that folk music truly came up from *below* in America, in full strength, played in the forties by Woody Guthrie, the son of a cowboy from Okemah in Oklahoma, and Robert (Bob) Zimmerman, or Dylan, as he called himself, using the name of his beloved Welsh poet. He was the son of an upstate Minnesota ironworker. They found that the guitar, a humble instrument, could capture the love of enormous numbers of the young. We heard what these folks had to say in their songs. What exactly was going on? They were like Old Testament prophets. They couldn't be termed dangerous communists. Yet, ultimately, it may be found that they will prove the down-falling of the fat corporations.

Folk music resulted in a communitas of the young that flooded the entire age. Power was hidden in the folk song—the ephemeral but powerful "Blowin' in the Wind." The newly enlightened world of the youth had the corporations heavily sitting on them—but they were *aware*.

So here I back-step in time to catch something growing that was in a class all on its own:

> This land is your land, this land is my land
> From California to the New York island
> From the redwood forest to the Gulf Stream waters
> This land was made for you and me.[22]

[After some of the sweetest most poetic lines in America the voice turns sorrowful.]

> In the squares of the city, in the shadow of a steeple;
> By the relief office, I'd seen my people.
> As they stood there hungry, I stood there asking,
> Is this land made for you and me?
>
> There was a big high wall there that tried to stop me;
> Sign was painted, it said private property;
> But on the back side it didn't say nothing;
> That side was made for you and me.
> —Woodie Guthrie 1940[23]

In the days of Gandhi and Martin Luther King Jr., and in parallel with them, a popular art was flowering in the United States, a spontaneous art using a portable instrument, the guitar.

In the mid-forties to the sixties, this company of popular folk singers and their fans created a cultural genre of communitas music that represented a hurting generation. Ordinary folks were seeing the advance of capitalism upon the fields of America. They saw the automation of factories on the one hand and a greedy class rapidly grabbing all good things such as waterfront real estate, on the other.

What was happening in the songs of the folk singers was a trend toward the human being, simple and good, communitas coming into the light.

Bob Dylan followed, with some inversions:

The Times They Are A-Changin'

...The slow one now
Will later be fast
As the present now
Will later be past
And the first one now
Will later be last....
—Bob Dylan 1962.

For, yes, the times they certainly are a-changin'. This well-known song shows several inversions: loser/winner, activity/inertia, slow/fast, present/past, and the prime one, unashamedly Biblical, "the first will be last."

Dylan, greatly beloved by millions of the young, was singing for the ordinary natural person, the poor, and the sufferers; he also sang the call to discard what was bogus. His song was a call from out of the crowd for change, like the cry of a prophet for the opening of the door. Dylan's voice, the music of real communitas, is still a vital part of our age.

The Chimes of Freedom Flashing[24]

Here's a story inside another Dylan song:

> Far between sundown's finish an' midnight's broken toll
> We ducked inside the doorway, thunder crashing

These are kids caught in a storm they never forgot. Those were thunderbolts, or were they bells?

> Seeming to be the chimes of freedom flashing

Huddled there and looking out—

> Through the wild cathedral evening the rain unraveled tales

—tales of the whole era of the nonviolent struggle for justice and mercy—

> Flashing for the warriors whose strength is not to fight
> Flashing for the refugees on the unarmed road of flight
>
> Dylan's heart went out to those with no help at all—
>
> Tolling for the deaf an' blind, tolling for the mute
> Tolling for the mistreated, mateless mother, the mistitled prostitute
> For the misdemeanor outlaw, chased an' cheated by pursuit
>
> —And a line for us anthropologists, social scientists—
>
> Tolling for the tongues with no place to bring their thoughts
> An' we gazed upon the chimes of freedom flashing.

These lines give me cold chills. Dylan's songs have curious features of communitas. The man stood up and let the songs flow, slowly letting the thoughts flash out when they would, without expression in that pale flawless face. He used the hoarse sounds of his empathy like a chant. And within the dark words there come the flashes.

How is this connected with communitas? He did the only thing he could—he spoke with spontaneity. I learned to pay attention to the look in the corner of his eye when he threaded his way through his performance, to where the flashes of communitas arose. Some spirit permitted him to make a person ache with nostalgia for a bit of real moss, grass, or weeds covering the earth.

In honor of that nostalgia, I present in this part of Chapter 7 stories of nonviolent revolution in our more recent world—as disturbed and bewildered as it is. Such revolutionaries are anxious to keep tender care of fragile human life and yet fulfill their dreams. The gentleness of the stories are a reminder—since we are now living in the very future that their lives led up to—that we can expect to see anything happen at any time, including communitas.

We may find the unexpected in a tale out of the blue, in, for instance, 1989, in Leipzig, Germany. This is a story few have ever heard.

Leipzig in 1989: "Nikolaikirche, Open to All"[25]

Since 1945 and into the eighties, Eastern Germany was known as the German Democratic Republic (GDR) and under the rule of Communist Russian. Those rulers seemed to think that punishing that country by means of leaching it of its wealth—"needed for the glorious Soviets"—would cause the Germans to be humble and penitent about their participation in Nazi ill-doings. A story surfaced about the longing of the people of Eastern Germany for a milder regimen. They ached to be free of the oppressive secret police agency known as the Stasi—to be able to think as they chose, and to be in a world where they could speak freely.

That place of freedom was St. Nicholas's Church in East Germany's Leipzig. In 1989, although this church was under the control of the GDR, it was known as "Nikolaikirche, open to all," for it had become a central meeting place for free conversation. "Nikolaikirche, open to all," became a slogan with a meaning similar to that which stirs the hearts of Americans: "We the people." The very mention of "Nikolaikirche" in early 1989 disturbed the Communists in power, because the Communists believed *they* were the people.

A packed meeting took place every Monday in the church. The nonviolent character of this movement was the attraction. Nikolaikirche is a large, old church, anciently changed to the Lutheran communion. A picture of the angel of peace has pride of place above the altar, a rarity as an altar symbol. To the right of the altar stands a large cross made of rough half-burnt wood brought from Coventry Cathedral in England after it had been bombed by Nazi Germany in 1940. It was presented in friendship by the people of Coventry to Nikolaikirche.

The Monday meetings in this church originally began in the early eighties in the Cold War during the years that folks called the "peace decade," when there were huge demonstrations throughout Western Germany, the Federal Republic, to protest against the arms race. Nevertheless, the arms race continued. The only chance the people of East Germany had to discuss and reflect on this burning issue was at meetings held in churches, because the GDR authorities forbade any secular meetings that they themselves did not sanction. The church meetings were held by peace groups comprised of former "Bausoldaten" ("construction" soldiers), environmental activists, and people interested in third-world issues.

Every Monday from May 8, 1989, onward, the road entries to the church had been blocked by the Stasi. The roads and motorway exits were subject to large-scale checks or were even closed during the prayers-for-peace period. According to the laws at the time, these discussions gave the Stasi an excuse to arrest people, which they did, yet the two thousand seats in the church were not enough for the numbers that wanted to come. In September 1989 the number of arrests climbed.

Thanks to the church venue, many of the Stasi discovered what the Sermon on the Mount really said and also heard prayers for peace for the first time. The windows were decorated with flowers; every night there were numerous lighted candles and songs about fundamental change. What was notable was the feeling of peace that pervaded the place. The peaceful attitude spread to the thousands who gathered at the same time in the dirty squares and streets.

On October 7, which was Remembrance Day, the fortieth anniversary of the GDR, for ten hours uniformed police battered defenseless people who made no attempt to fight back. The police took them away in trucks. Hundreds were locked up in stables in Markkleeberg. The press said it was high time to put an end to the counter-revolution, if necessary by armed force.

Two days later, on October 9, there was a massive show of force by soldiers, industrial militia, police, and plainclothes officers. This time, some 1,000 members of the communist governing Socialist Unity Party (SED) had been ordered to go into the church. Six hundred of them had already filled up the church nave by 2 P.M. Their job was similar to that of the Stasi. What had not been considered was that the Communist party members were now exposed to a gospel about which they did not know the least thing, in a church they were unable to bring into line. They heard Jesus's words—the inversions:

> "Blessed are the poor." And not, "Wealthy people are happy."
> "Love your enemies." And not, "Down with your opponent."
> "Many who now are first will be last." And not, "Everything stays the same."
> "Whoever will save his life will lose it and whoever will lose his life for my sake will find it." And not, "Take care."
> "You are the salt." And not, "You are the cream."

The prayers for peace took place in calm and concentration. Shortly before the end, the bishop gave his blessing, and the leaders appealed for peaceful conduct and dialogue afterward. As the crowd of more than 2,000 people left, they were welcomed by some 10,000 people outside with candles in their hands. Two hands were necessary to carry the candle and protect it from extinguishing, so it was impossible to carry stones or clubs at the same time.

This is what occurred. Troops, military brigade groups, and the police were drawn in among the people and became engaged in conversations. Then they withdrew. That evening, 50,000 people marched unimpeded through the town chanting, "We are the people."

The event united the whole of the GDR—those who wanted to leave the country and those who were curious: regime critics and

Stasi personnel, church and Communist members, Christians and non-Christians. There were no winners and no defeated; nobody triumphed over anyone else; nobody lost face. There was a tremendous feeling of relief.

After that, the nonviolent movement was only necessary for a few weeks before it caused the party and ideological dictatorship to collapse. Not a single shop window was shattered. This was the experience of the power of nonviolence.

Horst Sindermann, a member of the Central Committee of the GDR Communist party, said before his death, "We'd planned everything. We were prepared for everything. But not for candles and prayers."[26]

The effects throughout Eastern Germany were sudden, the talk was rich with inversions, and indications of communitas had appeared—those of the disappearance of rank and the sense of liberation.

The Increments: after a month, on November 9, 1989, the Berlin Wall fell. Eastern Germany regained its autonomy and was reunited with Western Germany.

The Fall of the Berlin Wall

This is the story of a trip from Denmark to Berlin made by Andreas Ramos,[27] an American writer and observer, from November 11 to 12, 1989, thirty-four days after the Nikolaikirche event on October 9. Below, he paints a word picture of the fall of the wall that shows continuous scenes of communitas in the city, all along the line of the crumbling barrier.

> On Thursday, the 9th of November, 1989, and Friday the 10th, the TV and radio in Denmark were filled with news about the events in Berlin. The Berlin Wall was about to fall. On Saturday morning, the 11th of November, I heard on the radio that East Germany was collapsing. At the spur of the moment, I suggested to Karen, my Danish wife, and two Danish friends that we should go to Berlin. Forthwith the four of us packed into my 25 year old Volkswagen bug and we drove off.
>
> It's normally an eight-hour drive from Aarhus, Denmark, to Berlin. After a pizza in Brunswick, we drove towards the German/German border. It was about 11 P.M. at night now. The traffic began to slow down. Soon there was very heavy traffic. No one knew what was going on. People were walking along, all heading towards the border.
>
> We finally reached the border just after midnight. The East German border was always a serious place. Armed guards kept you in your car, watching for attempts at escapes. Tonight was a different

country. Over 20,000 East and West Germans were gathered there in a huge party: as each Trabi—the comical cheapo East German car—came through, people cheered and clapped. The East Germans drove through the applause, grinning, dazed, as thousands of flashbulbs went off. Between lanes of cars, streams of people were walking, talking together. Under one light, a group of musicians were playing violins and accordions and men and women were dancing in circles. Despite the brilliantly cold night, car windows were open and everyone talked to each other.

We met people from Belgium, France, Sweden, Spain, England: they had all left their homes and come to see the wall being torn down. Germans were drunk with joy. Everyone spoke in all sorts of languages and half languages. French spoke German and Spaniards spoke French and everyone spoke a bit of German. We walked for a while with a French family from Belgium: the mother had packed her two young daughters into the car and come to see the German revolution.

At the checkpoint, which is a 25-lane place, people milled around. It was nearly 3 A.M. by now. Everyone had their radios on and everywhere was music. People had climbed up into trees, signs, buildings, everything, to wave and shout. People set up folding tables and were handing out cups of coffee. A Polish engineer and his wife had run out of gas; someone gave us some rope, so we tied the rope to his car and pulled them along.

We walked through the border. On both sides the guard towers were empty and the barbed wire was shoved aside in great piles. The East German guard asked if we had documents. I handed him my Danish cat's vaccination documents, in Danish. He waved us through. We drove along, listening to the radio. The only thing on was Berlin. There were reports that at one point in the wall, the crowd had begun to tear down the wall. They had succeeded in carrying away a 3-meter-tall slab.

We arrived in Berlin at 4:30 A.M., first to Brandenburgerplatz, where the statute of Winged Victory stands atop a 50-meter column. Over 5,000 people were there. We left the car and began to walk through a village of television trucks, giant satellite dishes, emergency generators, coils of cables, and tents. Cameramen slept under satellite dishes. At the wall, West German police and military were lined up to prevent chaos. On top of the wall, lined up at parade rest, stood East German soldiers with their rifles. Groups of West Germans stood around fires that they had built. No one knew what was going on.

After a while, we walked to Potsdammer Platz. Nearby was the mound that was the remains of Hitler's bunker, from which he commanded Germany into total defeat. We talked to Germans and many said that the next break in the wall would be here. Perhaps 7,000 people were pressed together, shouting, cheering, clapping. We pushed through the crowd. From the East German side we could hear the sound of heavy machines. With a giant drill, they were punching holes in the wall. Every time a drill poked through, everyone cheered. People shot off fireworks and emergency flares and rescue rockets. Many were using hammers to chip away at the wall. There were countless holes. At one place, a crowd of East German soldiers looked through a narrow hole. We reached through and shook hands. They couldn't see the crowd so they asked us what was going on and we described the scene for them. Someone lent me a hammer and I knocked chunks of rubble from the wall, dropping several handfuls into my pocket.

Everything was open: restaurants, bars, discos, everything. Yesterday over two million East Germans had entered Berlin. The radio reported that over 100,000 were entering every hour. With Berlin's population of three million, there were over five million people milling around in delirious joy celebrating the reunion of the city after 21 years.

We left our car in front of the Church of Remembrance, the bombed-out ruins of a church left as a memorial to the victims of the war. We walked into a bar. Nearly everything was sold out. A huge crowd was talking and laughing all at once. We found a table. An old woman came up and asked if we were Germans. We said no, Danish, and invited her and her family to our table. We shared chairs and beer. They were East Germans, mother, father, and daughter. She worked in a factory, her husband was a plumber, and the daughter worked in a shop. They told us about the chaos of the last few weeks. The family had chased a cat in an alley and they had eaten a dinner of bananas, a luxury for them. The father was very happy at the idea of being able to travel. He wanted to go to Peru and see Machu Picchu and then to Egypt and see the pyramids. They had no desire to live in the West. They knew about unemployment and drug problems. Their apartment rent was $2 a month. A bus ticket cost less than a penny.

At 7 A.M. or so, we left and headed back to the Potsdammer Platz. Everything was out of control. People were blowing long alpine horns which made a huge noise. There were fireworks, kites, flags and flags and flags, dogs, children. The wall was finally breaking. The cranes lifted slabs aside. East and West German police had traded caps. To get a better view, we scampered up a nine-foot wall. People helped each other; some lifted, others pulled. All along the building, people poured up the wall. At the Berlin Wall itself, which is 3 meters high, people had climbed up and were sitting astride. The final slab was moved away. A stream of East Germans began to pour through. People applauded and slapped their backs. A woman handed me a giant bottle of wine, which I opened and she and I began to pour cups of wine and hand them to the East Germans. Packed in with thousands, I stood at the break in the wall. Above me, a German stood atop the wall, at the end, balanced, waving his arms and shouting reports to the crowd. With all of the East Germans coming into West Berlin, we thought it

COMMUNITAS OF NONVIOLENCE 131

was only fair that we should go to East Berlin. A counterflow started. Looking around, I saw an indescribable joy in people's faces. It was the end of the government telling people what not to do; it was the end of the Wall, the war, the East, the West. If East Germans were going west, then we should go east, so we poured into East Berlin.[28] Around me, people spoke German, French, Polish, Russian, every language.

Near me, a knot of people cheered as the mayors of East Berlin and West Berlin met and shook hands. From some houses, someone had set up loudspeakers and played Beethoven's ninth symphony: *Alle Menschen werden Bruder.* All people become brothers. On top of every building were thousands of people.[29] Berlin was out of control. There was no more government, neither in East nor in West. The police and the army were helpless. The soldiers themselves were overwhelmed by the event. They were part of the crowd. Their uniforms meant nothing. The Wall was down.

This account gives what mere words of praise and wonder do not: this is the panorama of a city in glory, at one with itself, in a fervor of surprised *knowledge* of itself—a whole at last. The city is just happy! First, there is the cheerful ironic tone, actually joyous, while dwelling particularly on such items as the popularly known symbol of cheap communism, the Trabi. Throughout the story, the writer revels in the incongruity of the entire scene. There are people milling about and talking out of car windows and engaging everywhere. The great "mix" is an obvious feature—the mix of many European nations and their languages. It was a Pentecostal scene of all languages—the "no ranking" of communitas. No military power made itself felt; on the contrary, a joy was felt each time the giant drills poked their way through the wall—"We reached through and shook hands." The prime symbol was the destruction of a physical barrier between human and human—the wall. People sat on it, symbolically and physically putting it beneath them. Food and drink were shared.

This was a glorious natural communitas, the falling away of barriers, a liberation like heaven. It was a scene almost beyond words.

Next, we transport to another part of the world, to South Africa, and the date is April 27, 1994—a time of great communitas. This was the fruition of the black people's long struggle for democracy—the first general election after the people's liberation. Nearly twenty million people voted.

In 1990, Nelson Mandela had emerged from jail a free man. He had been imprisoned since 1962 when the American CIA falsely engineered his arrest and trial as a Communist.[30] Mandela believed in nonviolence; he, too, found Gandhi a source of inspiration. At the first general election after his return, South Africa saw many scenes of emotion—those of a people awakening from a past of subjection that had lasted for 342 years, since the coming of the Dutch in 1652. Now the people in lines waiting their turn at the polls realized for the first time, it was they who would decide the future of their country.

Miracle in Natal: Revolution by Ballot Box

The following account is told by Alan Thorold, an anthropologist teaching at the University of KwaZulu Natal, with accounts from four other voters.[31]

> Nelson Mandela's peaceful revolution in South Africa is potentially as important an event for the end of the twentieth century as the Russian revolution was for its beginning. A world which has been racked by division, war, and endless confrontation at every level has been offered an alternative vision, one of co-operation and consensus, the politics of affection rather than opposition.
>
> The Province of Natal (now KwaZulu-Natal) was further from consensus than any other, owing to the brutal war which was waged for several years between supporters of the Inkatha party in Natal and the ANC [African National Congress]. Then, eight days before the election date, Buthelezi, the head of Inkatha, was persuaded to take part. The transition from war to peace was virtually instantaneous. Even more remarkably, Mandela secured the agreement of his ANC followers to an Inkatha victory in a province which they were convinced they had won. When it came to the election, one woman said she voted for the ANC at the national level and for the IFP [Inkatha Freedom Party] in Natal because she did not want Buthelezi to come away from the election empty handed.
>
> It was a moment that was filled with wonder and grace, a time of dreams and wishes and miracles. After so much brutality, the spirit of the election emerged as something that transformed us all. The event itself had the substance of a miracle. For most of us the transition to democracy in South Africa was in the realm of the unthinkable.

Seeing Heaven's Door Open

Ntombikayise Shangase of Bethlehem in the Valley of a Thousand Hills
> When Nelson Mandela came out of prison I was more than excited. It was like seeing heaven's door open. To me Mandela was like a redeemer without any weapon, offering himself. He looked very old but our eyes and trust were on him. Silently we were begging him to help us. Talks began. My eyes and ears were open. The election campaign began. Everybody was excited. I was dancing and singing.

My family joined me in the celebration—and of course our neighbors. It was like New Year's Eve. We were going to start a new life. I knew Mandela was the next president.

About eleven in the morning we were standing in a very long line. Not even one person gave up and it was hot, really hot. Where I voted there was not a single person who did not look happy, even though there was only one tree for shade. Nobody seemed to notice that, for we kept encouraging one another.

When I got in to the polling booth I did what I had to do with great excitement which I cannot describe. We talked freely about who we voted for after we gathered outside. Most of my friends voted the ANC. We took a bus home that was free of charge.

The Old Man and the Smile

Nozipho Vilakazi of Edendale

As I walked out of my yard heading for the polling station my unsteady legs could not coordinate their movement—not due to the fact that I was weak but I was totally ignorant about the procedures at the polls. I did not know what I was going to do at the polling station. Fear had taken control of me but I did not want to expose that to my children, as they told me that my vote would bring about a good life for us and that was my greatest concern in life. I took up my walking stick and headed for the polling station. I could see some policemen and soldiers and I started to feel threatened thinking about the violence in the area. One young boy took me by the hand and told me that if I had any problems I should let him know. He escorted me to a table where a white lady was sitting. She smiled at me, and the young boy told me to give her my dompas, my papers. Never in my life have I seen kindness and warmth, and confidence started to spring up in me. With my imperfect eyesight I called the voting officer and I said the old man's name. He politely took me towards a bright booth in the hall and at last there I saw my man and without wasting time ticked inside the space next to the old man's kind smile. I asked what next and was told that I could go home. I was very happy as I came out of the hall with my dompas in the air. Happy because I've taken part in the elections. I shouted to my God to take me as I've done my work.

Three Stars Shining

Benzangani Machi of Nqabeni

During the election day, as early as six o'clock, there was already a long queue in the polling station. This was not what I had expected. I felt that it was up to each individual to either liberate or betray the nation. When I entered the polling station for the first time my heartbeat started to strike hard as if I had done something wrong, and my hands were trembling. As I entered I was struck by blackout and for the first few seconds I could not identify the political party easily. By that time I felt like collapsing because my heartbeat was striking much harder and at the same time I was perspiring a lot. It was just after a few seconds that I started to cool down. As I voted I made sure there was nobody who could see what I voted for.

As I went home I was filled with pride and confidence. What I noticed from the first day of the elections is the fact that the violence in our area and in Natal as a whole decreased greatly. This was very surprising to me.

One of the Heroines of African Liberation

Saraphina Ndlovu of Umlazi

I thought of all the people that had died for the struggle and felt an even greater urge to go out and vote for them, for myself, for my children, their children, the whole Nation, and for the Almighty. With tears in my eyes it was touching to see old people, some in wheelchairs and stretchers, all being ferried to the polling station. It was like the promised day, when Jesus would come back, and he had finally come. Once there I quickly made up my mind. Mandela and his Congress deserved all the credit.

What I did wouldn't directly benefit me, but would benefit my children in turn and, God knows, maybe one day I will be called one of the heroines of African liberation.

Thorold's account concluded, "Whatever happens in the future, that moment of quiet revolution when racial domination was overturned was a precious achievement for all humanity."[32] One can sense the strong communitas in this event; some of the new voters could hardly believe their luck. An election? It was unthinkable. It was a miracle. There was no ranking, no strong sense of political rivalry. Mandela allowed the IFP more votes to encourage them. This was *ubuntu*, African human-kindness. The man who experienced the blackout moment felt the strong individualism implicit in the election. Voters felt they had a responsibility as individuals to hit on some mysterious truthful candidate. From my anthropological work, I have learned that such extreme individualism is not a normal African experience; it is frightening, like witchcraft. Being African is social. As in communitas, Africans are rooted communally—one lives because others live. The lonely person is a tragic person. In one village folktale, a lonely grandmother is heroically saved from Giant Chishimukulu by her grandson. The message of the story is that she should never have had to live on her own.

Westernized African philosophers often start their theories with "the individual." But Desmond Tutu said in 2008:

> One of our sayings in our country is *ubuntu*—the essence of being human. *Ubuntu* speaks particularly about the fact that you can't exist as a human being in isolation. It speaks about our interconnectedness. You can't be human all by yourself, and when you have this quality—*ubuntu*—you are known for your generosity.
> We think of ourselves far too frequently as just individuals, separated from one another, whereas you are connected, and what you do affects the whole world. When you do well, it spreads out; it is for the whole of humanity.[33]

The Zulu say, "*Umuntu ngumuntu ngabantu*" (a person is a person through persons). Just as a person becomes a person through the natural process of living with and for other people, so, when a person dies, each becomes an ancestor spirit. They will still be with and for other people—they are not gone. The *ubuntu* of an African village literally means, "We-the-people-ness." With *ubuntu,* people are naturally welcoming, hospitable, warm, and generous, sharing their food, as Mandela put it. You're glad when others do well, sorry for those who don't, and easy in yourself. And you know when *ubuntu* is absent.

The woman voter who wanted to be a heroine of the African liberation wept, voting for the people, for her children, and for their children. Thomas Paine, too, long ago, had appealed to the colonized Americans to bequeath to their children something worthwhile. Children have a curious spirituality here, throughout the unfolding of the history of revolution. We do it for the children. The communitas running through the heart of the revolutions has this curious knitted-together character.

The Increments. The establishment of a precedent, another incremental shift: the first general election after the people's liberation, held on April 27, 1994. The results for the ANC were 62.6 percent; for the (white) National Party (NP), 20 percent; and for Buthulezi's IFP in the Natal area, 10.5 percent. After the election, the ANC, the NP, and the IFP shared executive power, with Nelson Mandela as president.

9/11: A Scene of Communitas, Harvard Yard

On the late afternoon of the tragic destruction of New York City's twin towers, part of the Pentagon, and the airplanes that had caused the crashes, September 11, 2001, I sat on the steps of the Memorial Church in Harvard Yard and watched. Between the steps and the Widener Library is a space almost as big as a football field. It was packed. Rev. Bryan Hehir, dean of the Harvard Divinity School, led a meeting, with clerics from the Christian communions, from Judaism, Buddhism, and Islam, who came forward and called for no revenge on Islamic people for the events of that morning. The whole company assented.

Shortly after this gathering, Hehir was no longer dean of the Harvard Divinity School.

Later we heard that similar meetings had happened all across the country at 140 colleges and universities—without much media coverage. There were some public calls for tolerance, for seeking a new way, but the old ways prevailed. And subsequently, there was revenge. war and the resulting victimization of many innocent people.

The Living Wage Protest, University of Virginia, 2006

The basic tenets of human rights instruct all nations to adhere to the principle that one's labor should be compensated with a fair wage. Where this principle is not respected, campaigns arise in protest. Campaigners sometimes take up the task of nonviolent civil disobedience when there is no other way to emphasize the message.

Behind the scenes at the University of Virginia, unnoticed by faculty, the student body, and many sectors of the administration, the university was not paying its lowest-paid workers enough, and poverty was the result. Those who were aware of this knew they ought to bring it into the open. But their pleas went unnoticed by the higher administration, so a campaign began to form, the Campaign for a Living Wage. The campaigners kept seeking a solution to the problem of poverty, but they were obstructed by the higher administration at every turn.

The decision was made to mount a protest that would include civil disobedience. Such a path can be hazardous and dangerous, as Martin Luther King Jr. found in the fifties when he and others such as Rosa Parks began to train in the art of this kind of protest. The training included using care and good judgment, both in behavior and instinctive reactions—the way of firmness and well-nigh saintly gentleness that is the nonviolent way. In Virginia in 2007, students, ready to enact the protest when the time was ripe, began to volunteer for this training.

Martin Luther King Jr. taught that the philosophy and practice of nonviolence has six basic elements:

> First, nonviolence is resistance to evil and oppression. It is a human way to fight.
>
> Second, it does not seek to defeat or humiliate the opponent, but to win his/her friendship and understanding.
>
> Third, the nonviolent method is an attack on the forces of evil rather than against the persons doing the evil. It seeks to defeat the evil and not the persons doing the evil and injustice.
>
> Fourth, it is the willingness to accept suffering without retaliation.
>
> Fifth, nonviolent resisters avoid both external physical and internal spiritual violence—they not only refuse to shoot but also refuse to hate their opponents. The ethic of real love is at the center of nonviolence.
>
> Sixth, the believer in nonviolence has a deep faith in the future, and the forces in the universe are seen to be on the side of justice.[34]

The training has its own style and philosophy, interlaced with communitas.[35] The Virginia students learned to help one another build the sense of community, solidarity, vision, discipline, and organization that they would need to sustain the practice of nonviolence.[36] They got to know each other and felt their affinity. Of the seventeen in the training, two of them were my own students. They learned what to expect from police, officials, other people in the action, and themselves. They learned that the strength of nonviolence would come from their willingness to take personal risk without threatening other people.

"Get your opponent talking and listen to what s/he says. Encourage him/her to talk about what s/he believes, wishes, and fears. Don't argue but at the same time don't give the impression you agree with assertions that are cruel or immoral. The listening is more important than what you say—keep the talk going and keep it calm."[37]

They were trained in arrest, courthouse, and jail procedures, for which they organized into support groups. On the occasion of actual arrest, the protesters might decide to show noncooperation by going limp or refusing to participate in arraignment during arrest—keeping all together in this and always communicating with the human beings behind the helmets, uniforms, and roles. They would talk to the police and perhaps befriend the prison guards.[38]

Wende Marshall, an African American professor of anthropology at Virginia, was a major figure in the campaign. On Wednesday,

April 12, she was outside the Madison Hall administration building with the crowd of supporters. They all took hands; there were enough of them to circle right around the building. She related, "It beautifully expressed the communitas. It was an amazing moment, the best moment at the University of Virginia—transcendent." When Wende told me this story I hugged her.

"We *have* to love," she said.[39]

The next day, the seventeen students entered and occupied the administration building. Wende went with them and was arrested for trespassing. The students stayed until the evening of Saturday, April 15. In spite of their messages to the president of the university inviting discussion, there was no sign of rapprochement.Later, my student Lauren Jones shared her videotape of the events and told my class, a seminar on communitas and sociality, what had happened. She said, "That evening, Saturday April 15, right before the arresting, when we knew it was going to happen, we all went into a circle holding hands, and we faced outward. It was communitas! We could feel the heat of each other's bodies. One current went through the ring, through all the people at the same time. It was *intense*, vivid. Then we were separated by the police, and we all went limp."

I took Lauren's hand and with my other hand enacted pulling the two hands apart. "Do you mean, like this?" I asked."No," she said, "they *wrenched* us apart, and it dislocated our arms." On the videotape, I had seen her crying when this took place.

> At this moment in the classroom, with her and my other students, we cried together.
> She went on, "I haven't thought about it much since. I feel guilty. But you have to go on with your life. I've a pit in my stomach right now, remembering it. We had been really, really connected—and then this bad moment, the hands put on to separate us."

Lauren told us how the student Kevin Simonwitz, one of the seventeen, had fared in the actions by the police, at that swift and terrifying moment. The police had bodies lying on the floor. One of the police seized Kevin's arm and gave it a mighty tug, in the wrong direction. Kevin was in agony from the pain and stiffened involuntarily. The officer felt the arm move and said, "He's resisting me." He docketed this as evidence of resisting arrest. Another cop stumbled over a couch leg and broke it. This was put down as vandalism by the students.[40]

On Monday, May 22, 2006, the courthouse was crowded with supporters. The seventeen students were found not guilty of trespassing because the police had been faulted in their actions—they had not given sufficient warning. Wende's charge was dropped, but she had notice to leave the department of anthropology—she was fired.

Implicit in small-scale efforts such as the Living Wage Campaign is a potential for a politics of communitas, and that potential is growing. It could be one of watchfulness. It was the threatening state that closed around the protestors, and it was academia that halted generous political moves by threatening jobs. Political communitas is not safe; it is the nature of communitas to break out and flourish, because the objective of small-scale face-to-face politics is precisely not the dictatorship of the proletariat nor the dictatorship of anyone; the objective is for little human communities to be honored for what they are, by means of their simple humanness, together in friendship and courage. And it is in this manner that many of these little groups claim our cooperation. It is what Francisco Suarez saw in the sixteenth century.

The Increment. After a year, another small incremental shift was achieved: the minimum wage at the University of Virginia was raised to $10.14 per hour.

Victor Turner's analyses of local level politics peopled by named personalities was shared by small branching combinations of groups.[41] Turner found the same view in Martin Buber. Turner and I were interested in the fate of communitas as it manifested itself in social life. In *The Ritual Process*,[42] Turner noted the joy of pristine small-group communitas in Buber's idea of a kindly small-scale society. We can see a current example of this on the Internet, in the exponential effect of the rapid coming together of groups akin to Buber's ideas of organic growth. Such interactions show how humans humanize technology. Technology does not necessarily dehumanize humans.[43]

Turner quotes Buber in a passage on "the organic commonwealth," and here I paraphrase Buber's quote slightly. It describes what a true extended community might be like:

...an organic commonwealth, built out of small and even smaller communities. Only such commonwealths can join together to form a shapely and articulated human race. Those in them use great spiritual tact to inform the relationship between centralism and decentralism, with the constant and tireless weighing and measuring of the right proportion between them, true to the processes of organic growth, preserving the concreteness of the relationship even in the larger social units. If the authorities responsible for the drawing and re-drawing of lines of demarcation keep an alert conscience, the relations between the base and the apex of the power-pyramid will be very different from what they are now.... There will have to be a system of representation, too; but it will not, as now, be composed of the pseudo-representatives of amorphous masses of electors but of representatives well tested in the life and work of the communes. The represented will not, as they are today, be bound to their representatives by some windy abstraction, by the mere phraseology of a party program, but concretely, through common action and common experience.[44]

"Buber's phraseology," commented Turner, "belongs to the perennial speech of communitas, not rejecting the possibility of structure, but conceiving it merely as an outgrowth of direct and immediate relations between integral people."[45] It is this vision of Turner's (and before him, that of Sartre about the natural origin of structure) that has influenced my picture of nature, communitas, and nonviolence in this chapter.[46]

There exists a direct link between Thoreau and Buber. In a passage on Thoreau's *The Duty of Civil Disobedience*, Buber said,

> I read it with the strong feeling that here was something that concerned me directly.... It was the concrete, the personal element, the "here and now" of this work that won me over. Thoreau did not put forth a general proposition as such; he described and established his attitude in a specific historical-biographic situation. He addressed his reader within the very sphere of this situation common to both of them in such a way that the reader not only discovered why Thoreau acted as he did at that time but also that the reader—assuming him of course to be honest and dispassionate—would have to act in just such a way whenever the proper occasion arose, provided he was seriously engaged in fulfilling his existence as a human person.
>
> The question here is not just about one of the numerous individual cases in the struggle between a truth powerless to act and a power that has become the enemy of truth. It is really a question of the absolutely concrete demonstration of the point at which this struggle at any moment becomes man's duty *as man*.[47]

Thus, in the thinking of Thoreau, Buber, and Turner, one sees an awareness of truth, real communitas, false communitas, and the difference between natural and toxic structure. In Turner's terms, the sense of the antinomies "antistructure" and "structure" is sharpened in capitalism through the awareness of the nature of the state and its ever-present temptation toward control for the sake of control. The state holds the conviction that communitas, a sentiment it covets, can be created by means of law, whether that based on Marxism or by such developments as neoconservatism. But communitas cannot be created. The modern state can at best protect it, set up the conditions for it to flourish, and leave it to itself. Otherwise the nature of the state will produce false communitas.

Along with the political vision, there is, as we have seen, a long and sacred tradition of peace-loving from before the biblical stories to modern nonviolent movements. The power of the weak shines out. The willingness to suffer also comes down clearly through the stories of the multiple French revolutions and the people's consciousness of their connections with one another.

In Chapter 6, communitas entered the great Événements of Paris—the true feeling, a true phenomenon. At the Événements, there was the vision of the piano, played in the yard amidst the pressing crowds;[48] there existed a spirit of which we see flashes. In such eras, we may find communitas, running wild.

But concerning the crimes of Stalin, the Myanmar generals, the Pol Pot killers, Milosevic and his racial cleansing, how does one achieve justice? The answer is: very civilly. One disobeys without violence, in passive resistance, in weakness, in the name of God or Buddha or anything sacred—with love. I watched a video on the Burma demonstrations, and saw the people mass around the humble marching monks dressed in red, hugging close to them in their defense. The people held hands all down the lines beside them, protecting their holy men from the armed police of Rangoon. I saw the urgency and care of the crowd, as if they were rescuing people in a disaster; I saw communitas in action.

As I wrote these two chapters on communitas in history, I participated in moments of déjà vu, seeing the past in the present and sensing echoes and resonances. The theme plays on, with the vision of the future child that draws us toward it, although it does not yet exist. That vision of hope for the future is itself the energy source of the revolutions through history, revolutions that shape themselves for the human rights of the unaccommodated human being and its unpredictable communitas. This becomes, paradoxically, a tradition of the new.

Finally—all comes down to rest like a flock of doves, to the communitas of nature.

Chapter 8

The Communitas of Nature

Nature doesn't "do" pride. Nature will do all kinds of things for those who listen.[1]

Anthropology is learning a better way of looking at the nature/culture dyad than the twentieth century version that implies humanity's fear of nature, the power of culture over nature, and hostility between them. There is a way of framing existence that addresses the respect we have learned for nature and the mystery of our sense of it. Nature not only comprises humanity, living things, and objects but also the way human beings act in producing the richness of their culture. It is their nature to do so, and therefore nature *includes* culture. Furthermore, the evidence of humanity's wide community of spirits and the consciousness of them that appears among humans are coming to be accepted. There are spirits, shamanic helpers, angels, and gods, and they have talked to people or had effects on them. I can have a sense of my soul. This is not outside of anthropology. Neither, then, are these things outside of nature, because I am biological, and we who feel the spiritual are flesh and blood. The body is made that way. Let us try out the thought that the spirits outside ourselves are part of the world, open to anthropology, and also, therefore, are part of nature—that is, if we dare to expand our ideas further.

Thus, this chapter entails the removal of previous theoretical distinctions between culture and nature, for a start. For some, these distinctions are on their way out, but impaired Western attitudes of mind are still strong. They still confront an obdurate nature that ought to be subdued, that ought to respond to our will, and become tidy and preferably insect- and bacteria-free.

The way we have been looking at nature is not natural. Among theologians, a similar point of view declares heaven to be separate from earth. The way we have separated God from fallen nature is even less friendly; it is pathological.[2]

All the while, we have seen communitas coming up from below, fresh and active. It occurs in wide ranges of experience, and now in this chapter we recognize it in the very environment. It is in the universe. Science agrees that there are certain affinities out there, even chemical ones, among oxygen, hydrogen, and carbon, for instance.

"The Soul of All the Worlds"

> There is an active principle alive
> In all things, in all natures, in the flowers
> And in the trees, in every pebbly stone
> That paves the brooks, the stationary rocks.
> The moving waters, and the invisible air.
> All beings have their properties which spread
> Beyond themselves, a power by which they make
> Some other being conscious of their life,
> Spirit that knows no insulated spot,
> No chasm, no solitude; from link to link
> It circulates, the Soul of all the worlds.[3]
> —William Wordsworth 1797–1800

Wordsworth was pointing to the truth, step by step—to the distinct form of the communitas of nature.

The power of the land was also experienced by the anthropologist Henry Stephen Sharp, who revealed how the Chipewyan sense their land, the northern Canadian tundra. Sharp, who married into the tribe, has internalized their sense of mystical participation with the land. He describes

> ...the people's awareness of its beauty and of its bounties. It is a pervasive aspect of the sense of place held by a people living in an active sensory and aesthetic interaction with their world....[4]
>
> They exist in a constant communication with the living beings surrounding them, a communication intensified by an order of magnitude every time they move more than few hundred feet away from their camps. Their universe is animate and filled with sound. The ice sings to those who travel upon it; the snow has its own songs to reflect its temperature and moisture content; the ground underfoot speaks with the passage of animate beings; and the muskegs protest the intrusion of a footfall. The plants, the lakes, the streams, the wind, and the animals, sometimes even the rocks and the earth itself, engage in constant communication with those who choose to listen.[5]

This is the natural state of affairs. It is part of Sharp's before-and-after account of this experience of awareness—first, this passage about the people's own habitual feel for the land; then the change when a posse of Royal Mounted Canadian Police arrive, having mistakenly suspected conflict and criminal assault in the small Chipeweyan encampment. Sharp describes how the old awareness winks out, replaced by the cold shadowy world the police brought with them.

> I was suddenly struck by waves of disorientation. The entire world in which I was standing...became out of alignment....The rich and fecund landscape was noticeably dryer and harsher....Grays predominated where had been rich dark green. The very colors of the world had bleached. Fewer birds were singing, their singing was thinner, as though most of the overtones were absent. What had been a background symphony was now an unorchestrated and disjointed series of individual performances. A presence that had been there was no longer there.[6]

Both Wordsworth and Sharp knew of this membrane between the visionary and the banal. They had a sense of alignment with ordinary community life that was in tune with the interdependency of nature.

South of the tundra, on the South Dakota reservation, the villages are hardly more than a scatter of tar-paper shacks, rusty house trailers, disintegrating log cabins, and toppling privies.[7] Some of the people even live in abandoned auto bodies. The far countryside, on the other hand, consists of beautiful prairie meadows and bluffs that support horses and white-faced cattle. Richard Erdoes, who collaborated with Lame Deer on the book *Lame Deer,* tells of his first experience of South Dakota:

> Before me stretched an endless ocean of hills, covered with sage and prairie grass in shades of silver, subtle browns and ochres, pale yellows and oranges. Above all this stretched the most enormous sky I had ever seen. Nothing in my previous life had prepared me for this scene of utter emptiness which had come upon me without warning. I stopped the car and got out. There was emptiness of sound, too. The calls of a few unseen birds only accentuated it. I found myself overwhelmed by a tremendous, surging sensation of freedom, of liberation from space. I experienced a moment of complete happiness....I kept singing all the way until we hit our campsite.[8]

Despite their poverty, the Oglala of South Dakota have a sense of the "Great Spirit," *Wakantanka.* The Great Spirit is with them always; his power is seen in the thunder, in the eagles, and in the mountains.

Erdoes records how, when Lame Deer was young, he asked a medicine man, "Tell me about the Great Spirit." "He is not like a human being, like the white god," said the medicine man. "He is a power. That power could be in a cup of coffee. The Great Spirit is no old man with a beard." This answer made the young Lame Deer happy. Lame Deer gradually learnt how to sense *wakan*, the power, as his people did.[9]

Communitas with the land is a recognizable, palpable concept. Even when I merely describe around it, it sets off affirmation.

I began experiencing the communitas of nature without knowing what it was. This was in 1939 when I worked on a farm, with cows and the smell of dairy milk, green grass, and mud. Cows were warm and peaceful to milk at 5:30 A.M., while they munched hay and cow cake. In the reality of the farmyard, my memory of the English painter John Constable, the equivalent of Wordsworth in art, came peacefully in. Many times I brooded over picture postcards showing his magical canvasses. In daily life his scenes appeared along the hedgerows and particularly in the form of an ash tree that grew a little north of the farm. Its leaf clusters waved in hypnotic beauty—just as forty years later in Sri Lanka I saw the clusters of the Bo tree in Ceylon wave. I would walk past this ash tree and then come back and stand and look at it again. It had a presence that spoke to me.

We take these details seriously. The presences are real spirits: *kami* in Japan may inhabit a huge rock, or a great hero or artist, or even the sea; the *inua* in the Arctic is the spirit in all of nature; the *akishi* in Africa are people, the strongest spirits—their own attentive dead, the ancestors; and so on, in many other languages. They have real purposes for the soul. This is also true for the animals with which we interact. My conversation with a friend from Point Hope, Alaska, elaborates this point.

The Animals and Global Warming

I had news from Point Hope, Alaska, on June 17, 2007.[10] Quite by surprise, at 11:40 P.M., Niguq and her husband, called, waking me from sleep. It was 7:40 P.M. there, four hours earlier. Though it had been fourteen years since I had seen them, far on the north slope of Alaska at Point Hope, their familiar voices filled me with joy. Jeff said, "Hullo, *Edie!* Happy birthday," in his Native American voice I love so much.

"Jeff! How are you?" I was excited. I sat up in bed to hear that familiar voice better, that hesitant voice with eagerness in it. "How's Nijuq?"

"Niguq's quite professional now. Though she's aching, tired. They've been boating." That is, they'd been out in boats among the floating ice catching the seals. Niguq had been cutting up ugruk, the bearded seal, meat to hang outside to dry.

He said, "Andrew [his son] and Her [Andrew's wife] have got their own boat. Andrew was out this year after whales."

What this means to the family! Andrew, who as a teenager in 1991 got into trouble for fighting is now a whaling captain, an *umialik*, the owner of a sixteen-foot whaling boat. When Andrew came home after his trouble, Niguq and the others worked on the school computer and created a huge paper banner that said WELCOME HOME ANDREW. They strung it across the entrance of the house. Back to the phone conversation.

"We're down getting ugruqs. You know how it is. But there're a *lot* of animals. A lot. It's the blubber. There's nowhere for the blubber to go...."

He meant that when they had finished the recent whaling they left the blubber there as it was, because there was no permafrost in the ice cellars where they had always stored the blubber and meat. Now, animal marauders were coming after the fat. That was why they were cutting up the meat and drying it on high lines, instead of putting it into ice cellars. The order of things was upset. There were too many scavenging animals coming around.

He said, "The harmony, harmony—" hesitating. "You know what I'm going to say before I say it."

"Yes, but say it."

"It's too warm. There are too many animals. People are saying this."

"You know...I've got goose bumps now," I told him.

He said, "Me, too."

"That shows how we feel," I said. "We don't have to say anything—go on."

"We've had the whaling festival. We had three whales." But despite this happy occasion, he was suffering from something. He continued, "We have to—The Animals—." His entire world, the arctic and all its inhabitants, was showing the first impact of global warming.

We discussed the activities of former Vice President Gore and the growing concern for environmental conservation. Jeff's concerns remained substantial. For him, the environmental problems, the animals' problems, and the young people's problems were all linked.

"It's a gift to us, from our maker," he said, speaking about the environment. A biologist, he conveyed his intimate understanding of their shared plight, trying to explain his communication with the land and the animals. "I could tell what—they're saying." The seals had been talking through him, as in the old days. The animals were speaking, and Jeff was their mouthpiece. Over the telephone, I heard their plea.

He advised me how to write my book on communitas: "It's not having a method. It's like putting the skin on the hull of a whale boat. You think you can't do it. When you have the skin laid out, you have to start with a bit of it, and work at it at one place and go on, and you find out how to do it—and then you do it."

"The boat skin. The way to work. I'll remember that. Goodbye, Jeff. We'll keep in touch."

This experience of communitas with animals is found not only in the arctic. The anthropologist George Mentore was in Guyana among the Waiwai hunters of Amazonia and, like the Waiwai, he experienced strong unity with the animals.

Mentore was in the forest with the Waiwai hunters when an event occurred that opened up the whole community for him. While chasing a herd of peccaries (*poniko*), there came a moment when the animals ran off with the Waiwai following them, leaving Mentore alone in the forest.

"It's hard to explain," Mentore said. "The body of a poniko is a gift to you."[11]

The Peccary Hunt[12]

I had been following the tracks for a while. I do not know for how long, because all sense of time seemed to have disappeared. Daylight remained and I could still hear the herd up in front of me. All of a sudden a calm came over me: a peaceful comforting composure of body and mind. It came from nowhere, unexpectedly. I stopped. I thought clearly, as if I were poniko. I was poniko. I became the whole herd up ahead. Before us, on a lower level of vision, the forest floor appeared in panorama. Shoulder to shoulder we trotted between the trees. We had eluded the two predators behind us. We refused to give up any of our kind today. We wheeled in one wide arc, doubling back upon our tracks, leaving the hunters to the east. Something seemed to be pulling us in the direction from which we had just come. We were approaching a tall dark hunter who stood in our path. By the time I had convinced myself that I had somehow willed the herd to return, they were pounding down the trail in front of me, intent on trampling me into the dirt. My bow came up, arrow notched. As my arrow left its string, the herd fanned out, dispersing on either side of me. There on the trail before me lay the gift of death from Poniko-yim: arrow piercing its heaving breast. The sudden strange feeling of perfect composure had not left me. I could still feel the sensation of thought outside my body. I could move my fingers and arms expertly to cut, weave, and load the carcass of the hog while my conscious self skillfully directed my every action from just little beyond my body. I did absolutely nothing wrong. I felt centered, balanced, clear, and accurate. I packed the hog and made my way back to the canoe without a single detour. It was as if I had been filled with a knowledge that could not be falsified. Wherever my feet fell was where I had to go. Where I had to go became where I was supposed to be; not a scratch from the abundant razor grass around me; not a single thorn found embedded in my flesh. No even tiredness from carrying the heavy corpse of the hog. My body and my mind had never before been this keenly vigorous and translucent. As I laid the hog in the canoe and sat to wait for the brothers to return, the helmsman and his son looked at me and smiled knowingly....

As I would later learn, mine had been an encounter with the spiritual vitality of *poniko-pen*—the collective spirit of peccaries. The Waiwai's term, *titpe* (calm or quietness), was expressed in the gift of translucency. *Titpe* directly refers to the sensation of translucent physicality which makes possible the heightened lucidity of human thoughts and action. It occurs as such when the sacred and secular entwine. With the rapture of entwinement, boundaries between differences and between separateness disappear. This eradication of difference, this assimilation of totality, this oneness of being precipitates the resultant accuracy of thinking and doing....

In what I have just written in an attempt to describe and interpret my experience of spirit, I have admittedly repeated much in the formula of theodicy constitutive of the Western tradition. This, of course, is predictable. Nonetheless, the formula was personally disappointing and inadequate. Succeeding finally to objectify my experience here in textual form, I have merely followed the hallowed Western paradigms for reducing a personal numinous experience to the historical and cultural discourses of its forms, contents, causes, and principles. Yet what Waiwai ideas have taught me more poignantly perhaps than my anthropological training is that no kind of description or interpretation can adequately explain the immensity of religious experience and, indeed, that any such attempt may even be an offence to religious mystery. And yet because "the *word* does not cease because there, before it, is the *thing*," care has to be taken as to how the offensive talk is expressed....[13] To keep the anthropological discipline from appearing so plainly offensive when it tries to explain such intimate and personal experiences of the numinous, alternative ways have to be created without falling back upon the scientism of inspection, measurement, and evidence. It seems to me the most obvious place to begin and the place with a legacy already anthropological has to be exactly that at which the awe-inspiring wonder occurs—at the sense of otherness our informants provide. I am not here arguing for a definitively "true" description of religious experience. Nor am I advocating any predominating means for justifying the presence of the divine.... The Waiwai framing of religious temporal space refuses to allow forces of coercive dominance to take over. Sacred communion instills wondrous courage rather than fearful subordination. It is one means of gaining access to heightened spirituality without the unseemliness of religious prestige. Relations with the divine empower, but they never become a power that can raise one human above another in righteousness or in law. No one, for example, can build up their experience of communion with spirit to become a paramount shamanic priest. Counterfoils exist throughout Waiwai society to balance all spiritual experiences among recipients. To speak boastfully or piously about such experience will not gain anyone privilege, in fact to do so defiles both deity and its wondrous gift.... The Waiwai experience of spirit cannot become a time of individual self-aggrandizement. I could not have used my personal encounter with the spirit of poniko-pen to claim something akin to an Abrahamic covenant with God. In the Western tradition, the faithful and obedient servant of the Abrahamic God dutifully accepts the gift of an abundant progeny (Genesis 22: 15). If we were to transfer the Waiwai logic to the Western procedure, we would find that divinity could easily have accepted the sacrificial gift of Isaac the son of Abraham and, in so doing, have reversed the order of hierarchy between them. Hence rather than an obedient and fearful human servant in debt to divine largesse, it would instead be a case of a sublime subordination by God who would be owing humanity for having received in blood sacrifice his highly valued son. In other words, by the force of obligatory reciprocity, set in motion by the destruction of the offering and therefore the impossibility of its refusal, divine dominance would have been made to seek a balance with humanity. Thus does the Waiwai *čew-yarano* (the bliss of goodness) experience divine spirituality as the Godhead.

My own sustained elation and enhanced lucidity faded. And this is the way it is supposed to be.

This humble theory accords with the idea of philosopher Emmanuel Lévinas, that God has enormous need of the prayers of humanity in order to bring the worlds into existence.[14] If one can be the receiver of a gift from God one is then setting the creation of things in motion. It is harder to give and have the gift accepted than to receive it; therefore, the giver gives thanks and the true receiver becomes one with the gift and giver. Mentore implies also that, although Abraham was saved from having to kill his son, the Christian God was not: his son was sacrificed. So that here, the giver's unity with us is on a surprising "reverse tilt" of the obligation—on the level of the giver's longing for our acceptance of the gift, moving to the level of interior translucency where there is no political predominance at all.

The story thus shows the Waiwai comradeship into which Mentore has entered by his understanding of the special moment with the peccary—his communitas with the animal and with the people. The features of the communitas moment are liberally present: the unexpectedness of the shift of the animals and of the whole event; his change from person to animal to person that happened in a flash; moreover—"something seemed to be pulling us around"—the sense in communitas that something is engineering all this; and he saw himself from outside himself—this is a true out-of-the-body experience, even one of *satori*, the flash of sudden awareness or individual enlightenment.

In Mentore's discussion of the event, it is clear he would not have wanted to be anywhere else. His story glowed with the pleasure of communitas and the entwinement with another being. There was entanglement, empathy, unity, and (with his arrow shot and in his actions afterwards) accuracy, which are givens in such a moment.

And thus, we hold this moment sacred. Analysis itself is an offense against its sacredness, because there is no ranking in communitas. It cannot be treated as higher or lower, and there is no work the social scientist can do to reduce the episode to its parts. The social scientist has no power to handle this "material."

Turner said, "Spontaneous communitas is always completely unique, and hence socially transient.... It can never be adequately expressed in a structural form, but it may arise unpredictably between human beings."[15]

Communitas turns out to be a major biological characteristic of things, like Trevarthen's sociable baby with the outstretched arms (see Chapter 1). It is written into the equation. We cannot shake it out.

The Nature of the Brain

> Democracy is trusting the human brain. The converse of this is not trusting the human brain and therefore enacting many laws, which accumulate in a stranglehold on community life and are recognizable as neoconservative, or neoliberal, or as actually fascist systems. On the contrary, the brain only needs a few principles. Then *it knows what to*

do. This goes back to how you develop your integrity, your morality, as a child.

—Irene Wellman 2007[16]

Our biology provides evidence of our mutual awareness of others—evidence found in the intuition of someone's unseen presence; in the gift of our pleasure over food, freedom, sex, and family love; and in a whole range of skin and bodily reactions to great beauty and divinity, such as goose bumps, dances of delight, and falling in worship. Everybody counts at these moments. Everyone mutually embraces the others' quirky personalities and has total support for them—as in Shakespeare's scenes where he brought in Falstaff and his disreputable pals.

The Brain

How does the brain learn in the first place? Myelinization is the process of the inception of our nerves whereby, when a nerve is first used, myelin builds up around it and facilitates all future use of the passageway. Thus the nerve is "learning to remember." This happens even early in life. For example, the mother is seated at the table with the baby on her lap. The mother takes a spoonful of apple sauce and lifts it to the baby's mouth; the baby tries it. It is the baby's first taste of apple sauce. The baby is obviously sensing that apple sauce. The build-up of the nerve has begun. The baby will never again be ignorant of apple sauce.

That one was easy. The brain now assesses what it needs by means of its basic knowledge—that is, its primal natural education. It has experienced this, and it knows about this "acquiring of knowledge." In its "theory" brain it only establishes a few things, then it "takes off running, on its own." The "good" in the brain is doing this. The brain adjusts, and finds what it needs for itself, "hunting" for the appropriate means to develop. It knows. This kind of knowing occurs because of the love of the family, because of the communitas of mother and baby. Nowhere does structure enter this process. It is organic.

There is new research on activity in the brain concerned with goodness and ethical behavior. This good has a specific site in the brain. Shankar Vedantam's account in the *Washington Post*, presented in the next section, describes new studies of brain scanning that show how making ethical decisions lights up in the brain in the same area as food and sex (the ventromedial prefrontal cortex). Goodness is therefore not merely a product of culture but is hard wired, intrinsic to the human brain.

Shankar Vedantam on Brain and Altruism: "If It Feels Good to Be Good, It Might Be Only Natural"[17]

The e-mail came from the next room.

"You gotta see this!" Jorge Moll had written.

Moll and Jordan Grafman, neuroscientists at the National Institutes of Health, had been scanning the brains of volunteers as they were asked to think about a scenario involving either donating a sum of money to charity or keeping it for themselves.

As Grafman read the e-mail, Moll came bursting in. The scientists stared at each other. Grafman was thinking, "Whoa—wait a minute!"

The results were showing that when the volunteers placed the interests of others before their own, the generosity activated a primitive part of the brain that usually lights up in response to food or sex. Altruism, the experiment suggested, was not a superior moral faculty that suppresses basic selfish urges but rather was basic to the brain, hard-wired and pleasurable.

Their 2006 finding that unselfishness can feel good lends scientific support to the admonitions of spiritual leaders such as Saint Francis of Assisi, who said, "For it is in giving that we receive...." The results are showing, unexpectedly, that many aspects of morality appear to be hard-wired in the brain, most likely the result of evolutionary processes that began in other species. It is known that animals can sacrifice their own interests: one experiment found that if each time a rat is given food, its neighbor receives an electric shock, then the first rat will eventually forgo eating.

What the new research is showing is that morality has biological roots that have been around for a very long time, indicated in the reward center in the brain that lit up in Grafman's experiment. The more researchers learn, the more it appears that the foundation of morality is empathy. Being able to recognize—even experience vicariously—what another creature is going through was an important leap in the evolution of social behavior....

A number of experiments such as the one by Grafman have shown that emotions are central to moral thinking. In another experiment published in March 2007, University of Southern California neuroscientist Antonio R. Damasio and his colleagues showed that patients with damage to an area of the brain known as the ventromedial prefrontal cortex lack the ability to feel their way to moral answers....

Joshua D. Greene, a Harvard neuroscientist and philosopher, said multiple experiments suggest that morality arises from basic brain activities. Morality, he said, is not a brain function elevated above our baser impulses. Greene said it is not "handed down" by philosophers and clergy, but "handed up."

The research above confirms that there is a basic goodness in the biology of our brains, upholding the curious Amazonian insight that there is *ekati*, spiritual energy, in everything. The same insight regarding goodness is found in varying degrees all over the world. Furthermore, goodness and generosity are pleasurable—a big element in communitas. Thus, the principle behind our entire economic system—"first and foremost seek profits"—is not in accordance with the inborn nature of humanity. The kingdom of God is within you, say those religions that have a sense of God *in* the human being. It is not necessarily in the structures. This principle of goodness, deep in creation, explains the communitas in the heart of revolutions and the remarkable historical progression of democracy unfolded in Chapter 6.

There has never not been goodness. We *know* when we are in touch with goodness and communitas. We are comfortable when we are aligned with it.

At the Max Planck Institute, Leipzig, in 2010, where neuroscientists have been carrying out brain research with magnetic resonance imaging, it has become fully accepted that the human brain is primarily a *social* brain. Everything about it is social. A cognitive neuroscience that regards the brain as a solitary organism looks at something that does not exist. Colwyn Trevarthen, the child neuroscientist, has become the great authority on the social brain, and his star is rising, while the star of the cognitive neuroscientists is setting.[18]

This section, on how the human being is naturally social, turns to the kindly, shadowy figure of Emmanuel Lévinas—a philosopher who recognizes that a person naturally gravitates to another and needs to do so, and that this happens directly from the inner self in a primary way.

Empathy

Emmanuel Lévinas[19]

The French philosopher Emmanuel Lévinas (1906–1995) was born in Lithuania and received a Jewish education. His first formative influence came from the Talmud. Next it was the Russian classics: authors such as Pushkin, Dostoyevsky, and Tolstoy. He experienced the Russian Revolution in the Ukraine, where he became a prisoner of war. He later studied in France.

The following is a brief interpretation of the work of Lévinas, which was originally written in a hesitating, wordy, and deeply philosophical way; to note, "the Other" indicates "other people." With sympathetic interpretation, one can see that he is saying something about the mysterious propensity that brain researchers have discovered. His work is based on the sense of goodness and sociality in one's relation to one's fellow human being—which, he implies, is one's first and basic consciousness in life outside of oneself,[20] one's first handhold on the outside world and consciousness of oneself in relation to it. This is a consciousness of *people*, usually one's mother. Lévinas proposes that one cannot truly *know* other persons by means of analysis and comparison, as if they were objects viewed by a "self." Rather, the whole of one's consciousness of what the Other is starts with love and the sense of goodness. Thus, the other person is and always has been one's greatest care or responsibility. The other person *is* ourselves; this precedes any "objective searching after truth."

This love is already rooted within our subjective constitution and does not need morality talk to make it so, says Lévinas. As we have a sense of love for another person, mother or sweetheart or comrade, our delight in ourselves is primordially inseparable from that sense. It is not taught. The sense of "the holy" is the feeling of deepest respect for relation. If we are the relatives of all things, of infinity, we will have respect for the extraordinary variety of the people and the universe outside ourselves, without being bewitched by it. This is because we welcome the loved one—God, or any human—and our marvel goes on into infinity. Lévinas thought that having a simple face-to-face relation with everything was not what is called "participation," but was the normal action of love itself.[21]

This is my sense of Lévinas's meaning: I am born to respond to that mother, that lover, children, all persons, to be there for them, and love and work for them, without waiting for reciprocity, were I even to die for it. Reciprocity, their loving me, is a matter of their own consciousness. Meanwhile, I am there for them, and I will not fail them. There is no discrimination in this direct relationship. This is unconditional love, and it is our first, our primary nature. Also, because I am responsible toward all outside persons ad infinitum, says Lévinas, I am called to guard them against the systematic structurization of moral law. In Lévinas, we encounter a passionate denunciation of dead structures and law. Lévinas sees there is violence in sets of moral principles. For Lévinas, love lives in active friendship.

I see Lévinas as saying that love is universal. It is not made up. Love "grasps" nothing so does not have a theory. It doesn't *have* this and that, does not work busily in that way, and does not have a subject–object structure. The real Eros does not "collect conquests." Without thinking, it simply goes beyond the possible—which is what real love is like.[22]

Furthermore, Lévinas wants to extend love to the stranger, to others as neighbors and fellow humans, which is love without wanting to dominate. He says that all indigenous people know how to give hospitality to the stranger; they let strangers enjoy the rights they have. Civilized people think we have to establish institutions to guarantee justice. Therefore, we have to employ knowledge and wisdom. But this knowledge and wisdom are provided in the service of love; love is not in service to knowledge and wisdom. For Lévinas, love is prior to knowledge and wisdom.

I believe that there is something more to be added to Lévinas's philosophy, and it is communitas with many, not simply one-on-one, or self and the Other. I have been in the middle of the African phenomenon of communitas in the ritual of Ihamba, when everybody gets the spirit together—we all did (see Chapter 10). We hear it in Hinduism in the story of Krishna and the milkmaids. And it is in many homes at the Jewish Seder dinner. And communitas was there in the Pentecost scene, in the first verse of Acts 2.

Pentecost[23]

The following words exploded from my friend Dawn Hunt when she saw what I was trying to say:

> Communitas was there in the Pentecost scene, here, in the very first verse of Acts 2: 1: "They were all with one accord in one place"— with one accord, like communitas. And when describing the tongues of fire it says, "*It* sat upon them." It is singular. It was one fire with many tongues, not lots of tiny little flames over the head of each one as some paintings show. And then what happens? Everyone there from countries scattered far and wide can understand what they are saying. They can all hear the same message right where they are—one message in many tongues. They can understand each other; all are connected. Many are deeply touched. They throw in their lot with this scruffy band of fishermen and tax collectors—thousands of them. And here's the kicker: "And all that believed were together *and had all things common*. And sold their possessions and goods, and parted them to all men, as every man had need. And they were continuing

daily with one accord in the temple, and breaking bread from house to house, did eat their meat with gladness and singleness of heart" (Acts 2: 44–46). Wow! Sounds like a revolution; sounds like socialism; sounds like communitas. And miracles came springing out of that outpouring of the spirit that drew them all together.

Jesus told them that to be leaders they had to be servants, as *he* was, always inverting the power. And they did serve, healing, helping, supporting widows and orphans—maybe even up until the time when Constantine pulled the church right off its marginal tracks, the tracks Jesus had in mind for the church, and into the heart of the establishment, causing a train wreck when it came to what the true message of the church was intended to be.

This rang bells. I remembered the instruction, before Pentecost, "Wash each other's feet, as I would do for you. Care for each other as I have cared for you. Bind each other's wounds." The apostles went out from Pentecost glorifying. Are not collective hugs like this? Was our "childbirth" march in Ndembu girl's initiation—which I shall describe in Chapter 9—merely a savage rite? When I thought of my friend Dorothea praying for me, my acid reflux stopped. It was cured when she prayed for me personally—so that the spirit of love came over me in marvelous peace, because...because it's me she loves—my god. Is that not the miracle we all know about—the loving presence of others even if they are far away? In Dorothea's case, it was her infinitely sincere hug—joyous. It also occurs when we all have our hands clasped in a circle or laid on in healing. Here, the Pentecost story shows communitas, the *multiple*, at work.

The African concept of *ubuntu* is also related. As we saw in Part 2 of Chapter 7, when considering the social person, the *muntu*, we began to understand how the muntu would naturally grant human rights to the other person, thus practicing ubuntu. This is because all people are our kinsfolk, and we become persons, *antu*, by virtue of their existence, nested in this world with us.

Furthermore, according to Lévinas and ubuntu, one is a person through the natural process of living with other people. This is the "man" to whom the Rights of Man applied. A person adhering to those rights for others is a true muntu, by whom and for whom the human rights document is written.

We can see that nature encompasses more than just elements and matter: it includes organic society and our dynamic intermingled relationships. Here is a translated passage from Professor Tshiamalenga Ntumba, the head of the Department of Philosophy and African Religions at Kinshasa B. P., Kinshasa, Congo. He is one of the few

African thinkers who base work on the African view of society, not the Western. His thesis has strong connections with ubuntu.

In the following section, Ntumba starts with a critical reference to earlier sociologists, Talcott Parsons and Niklas Luhmann, who derive society from a "feedback-system-in-evolution," the complexity of which can be reduced back to its original basic functions.

Tshiamalenga Ntumba on Language and Sociality: The Primacy of "Besoity," "We-ness," over "Subjectivity"[24]

Contrary to the reductive, reductionist, and positivist tendency among sociologists, I embrace for my world view a different system: human society is a *dialogical community* and, at one and the same time, an *ethical community*, that is, a society which is not simply given,[25] but in which—as in an ideal society—an ethic has been there from the beginning, from necessity, and has already long been the precondition of every act of speech, in fact, of every communication worthy of the name. Hence derives our foremost thesis: language, from the beginning, in any communication worthy of the name, already necessarily presupposes, postulates, and anticipates human sociality itself, governed by authentic ethical norms, and not simply by some contract, constitution, or other convention. Sociality, in fact, transcends all such conventions. It is not a simple artificial object at the mercy of sociologists and politicians....

For speech to happen, there exists beforehand the We. For us, society—postulated and necessarily anticipated and, above all, always and already in argumentative and auto-reflexive communication—this society is naught but the resulting sociality that necessarily and always is already the We, *Biso*[26]—and has first place with regard to individuals and to that encounter of individuals which is termed "intersubjectivity." Hence there already exists, necessarily, the primacy of *bisoity, biso* sociality, We-ness, over intersubjectivity (interindividualist sociality, intersolipsist, intermonological, interpersonalist, and therefore associationalist). Thus, human society as *bisoity* and We-ness transcends simple interindividualist and associationalist sociality.

We need to ask, has the I been devoured by the We? Can the We exercise political power? Can the We think, create, invent? And what can we say about the Other? The Stranger? God? About the right to difference? About war? I and Thou, though second, are certainly not devoured or swallowed up by the We. Moreover, if the I, the Thou, and the He or She are always necessarily and already *included* in the We, it follows that, anthropologically speaking, the problem of the Other and Stranger is a false problem issuing from the western solipsist tradition. Besides, the We, being before all cultural differentiations and possible conditions, always necessarily and already accepts the right to difference and its immense span of different ways of relating, even through war, even in the destruction of communication. Hence our threefold thesis: without being devoured, the I, the Thou, and the He/She are always, necessarily, and already included in the We where they move freely, deferring in absolute respect to dialogue. Anthropologically, even God is *Bisoity*. The We has primacy, *he* is in *it*: he is not the Totally Other but is Immanuel, God-with-the-We.

Considering sociality through Ntumba's words, we might concede primacy to the natural We, and see it as communitas. "Autre," the Other, is no more. Its problem simply does not exist because the We includes the Other. Ntumba is careful to continually repeat his "necessarily, always, and already," knowing how prone we western individualists are to cite evolution, special cases, and/or the otherness of God to keep this problem away from us. Still, we are seduced by Ntumba's generous attitude to war, arguments, strangers, trouble with communications—he has not ranked these in terms of morality, but encloses them all in his embrace.

Ubuntu, then, and Ntumba's biso, simple yet profound, are the philosophies of communitas, which are cheerful, full of vitality, believable, what we actually experience, and what we have never thought to state as a philosophy—for philosophy, of all things, looks as if it ought to start with the "I." Ego consciousness itself is undermined by the knowledge (recently faced squarely by Thomas B. Fowler in *The Ontology of Consciousness*[27]) that the psyche, our permeable soul, is more continually present than ego consciousness, and holds primacy over it. Consciousness is sometimes aware of spirituality and sometimes is not, even though one may be in a spiritual milieu. What is interesting is that the psyche appears to be the home of sociality in societies where its spontaneous form has not yet been obliterated.

Ekatï

Let us then go to that Native American people half a world down to the south—the Waiwai of Amazonia in Guyana. Here, anthropology has identified a missing link in what you might call theology or cosmology—a thing called *ekatï*, a "spiritual force," says Mentore, something like the Iñupiat concept of *inua*.[28]

The ekatï of the Waiwai is the original vitality of the divine manifesting itself in the sustaining of human life. Spiritual vitality *is* the vitality that is everywhere. The orbs of the eyes themselves do not just see, "they are the very curvature of divine coherence and spiritual energies."²⁹ Moreover, the Waiwai say that living with other people in a particular settlement for a goodly period of time will make an individual not only smell like, but also look like the people he or she lives with. This is because space and time encourage the necessary exchanges of substances between bodies that allow collective community life to exist. Shared food, fluids, talk, and ideas all help in the daily production of community life and the very quality and features of individual being. All shared substances carry elements of ekatï. From a Waiwai point of view, the supple circuits and metrical rhythms of daily exchange actually assist in stabilizing the volatile spiritual vitalities that constitute the life-sustaining force of the body. In other words, human existence relies upon and is completely connected to the balance of this spirit force.

The ekatï existing in human sexuality, says Mentore, "needs" to materially manifest itself, in a balanced and harmonious way, "as the convivial goodness and beauty of the compassionate body." Thus it "accommodates its own transcendental potency in human sexuality. Without the effect of this accommodation, its force would be too excessive and, instead of being creative, would be destructive to humankind." It must "flow through the community of complementarily opposed individuals in passionate and compassionate love."³⁰

This sense of what is going through people results in what I see as the real spiritual/natural human being, and it makes rubbish of the nature–culture divide. It neatly confirms Lucien Lévy-Bruhl's thesis of 1910 that "natives" think in terms of a law of mystical participation—a law that still holds.³¹ These spiritual powers, ekatï, *wakan, shakti, chi, /num,* and many others, are known all over the world. Nature itself, the Chinese acupuncturists say, is thrumming with chi. In many circumstances, this energy also inspires the healer and heals the sufferer. The gift of healing and the practice of shamanism belong in nature. Nobody plans or constructs a healing; it is *given* to the healers. It feels as if the one that gives the power is the immensity of grace itself.

The Romanian-born religious historian Mircea Eliade, in a blinding illumination recounted in his book on shamanism, said that spirituality from primordial times was always there in full. "The sacred does not cease to manifest itself, and with each new manifestation it resumes its original tendency to reveal itself wholly."³² The sacred does not *evolve*. It has always been there. Similarly, looking through the eyes of the Iñupiat, everything in the universe has its inua, its particular soul—rocks, lagoons, as well as people and all the animals. Is religion, then, that same consciousness of a spiritual power that passes through and through everything in the universe—matter, living things, animals, and humans—and part and parcel of all of nature as a matter of course, already, always, and necessarily? Healing itself is an equiprimordial phenomenon, and similarly, "at each new manifestation it resumes its original tendency to reveal itself wholly." This confirms that this tendency toward spirituality is inborn, an endowment, a biological predisposition, a propensity, existing for just such a purpose, the communication with each other and with spirits.

From a scientific perspective, we may think of the way water exists—a substance consisting of two elements, hydrogen and oxygen, which have an affinity for one another and are naturally married to each other in a compound. This falls under the law of affinity or "chemical kinetics"—what one might call part of the law of mystical participation. But the law of mystical participation is immensely broad. It includes the energy especially felt by healers—the Chinese with their chi, the Lakota with wakan, and so on—and it appears to be a part of nature.

What is the Soul?

Jacob Levy Moreno, the founder of psychodrama, said that in a true psychosocial picture of a person, "the psyche appears as outside the body, the body is surrounded by the psyche and the psyche is surrounded by and interwoven into the social and cultural atoms."[33] The individual psyche is always intimately and naturally connected with other humans—that is, the "social and cultural atoms." The terms "psyche" and "human energy field" are synonymous here. What Moreno said points to the particular working location of communitas—that is, between people. Moreno discovered this while engaged with therapy and conflict resolution, and it took shape in the psychodrama.

Psychodrama involves role enactment of the conflict, where the protagonist takes on the character of the auxiliary, some absent person who is troubling the sufferer. With continual reverse role-playing, and friendly adoption of awkward roles by helpful participants, one can reach right into the working soul of the troublesome other and, marvelously, forgive him or her.

Another characteristic of the link of communitas through engaged healing is "sympathetic entanglement," where "sympathy" means literally feeling what the other person feels. The anthropologist Tenibac

Harvey explored this, in spite of himself, during his research in Guatemala, and it is recounted below.

Humbling, Frightening, and Exalting: An Experiential Acquaintance with Maya Healing, as Told by Tenibac S. Harvey[34]

Harvey had come to the highland farming town of Nima', Guatemala, to learn about Maya healing. He thought best to introduce himself as a researcher who wanted "to learn about healing and the care of the sick." Fine, but the Maya were taking that word "about" as a sign of a social and moral space that existed between him and themselves, suggestive of a kind of veiled detached inhumanity. It was as if he expected to remain safely untouched by the tendrils of life and death reaching in and out of it.

Soon after arriving in Nima', he set himself to the task of concurrently studying with several local healers of different therapeutic orientations, observing sacred mountainside ceremonies, recording cross-cultural clinical consultations with nonindigenous health professionals and Maya patients, and attending Maya bioenergy consultations with herbalists and their clients, which included both the physically present as well as the geographically distant sick.[35] He still wondered why his movements were perceived as suspect and his varied participation as near sinful. He openly explained he was not intent on *becoming* a healer with any particular specialty. But the Maya perceived this very thing as an unwholesome and potentially deadly duplicity (*perfidia*).[36]

Then Xuan, a high-ranking sun priest, asked him, "Are you of two hearts?" Harvey felt that the weight of this question was immeasurable and his response beyond any kind of valuation; the answer would be unredeemable. How should he answer? How could he respond when he did not know what being of two hearts meant? He said nothing.

Months afterward, the answer came in a darkened room, one late afternoon in the church parish room.

He was called: "Come, there's one sick. Miriam says come to the dispensary. Come!" When Harvey arrived at the dispensary and entered the ill-lit consultation room, he found a middle-aged man sitting across from the Maya theurgical herbalist named Miriam[37] and her assistant, Xper. The healer and her assistant ran the dispensary.

The man who sought the consultation had traveled in a rented truck over 200 miles on behalf of his father, who was near death back in the Alta Verapaz region of the country. The Keq'chi man had not come seeking treatment on his own behalf. When Harvey arrived at the clinic, his mostly silent expressions of concern for the sick man did not go unnoticed by the keen sensitivities of Miriam. In response to his concern, she placed a small wooden chair in the center of the room and, turning to Harvey, pointed to it and asked, "Are you of two hearts?" Here were those awful words again, deafening and deciding but not requiring a decision so much as an enunciation. Then, up from his heart through unwilling lips came a prayer, barely in words, a murmur in a creaky voice uttering, "I am not of two hearts." Miriam motioned to him saying, "Take your seat."

This was personal experience.[38] Though unaware of his new role, he willingly took the little seat between the healers and the sick man's son and, with it, he unwittingly left behind the vantage of detached observer, exchanging it for the inescapable close-up presence of the full-fledged participant. He was "sitting in," unbeknownst to him, for the suffering father—sitting in for his illness, while the father would gain substance through a sympathy perfected in sickness. But it entailed feeling the sickness. A slight faintness came over Harvey. He wrestled against a dizziness that was heavy, like unwelcomed sleep, then succumbed to the shivers of a sudden fever. And when he felt his forehead dampen and breath shorten, he became afraid. As he sat, Xper handed him a small crumpled piece of paper bearing the name of the Keq'chi man's father, Obispo. He was instructed to hold the scrap of paper in his hand and think on the ill man. He now wanted to heal him. But what would become of his own self? He whispered a prayer for the man's life and his own also. "God, help me."

Miriam took a shiny piece of metal and touched his shoulder with it. With the other hand, she held Xper's hand. Xper was reading the contortions unfolding between her fingers, the bodily sympathies for signs of sickness registered through to her by Miriam's other hand as it traveled across Harvey's body, making contact here and there through the tiny metal object.[39] These related to the absences of energies unfolding within and around the sick man. Miriam said, "It's like a cell phone. We're connected."

Harvey had been finding that, among the Maya, everyone is your companion. They live very little of their lives alone.[40] In some instances, the responses and narratives of the companions of the sick take the place of a sick person's own responses and narratives altogether.

They placed herb bags in Harvey's lap and checked the result with the metal object. Soon they had identified the right herbs for the absent father's sickness, herbs that they proceeded to send with the son to the sick man, for his good cure.

For the Maya, sickness and healing, and bearing and sharing the identities of the people involved in one's companionships, mean *feeling with* others, an emotional and moral bond that allows a companion to speak directly about sickness and, in some cases, seek care on another's behalf. This extends to the healers who take *feeling with* others into another intensity, with something which might be called "sympathetic clairvoyance." This was sympathetic in two interconnected senses. In the first, healers were sympathetic in that they were able to enter into or share the feelings of others. In the second, having shared and entered into the feelings of others, they themselves were correspondingly affected (and in some cases afflicted) by the suffering and sorrow of others. For the uninitiated sick person or participant in Maya healing, the effect of this sympathetic affect, of having one's feeling felt aloud, was a sense of the healer's clairvoyance, a keenness of perception that could make healers seem from another world, a sympathetic movement from the role and experience of observer to that of the participant and back again, in fact, "sympathetic entanglement."

The participant and observer can be one. To advance in understanding sometimes means not shrinking from human suffering and the moral bonds that such experiences entail. Indeed, shrinking and refusal often arises from a mistaken loyalty to an "objective" science. Stepping away from scientific medical perspectives with "one heart," as Harvey did, can be humbling, frightening, and also exalting.

Cultural anthropologist Roy Wagner made this comment on Harvey's experience: "Curing the companions of a so-called 'patient' as the principle mode of conceiving illness itself is tantamount to an open admission that the soul is precisely that part of us that we hold in common."[41]

Conclusion

Along with what we call nature, I see the entire range of human culture as natural, allied to spirits more or less consciously, in an affinity with spirits as in a compound—and *within* the natural world. Contemporary anthropology has led some of us to naturalize ourselves to the spiritual world of the people we study, so we and the people are no longer strangers to one another. Again, from this point of view, our relationships can no longer be structured nor can they be foreign to the truly human way of being. We are free to experience and recognize energy in nature as possibly something to do with religion. At this stage, the soul comes creeping back, with facts about healing, the communitas of the land, and our undeniable relationship with the animals and plants as well as with each other.

And now in Chapter 9, we embark on the changes in the human body, the nature of the human body. The anthropological study of bodily changes has lit upon the oddities and facts of human rites of passage throughout the world. The way people regard them flows from nature, their biology, and from the people's permeability to spirits, all of which has been expressed in their cultures and languages. The ritual of passage is something that indigenous and local societies will often say has been given by the spirits, by ancestors, especially the richness of symbolism and detail that has accrued from intuiting the nature of bodily change, both physical and spiritual at once.

We will examine the origin of the researchers' concepts of communitas and liminality; that is, the theory of the rite of passage, because the initiates experience many paradoxes that do not fit into life as the previous analysts saw it.

Chapter 9

Rites of Passage: Communitas in Times of Change

Communitas is closely linked to rites of passage. What we know now as communitas first came to the attention of anthropology indirectly, through the curiosity of the French folklorist Arnold van Gennep (1873–1957).[1] In 1902, van Gennep wrote *Les Rites de Passage*, laying out the results of his research, which consisted of accounts of passage rituals from around the world celebrating an individual's life change. These were rituals of birth, adolescence, marriage, group initiation, and death—mainly those of adolescence, the maturation of the human body. Van Gennep called the rites *liminal*, as in lintel. They were "doorway" rites, occurring when a person was in the middle of change, not yet settled but in between. Van Gennep found that differences in style and symbolism in the rites occurred cross-culturally.

The physical changes in the human life cycle trigger changes in human consciousness and in a person's relationship with others. They are stages of physical growth and expansion and also an increase of one's awareness, involving various readjustments in one's social niche. Such moments usually entail some cracking and breaking out of existing ways of life. We know how, from the point of view of the youth in the Western world, ordinary habits, training, and obedience to formality become something to break free from. These are commonly the structures of society. For the youth, a sudden and exciting view outside of the box may result in the liberation of communitas, joy. Victor Turner termed this liberation "antistructure." All of us experience those naturally occurring events of change, not only in ourselves but in our family and for people we know. They represent fundamental changes from the perspective of any given person in that family or group context. Thus, it can be seen that the processes of natural maturation are major events that jog our consciousness and also our memories of previous communitas. Consciousness is our good apple of knowledge. But we know only too well that this is not good from the point of view of parents in our present work-a-day world, in which the adolescence of children is often a disaster period, fraught with antagonisms. Since it seems a period of well-nigh violent disagreement between adolescents and parents, it often produces fear of this uneasy time. Nevertheless, when understood, the characteristics of rites of passage show exciting features. A person's awareness sharpens on the eve of a life change.

When complex rituals are involved—especially for the young the rites of passage inevitably display the three-stage dialectic of change:— the separation from the old, the betwixt and between stage, and the celebration of the return of the initiates into their new community.[2] The first stage ignites excitement and awe in the subject on entering the ritual mode. The second is the liminal time of tiptoeing across the threshold, a time of anomaly. This threshold time is unfamiliar to the novice, experienced in a strange land with—as it were—long avenues revealing not-yet-understood wonders. A god, or a spirit, or one of the dead may be involved. One could be in a ghost-land, or a wonderland, like an Alice-child or Harry Potter or the little girl in Hayao Muyazaki's *Spirited Away*, learning hand-over-fist about mysteries. This is what liminality is: a time of wide-open wonder and realization. The collective joy at these times can be unforgettable. It is communitas. In the last stage, a person is ushered into the new reality, adulthood. A person goes through it all and comes out different.

In this chapter, we have examples of these natural celebrations of change. Victor Turner and I joined the rites in our fieldwork in Africa and were the first to take notice of the signs of communitas. We looked closely at the in-between stage, the liminal or doorway stage, a time of process in action. We saw the alternation between fixed and fluid custom, where anything might happen, where the tight fit of systems was dissolving into something fluid and growing original unit by original unit, different from anything before as if a seed in the ground were unwrapping.. This is generativity itself, free, untrammeled like nature, and autonomous, open to the energy and spirit powers of primal existence. Also, liminality sometimes becomes a way of life, a much broader phenomenon, generating another whole genre of culture. People of all kinds populate its in-between world. This is how the anthropologist Barbara Myerhoff put it:

> All manner of possibilities occur: tricksters, clowns, poets, shamans, court jesters, monks, dharma bums, holy mendicants; even social movements such as millenarian cults, or social principles such as

matrilaterality in patrilineal systems, qualify for examination as liminal phenomena. They are astonishingly diverse but share some of the same characteristics of neophytes in the liminal phase of a ritual of transition: the symbols used for them are similar, emphasizing innocence, rebirth, vulnerability, fertility, change, emotion, paradox, disorder, anomaly, opposition, and the like. Underlying all these traits is lurking a sacrality and power that accompany movements toward the borders of the uncharted and unpredicted. The edges of our categories, as Mary Douglas has also stated in *Purity and Danger* (1996), are charged with power and mystery. The people, objects, or events that touch those margins may be taboo or polluted because they are out of place. They are sources of danger, a threat to our orderly conceptualizations and desire for form and predictability; but also, as Turner shows, they are sources of awareness, possibility, innovation, and creativity.[3]

Victor Turner and I explored the connection of liminality and "communitas," the state of oneness and unity that neophytes living outside the norms and fixed categories of a social system share during liminal periods. Equality, undifferentiated humanness, androgyny, and humility are some of the characteristics of this condition. Neophytes are symbolically represented as pure undetermined possibility, the very opposite of social structure with its emphasis on differentiation, hierarchy, and separation. The liminal person comes to stand for the sentiment of undifferentiated humankind: all that is innate, whole, and unified.

Adolescent Initiation

Evening in the Tent

In 1934 I was a thirteen-year-old in England, and a member of a Girl Guide camp. We pitched our bell tents on the sea coast of Sussex. Outside the tent at night the grass was dewy. There was a pleasure in feeling the prickly stubble with our bare toes and the dew coming up between them. We felt our way in the starlight back to our sleeping bags laid out on the groundsheet, and we snuggled in, about five of us, and lay there, grinning and talking.

"Why?" said one. "Why is it we can say anything here, we can talk about anything and nobody minds?"

"Not like in the dorm," I said. "Why's it different? You could never say things like this in the dorm."

People would have had little cliques in the dorm. Here, we were just happy and liked each other. We could all talk without embarrassment. Lying there we gratefully gazed up at the apex of the center pole. To this day I remember the sensation of freedom. We noticed the difference.

Twenty years after my break at the Girl Guide camp, I found myself doing fieldwork in Zambia with Vic, trying to understand tribal initiation. We had our two boys, eight and six, and Irene, four, with us, doing fieldwork en famille. I became very familiar with the girl's rite of passage.

A Birthing Symbol: The "Baby" is a Teenage Girl

The first rite of passage in which I joined was a girl's initiation called the Nkanga. It was said to be the greatest of the rituals. This one was for a thirteen-year-old girl named Ikubi. An older woman, Fatima, was her "midwife." Midwife implies the one to bring her into the world of adulthood, that is, the facilitator of biological change. First, Ikubi was to go back to "being a baby," and a "dead person," too. The women lay her passive body down on an antelope skin in the forest, in the bosom of nature, on a spot they called the "place of death," *ifwilu*.

The exact place was important. It was at the foot of a young tree that exuded milk from its leaves. There Ikubi lay, curled up like a fetus, and the women covered her from head to foot with a blanket. The milk of the tree, just by its presence, exuded its benison upon the "dead" body, fertilizing it, electrifying it with a new sexuality. She could not help but sleep—she was enchanted: she was "dead." She lay asleep in full daylight while high festival raged around her, with folks drumming, dancing, leaping from side to side, clapping, chanting boisterous and salacious songs, all the time keeping a circle of dancers moving around her.

Not until sunset did they turn to attend to her body lying in the *ifwilu*. Gathering around, her friends lifted her and placed her on her midwife's back. Then the crowd of women, myself included, pressed closely around the two and as one body; we all began to dance. Even the bearer of the girl, "heavy with child," managed to dance as well. Singing, we forged our way back to the village, smiling out in triumph at the world. There was love and excitement in every eye.

Now the crowd of women imitated childbirth. They periodically pressed themselves in toward the girl, just like the body's contractions in childbirth. We wanted this baby to be born. Women pushed me from behind and I pushed those in front. Push! Ahhh! All of us mothers knew those feelings. The men were waiting in the village with the drums. Our work showed them our power, our unspeakable muscles in action, unstoppable. We, plural, were that woman in labor, and dancing, in front of the men. We were in command. It was impossible to mistake the sense of being all one body—more than a mindless crowd. Our "body" was made up of conscious remembering individuals engaged in active communitas. We lunged forward together, enfolding the treasure of a new woman borne between us.

At last the crowd turned and pressed toward the initiation hut, a construction of thatch shaped like an inverted A. The front women pivoted around and quickly delivered Ikubi head first into the doorway, like a baby born into the world. They had done it. They had borne the body like a corpse and also like a womb-emerging baby, into its dwelling, far from its real mother.

Ikubi woke from her trance with twenty new mothers—which comprised the entire band of village women. Into the rafters of the new grass hut the women placed a small string of white beads.

"*Diyi mukishi*; this is the spirit of the mothers," said Fatima, my instructor in ritual. There were about thirty beads on the string. Any one of the beads could be the girl's future child—she could take her pick. But the girl herself was not permitted to look at them. The vitality of unborn babies lay in those tiny white beads.

At various times during Ikubi's three-month stay in the seclusion hut, the midwife and the women took her in private and laid her down on her side to practice the "dance on the bed." For this activity, the midwife herself lay down, facing the girl closely. To accommodate her teacher the girl's elbow was crooked out, and the midwife's head rested comfortably on the crook.

They began, side by side. Both bodies moved stomach to stomach, a belly dance for two, woman to woman. The heat in the two bodies on the mat grew. Very soon the midwife caused the young girl to flower open like a lily in climax; the eyes of both feminine beings fainted and their eyeballs rose to heaven. Meanwhile the sister–women and I gathered all around crooning a dance song in rhythm, with beauty in our voices and sheer delight in our souls.

I watched, sighing with the rest: a bride trained like this was guaranteed to make the shyest bridegroom grant his arrow, *nsewu*—his bride price for such a paragon. Privately the women know that the bow—the woman—gives power to the arrow—male—to make it fly.

After three months training in the art of Eros and the skillful coming-out dance of the moving breasts, there dawned the coming-out day. The women entered the hut and bore the girl away to a secluded spot to be anointed, coifed, and dressed, for her final display. Once her hair had been braided in sparkling cornrows, they hid the white beads in the part of the hair. Then, with breasts bare, enswathed with beads like a queen, she suddenly disappeared into the bush—only to emerge unexpectedly in the middle of the crowd. The entire population of the surrounding forest had gathered with drums in the plaza for her moment of glory. She charged in, struck the drum, rose in triumph and—look, she was full-breasted, naked to the gift of her swelling domes, fearless as a hunter with the gun that she brandished. She was black, in ecstasy, all a-dance from head to foot, with sussurating rattles harnessed on her back and calves.

None of the uninitiated girls could resist practicing this dance, riding in on this rite of passage.[4]

A process almost akin to flying takes place with adolescents, like a bird learning to take wing. A girl's initiation is a complex and mysterious performance, with a stage like the chrysalis stage of a butterfly. This African ritual woke up the memory of my old happiness in camp. I could see the commonalities between my Girl Guide nights and the Zambian girl's rite of passage. In both, we were away from the ordinary world of school, work, and mother in a liminal place. As teenagers, we were at the betwixt-and-between age. Both Ikubi and I camped out in a simple A-frame temporary shelter, near the wilds. Neither of us girls was involved in necessary duties: there were no exams for us at camp and the Kankanga girl did not have to dig. Our indeterminacy, the looseness of fit, and a space in which to change made it possible. Nature figured largely in both experiences, and in both we enjoyed a sense of wonder and freedom. We never forget those experiences.

Communitas can appear in its full glory anywhere. It does so frequently in rites of passage because here is the great mood of people celebrating a new stage, whether it is one's own marvelous marriage, the birth of one's baby, or solemnly—with tears all around—at the death of someone we value greatly. Where these occasions are not over-structured, they burgeon with communitas and generate effectiveness.

In our present culture, ideas about initiation are growing. There are books for teenagers, expressing the idea, "We girls know about girl talk." It is said that the most important rite of passage for the teenager is the secret illicit collective smoking of cigarettes or marijuana. A teenager is recognized to have grown up when making a conscious break from the square parents. The nature of these symbols compared to the richness of the Kankanga ritual is striking.

Nevertheless communitas does exist among college students. An African American woman student told a story. It was coming on to exam time, and she was in the library at 2 A.M., with a whole mass of other students, bent over their work. She was tired. She lifted her head and saw them, all the others. She suddenly *felt* how everyone else was tired, too; she *was them*. A unity. She will never forget it.

The jam session described in Chapter 3 is also a rite of passage. Inventing and finding their own tune, gathering it up into real music, gives the young ones a natural pride and gentleness. The group grows into independence by going into the music on their own initiative and being grabbed by it. The music initiates them and takes them through.

Among Iñupiat children of northern Alaska, the first product of their hands, whether it is beadwork, making a boat, or catching a seal, is entirely given away. This is their initiation. When a man catches his first whale, anyone can take his goods from him—TV, boat, gun, anything. The people are proud of this custom. They have tears in their eyes, both takers and givers. Among initiations, let us not forget bar mitzvahs, or the beautiful Muslim religious schools for children, chanting the poetry of the Quran.

Victor Turner felt the phenomenon of communitas—then not mentioned in the social sciences—among the boys in the circumcision camp in Zambia, the comradeship of those under ordeal together. A crack appears for humankind in its very biology. This is the chrysalis stage of puberty, when the child becomes different than before, finally unfolding into adulthood. There is no such thing as gradual development around the time of puberty. In Africa, there is a time of apparent stasis during the rite of passage when the young boys are secluded. But far from being a time of stasis, things are happening offstage that verge upon the eerie.

The Boys' Rite of Passage: Its Inversions and Comradeship[5]

The initiation of the young is likely to be peculiarly personal for the individual. Each culture has its own take on how physical it is. The boys' initiation in Africa has a blessedness about it because it is an act of inclusiveness. The particular ceremony in 1953, then, was the occasion when Victor Turner first realized that communitas was a phenomenon of prime importance for anthropology. His training in the past had attempted to teach him that all social facts, and especially all rituals, derived from the authority of outward society. That is, rituals were concerned with the various pressures laid on the individual about the way one ought to act. All this was learned. The teaching secured obedience to the mores of the society, and ultimately had a social structural rationale and was evolved for that purpose. This was Émile Durkheim's theory of functionalism.

But Turner saw the rite of passage as a phenomenon that had strength in its own right—that the rite was a pleasure and had great effect, while for the people it was located "out of this world" and in a place that was no place and a time that was no time, sacred, replete with inner rites, ending with a rite of homecoming and time's resumption.

A Rite of Circumcision

The forest villages had a problem. They knew the signs: for instance, the withdrawn air of Sakeru, the son of Chautongi. It was noticed how he went alone to urinate and seemed depressed. Moreover, certain other friends of his seemed to be in the same condition.

Sakeru knew what the matter was. Whenever he had the chance to see the beautifully trimmed penis of his elder brother he was eaten up with envy. Drawing back his foreskin, he gazed with dissatisfaction at his veiled acorn, still wet, immature, and unreleased from its curtain of flesh. That dirty mucus in the folds was what witches used, to kill a man.

It was not just Sakeru who felt this way about a foreskin. When Manyosa helped a little grandson to urinate, her lips quivered with disgust. "Hanging flesh," she said. "Not like a woman's labia." She grinned up at me and touched her lips; I understood the allusion to the ones she bore on her "lower face," as she called it.

In the Zambian village of Kajima, the circumcision ritual was only undertaken every eight years. Along with young Sakeru's depression, the growing number of uncircumcised boys in the neighborhood was a sign that the time had come around again. The villagers gathered together to mount their great rite of passage. Messengers were dispatched down the bush paths carrying information and plans, and these were communicated to Kanongesha, the chief. The date was fixed.

Shortly afterward, ten-year-old Sakeru set out on the trail to the village of Nyaluhana, the circumciser, situated beyond the confluence of the Kakula and the turbulent Mudyanyama River. When Sakeru arrived, he addressed Nyaluhana with the traditional words: "Old man circumciser, what's the use of you; you good-for-nothing, ham-handed old fool with the blunt knife? They'd never think of holding circumcision in your village!"

The old man nodded. He fully understood the meaning of this insolent greeting. It was inverted speech. This was the right way to open the ritual. From now on the participants would be in a different world, an upside-down world, in the time that was no time, and place that was no place. The curve of life would no longer rise on an even slope but would go out of this life in a strange fashion before proceeding, as in all situations of sudden change. Participants would find their ideas upside down and would see things from an unexpected perspective. They were going to exist in an unfamiliar world between one overlapping kind of life and another; a place where anything might happen.

It was a long way to Nyaluhana. Vic and I went on foot like everybody else. He was to write down the ritual, show its depth. I could not venture near the cutting area but could relate it as a story. The string of hamlets thickened as we drew nearer. We briefly paused at a large village surrounded by mango trees before passing on.

"That was Nyaluhana Village," said Vic, but we did not stop there, and instead threaded down a short trail and came out into a clearing; it was as if theater curtains had been drawn aside. A large crowd of people were present, clustered in groups, gesticulating, making fires, stirring cassava. I edged to one side, found a log to sit on, and stared. This was the place called "the Sacred Fire of Circumcision," the supply camp for the boys in seclusion. I could see the boys crowding the entrance of the clearing. Through them was pushing an old man who wore a large sun helmet, under which could be seen two hooded, sheep-like eyes in a withdrawn face. His waistcloth drooped down to his feet so that he appeared to glide without moving any part of his body. This was Master Nyaluhana, the oldest of the circumcisers, whose hand was said to be shaky. I rose and greeted him, but didn't look into his eyes.

Meanwhile, the boys clustered around their fathers and tried to straighten their backs. They were scarcely older than ten, one was only five. Each boy wore discs of white chalk beside his eyes, the blessed *mpemba* that strengthens the soul. Their young faces were expressionless, but their eyeballs swiveled.

People were busy tending fires. Women would be needed in this area all through the seclusion and healing period to cook for the boys, though we were not allowed in the lodge. In the middle of the clearing grew a wiry thorn tree, the spiny strychnine, from which the helpers had been making lotion. The Ndembu called it "The-Tree-of-Strength-that-the-Elephant-Fails-to-Break."

It was exactly eight years before, at the rising of the morning star, when the band of circumcisers had collected the most sacred of the medicines, *nfunda*, to be used this year for the boys. *Nfunda* was a black complex powder made from certain ashes and kept in black gourds shaped like bottles. The medicine contained the burnt foreskins of the boys of eight years ago, mixed with those of sixteen years ago, and so on back to the dawn of Africa. This year it was to be reinforced with a new supply of ashes from the present candidates; thus these children would be ritually included in the comity of Ndembu men, past and future.

There was a bustle of excitement, for the old men had gone to prepare. The thunder of drums arose, singing broke out, and each boy was swung upon the shoulder of the man who was to guard him in the lodge of healing. Then they whirled around the Tree of Strength, and outside them whirled the mothers. The drums beat louder, and into the circle ran the three circumcisers, each wearing red paint, with a red feather of war set upright in his hair. The men crouched down, rose, and roared. Each circumciser held high a striped basket, out of which projected two arrows. The basket contained the *nfunda*; the arrows guarded the basket that hid the black bottles of the ancient medicine.

> The song contained riddles:
> I am the lion
> Who eats you on the trail
> —*Kwalamo!*
>
> You sleep on your back
> You look up at the sky
> —*Kwalamo!*
>
> The high-flying kite has stooped
> To lay her eggs with the stork
> —*Kwalamo!*
>
> The lizard turns around
> Lays eggs in the mamba's hole
> —*Kwalamo!*
>
> Far from home in the lodge
> The child of the chief is a slave
> —*Kwalamo!*

In the morning came the circumcision. A scary figure called "the hyena" appeared and herded the children toward the path into the bush. There was a crashing from beyond, and down the path tore a throng of elders and guardians. In an instant the children's clothes were stripped from them and flung down. Then the spotted hyena came hunting in and out, driving the mothers off, back, back to the clearing, while the men drove the boys between them at great speed through the gate and up into the forest. Nothing remained but a host of little boys' clothes flung down: pathetic old ragged Bermudas, an ancient cowboy shirt with the check all torn, odd little yellow shifts, all the foolishness of boys' discarded lives. These were still part of their old lives, so that it would be dangerous for the boys if the clothes were left on the ground, the place of blood and death. The clothes were draped over the top bar of the gateway to the sacred lodge.

In the forest clearing of circumcision all was ready. Beside two small sacred trees, the milk tree and the ancestor tree, stood old man Nyaluhana, wearing only an apron, his chest withered inwards to the ribs, his eyes baleful with power. He wore marks of red clay beside his eyes, and his hand held the knife he had whetted until you could smell the thin acid steel. The circumcisers were ready.

Now came the crowd of victims, hustled by the men. For young Sakeru, it seemed as if all his friends were going to be circumcised before him. At last his turn came; he was lifted off his feet by two men, his naked body spread-eagle by their arms.

"To me, Nyaluhana," croaked the circumciser, waving him over with his knife. The men laid Sakeru down on the death-place; they wrenched his legs apart and held them tight. His penis lay exposed. It gave a little jerk.

Nyaluhana bent over. The drums bellowed and shouting arose, to drown out the feared cries of pain. But Sakeru was quiet.

Carefully Nyaluhana put his hand under the timid object, and then pulled out the fleshy sleeve that hid the acorn. His knife pricked one mark; did the body tense a fraction? Then another prick at the back. That was the line, all around. When the first spot of blood welled, he tenderly widened the slit with the point of his knife. The men and Sakeru himself held absolutely still, anxious that the work should be successful. Nyaluhana took the slit right around the sleeve and drew the sleeve off, leaving a ring of white that immediately turned red. Sakeru in his pain was lifted up, raised like a spirit over the ancestor tree, and then set down on his feet. Panting, he straddled toward the bleeding place and seated himself on a log. He was circumcised. It was beautiful. In a hoarse voice Sakeru growled, "Kwalamo!"

The log was full. Next to Sakeru sat a bawling child. Sakeru carefully held his own penis out to bleed into the anthill cup provided in front of him, where the blood combined with the seethe of ants. What was to come from his penis later would be alive.

Much confusion and much careful action were in evidence around them. Now Nyaluhana possessed a pot full of black wrinkled pieces, the ingredients for his new *nfunda* medicine. A guardian went down the row of boys and sprinkled them with thorn tree medicine and soothing herbs. The blood retreated and the flesh drew together.

In camp, Sakeru and the boys settled down to a new communal life. Their days were going to be carried on in nakedness, exposed to the wilds for three months before returning home. The guardians piled brushwood around to make a long oval enclosure for the boys at night. This was the lodge, called "The Elephant." The boys learned archaic words for familiar things: food had a different name and it was rolled in balls "like testicles" and was not sent in on a plate. They should not eat any salt, or any spotted thing.

The guardians and boys had a curious game, or custom, which often produced laughter. For a pillow at night each boy had a stub of wood, called "the mongoose." A mongoose is a rat-sized secretive animal related to the pole cats and wolverines, *muskelidae*. This animal is unbelievably brave and can kill a serpent. But this mongoose" was just a stub of wood. It was also the boy's chair which he sat on around the fire. Any stranger that came into the lodge was supposed to show his penis. In defiance, the stranger would grab a boy's mongoose and shout, "Lift a leg!" All the boys had to stand on one leg or else lie down with one leg in the air. The stranger then ran off with the stub to the death place of circumcision, the bloody ground, and until he returned and gave the stub back, the boys had to keep their legs lifted. This mad game was all part of circumcision, and they laughed like crazy.

When the boys' wounds had almost healed, a monstrous being appeared. Sakeru, always on the lookout, happened to turn and saw passing behind him a tall striped creature with an enormous head. He gasped and all the boys gathered to look. The thing groveled along the hedge; the drums beating loud. Where had it come from? Out of the ground? It lollopped and swayed and showed its great hands, bound around with knotted root fiber. Then it took a stick and advanced upon the boys, knees bent, rattles clacking on its calves, head held back in a majestic sunward gaze. From the back of its head rose a threefold serpent, thrusting its tail back and over and up until it stood on end, while the sun, blazoned over the brow of the face, faced up to the sun in the sky. Lightning lines lay across the brow, creating a frown in a jagged row. And tears came from the eyes—long tears. It was mourning for itself, with its little square mouth shaped ready to utter—but no sound came. As the creature drew nearer, the boys ran off squealing. It floundered at them and danced by to the singing of the elders. As it went by, a blow was suddenly felt on each back. Now the glade was full of crying, while the sorrowful figure wallowed in the center, seemingly hardly able to stand. It was *Ikishi*, the Mad Chief.

Not long before the end of seclusion, another bizarre figure strolled around the lodge. This was a tall woman with a heavy, crude face wearing a head cloth, a blouse, and a skirt, below which ugly muscular legs could be seen. The boys looked down at the ugly legs and laughed. It was the *Nyakayowa*, the Ancient Mother.

"You're to be married, you 'first wives,'" declared the guardians. "There's your husband."

The little boys held their heads, dizzy with the puzzle of it. Yes, as novices they were called first wives, but how could this woman be—a husband? Everything was topsy-turvy. To prepare for what followed, each guardian fed his boy with the oily meat of tortoises so that the "head" of his own penis would come out, long and enquiring. Then, one by one, each guardian led his boy up to the Nyakuyowa, who was now sitting entirely covered by a blanket with legs outspread.

"Eh! Eh!" said the child in horrified glee. Through a hole in the blanket he saw a black swelling.

"Go on. Touch her, touch her."

The child felt his own strong heat then, his own swelling, and without looking at his guardian he wriggled closer and closer to Nyakayowa and finally laid his tool against hers.

"You are a man," said the guardian, grinning cheerfully. "Take some *nfunda* now." The guardian had the black bottle open, and proffered some of the black substance on the end of the circumciser's knife. The boy ate solemnly.

"We give you back your bodies," the guardians said.

Now the taboos fell from them, one by one. They feasted on salted cassava and they spotted themselves all over with white clay dots. Their lithe bodies jumped about. They were caught and given grass skirts.

"Come on, wives," mocked the guardians. "We're off to scare the life out of your mothers."

They all lined up. Each guardian chose a boy who was not his own and lifted the child on his shoulder. Each one was a chief now.

"The return! The return!" They ran full tilt down through the forest into the open, into the public world that the boys had not seen for three months.

"Yey, yey, yey!" shrieked the women in joy, ululating their tongues. The boys were carried around the center thorn bush in a streak of black and white spots, each boy clacking a pair of sticks behind his head. The mothers ran around in an outer circle looking for their sons.

"There's his guardian, I see his guardian. But he's carrying someone else! Where's my son? He must be dead. Yey, yey! They've killed him. Eh! Why, there he is. Sakeru, Sakeru!"

"War Leader now, Mama!" called down Sakeru from his height.

Another voice cried, "That one must be mine. No, who's he? Ah, there you are, Sakwimba!"

And another—"Mukengi!"

"Mama!"

Vic was watching. He wrote: "It is impossible to describe adequately the ensuing scene of complete uninhibited jubilation. The guardians ran around in an inner circle and the mothers danced beside them waving scarves, cloths, anything they could lay hands on, while other women relatives and friends made up an outer ring of joyful chanting dancers. The men stood outside the whirl, laughing from pure pleasure."[6] The children were back again, safe and sound.

All that day, after the parents and children were sorted out, the celebration with feasting and dancing continued. The whole of Mwinilunga District seemed to be there to help drink the thirty-six calabashes of beer that had been assembled. Tirelessly they danced around the thorn tree, charged up with joy and relief.

Toward dawn, Sakeru looked around sleepily at the scene: the glow of the fires, the still shuffling dancers, and the brightening sky. There in the east....

"The star!" he cried. "The star is rising!" Over the treetops shone Venus, a pinprick of dazzling light. It was the star of beginnings, the beginning of the day and of arising; the star of the revelation of the glans penis. At every circumcision it was seen like this, and the old men's faith in its coming had never been betrayed.

At Sakeru's first call, the men rushed toward the lodge. Now a roar was heard, and another light rose furiously.

"The lodge is burning, *kwocha, kwocha!*" cried the women. "Hide yourselves, boys, hide your eyes, or you'll go mad."

Suddenly Sakeru's memory came back to him, that of the first touch of the knife. No, looking back was an impossibility, he couldn't do it. There was a blanket on top of him now, and a mat descended on top of that, and his mother was beating at the mat, crying, "Hide, hide," while he stuffed his mouth with the blanket, pushed it into his eyes, pounded and worked his hands, squeezed his eyes tight.

Then he could breathe more freely. The banging ceased; the roar lessened. He had come out the other side. He pushed the blanket away and stood up, finding his guardian waiting for him.

"Up on my shoulder."

The guardians bore all the spotted company down to the river, where they dumped them in the water. The grass skirts floated off and the spots were washed away with the uncleanness of childhood. Cheerfully they scrambled out to occupy themselves with the task of dressing up, which included hair trimming, oiling, and an entire set of new clothes to put on. Each boy was adorned with a band of beads around the hair line and over the top—a mess of little boys full of glee and fooling around.

Mwanta Kanongesha, the chief, arrived at the thorn tree. The boys, dressed in their finery, were carried by the guardians into the clearing amid hoots of triumph. A long mat was unrolled, and the boys were set down on it in front of the crowd. The chief sat before the thorn tree on a carved stool, wearing a white-and-black bead crown with many projecting horns, and around his waist was a leopard-skin apron. The drums and the royal xylophone began their unsteady syncopation. Sakeru the War Leader danced up to the chief and struck the chief's short sword with his knife, the circumciser's knife. The boy straddled, advanced, and retreated in his dance, elbowing and pawing with his feet like the bull buffalo, the strongest animal in Africa. Then each boy followed with his own war dance.

Finally the War Leader advanced and accused the chief:

"I am a man! You, chief, are a fool and a rogue, nothing but garbage. Hah! I, War Leader, command you, chief. Have better manners, do not be so greedy. Feed your children."

Kanongesha's face was impassive. He observed the strength of the boy and his defiance. It was right.

The senior guardian advanced and showed the children. "Look, *Mwanta*. We have guarded them well. Count them, not one of them is missing." It was seen to be true, and the feast began.

As shown in initiations and their time of liminality, the task for us was to "get" the experiences whole cloth. For the Mukanda boys, the three rites ran in this fashion: separation, seclusion, and reaggregation—that is, *kwingisha*, literally "the going in"; next, *kungula*, "in the lodge"; then *kwidisha*, "the coming out." It was the lodge stage that we later termed liminal, and from which we began to develop the theory. Here, in Mukanda, the limen, the gateway of the rite of passage, was marked as the separation place by placing the boys' old clothes over the lintel. At the lodge stage the change took place. Those particular little boys were not coming back. They were now men, and they came out as men.

Liminality and Communitas

In 1958, Turner wrote his account and analysis of "Mukanda: Rite of Circumcision."[7] It was a functionalist, sociological account of the circumcision in the factual style of a scholar. He also wrote a long essay, "Ndembu Circumcision Ritual: Three Symbols of Passage," in *Essays on the Ritual of Social Relations*[8] that focused on the analysis of the symbols in this rite—and gave a richer view of it. Turner was also a poet, and that sense in him informed his perceptions and sharpened his interest in symbolism. Even so, on the topic of Mukanda in that era, he did not deviate from his social science style—except for once, on page 255 of the sociological essay. He wrote the most emotional thing in all his doctoral research:[9] "It is impossible to describe adequately the ensuing scene of complete uninhibited jubilation."

What Victor Turner realized was that, owing to the destructuring and spiritualizing processes involved in rites of passage, a major exciting gift was unloosed, communitas: this is what he had seen. He realized that what may not be easily said may change one for ever—and I realized it on my side, too, thanks to my dear instructors in girl's initiation, Fatima and Manyosa. They taught me that the spiritual world did exist; that companionable love counted for everything and was not just an extra. Through these experiences we saw that communitas could easily flow from liminality. Vic had worked for months with those boys in the lodge and knew all about their suffering, their freedom, and their joy in finally belonging. He saw that this odd seclusion period was a crack in time and space when spirit beings and spirit materials got through.

First, there was the gate, the literal entry into liminality. Inside the lodge there was another world, inversions, a different way of looking at things, and scraps of another language. There was even death imagery. In this realm, there was no social construction of reality by practical adults intent on controlling the young. There was constant laughter and the company of their friends in equality. The circumstances of Mukanda positioned the ritual right across the gulf between child and man, leading to outlandish events having nothing to do with everyday life. The power of social structure was broken.

The Link with Liminality: What Does Our Own Society Look Like?

We can map out sections of society that are liberated from the usual hustle and competition of life, by envisioning a diagram. Take a large circle. In the middle is a pod-shaped ellipsoid containing novices in the liminality of a rite of passage. At the margins on each side are the pods of those near the outside of the circle; these are marginals. On the bottom edge is a hill-shaped pod, the abode of the inferior and the powers of the weak.

Communitas breaks into society through the interstices of structure in all these pods: within the circle, in *liminality of the rite of passage*; at the edges of structure in *marginality*; and from beneath structure, in *inferiority*. Almost everywhere communitas is held to be sacred or holy because it is accompanied by experiences of unprecedented potency.

The liminality of a rite of passage takes over the souls of those going through it. Their characteristics become ambiguous, for where they find themselves has few or none of the attributes of either the past or the coming state. They become the unaccommodated human being, betwixt and between the stages of life. Their secular powerlessness is compensated for by a sacred power, derived on the one hand from the resurgence of nature when structural power is removed, and on the other from the direct experience of the sacred at the key point, though hardly recognized as such. Much of what has been bound by social structure is liberated in liminality, notably this sense of comradeship and communitas. Examples of people in our society who are liminal are teenagers, students, trainees, travelers, those with new jobs, the sick, the dying, those in the army, or those in major disasters. In Western society, there is a paucity of ritual for these occasions; nevertheless, new and spontaneous rituals sometimes arise.

Marginals are often incomers or immigrants who often look to their group of origin for communitas, and to the more prestigious group in which they now live for their structural position. Certain groups of people prefer to be marginal, those who are critics of the structure. Many poets, prophets, visionaries, innovators, writers, philosophers, and contemporary artists are marginals.

Inferiority describes those on the lower rim of society: minorities, the immigrants of necessity, the poor, descendants of slaves. The unpredictable recrudescence of communitas teaches us the powers of the weak, powers countervailing against structural power, fostering continuity, with a vision of the wholeness of the total community whose units are total human beings. In hierarchic and stratified societies, the powers of the weak appear in women, original inhabitants, outcasts, holy mendicants, children, and human rights advocates. The very existence of the weak can remind humankind that in spirituality there is no ranking; there are no peripheries to humanity. Here flourishes communitas and with it the unsolvable mystery of the inversions.

All these groups, for one reason or another, are loosened from the power structure of society because they are different, other. Such folks can easily see their fellow human beings as themselves. They have a sense of the naked unaccommodated human being, the communitas person. Power structures tend to kill communitas. It is the fact of liminality, its aside-ness, its below-ness, that produces and protects communitas. These pods are where the domination system of the corporations and state power is not watching and appropriating all loyalty to itself.[10] The domination system cannot understand liminality. But the liminal desires the liminal, has to be out of the structure game, where it can have its ordinary people quality. There communitas exists, just as grass wants to come up between the cracks.

In the course of life there are multifarious changes, which are not scheduled but which one experiences as they fall out—love, marriage, and parenthood. I have indeed been in love, and the world knows the indescribable glory of sexual union, its gift of ease yet frantic urgency, its comical liberty of speech making everything wicked and happy. Its communitas of two. And being a woman, I know the mother and baby communitas. Trevarthen saw and proved it in Chapter 1. The mother–child relationship has a time dimension, due to the slow development of the infant, and there is no closer relationship. It becomes stacked and packed with memories, the source of billions of little family stories all over the planet, fond looks, shared consciousness, laughter over some ridiculous misdoing.

But how about the father/baby connection?

The Ecstasy of Fathers

Regarding the father's relationship with his child, the men involved seem to have few words to describe it. I heard a father say, "When my baba was a week old, she recognized me as Daddy. Now *that was it!*" It was the communitas between father and baby. Both may sense the "I–Thou" of supreme delight.

Curiously, the relationship does not seem to be a superimposed cultural feature of family life. The explanation is not that cultures teach that the father ought to be protective and kind, so that they are, but rather the reverse. We find that when men have strong feelings they tend to hide them. This moment of love can come unexpectedly.

Wellman among the Fathers[11]

Irene Wellman had been undergoing physical therapy for a frozen shoulder at a small physical therapy clinic in Bedford, New Hampshire. This clinic looked like a cozy house, with a fireplace and small rooms. Her physical therapist, Jake, was a young man in his early thirties. His wife was pregnant with their first child.

Wellman's treatment was scheduled for 7 P.M. It was quiet in there at that time of day. The room had several treatment tables and was not brightly lit. Jake started to work on her arm and the other therapist was treating an older man in his sixties who had a bad back. The older man's therapist was also a young man, with two young children.

Jake was a gentle soul, with leadership qualities. He had a strong, fit body and a healer's firm touch. As he was moving Wellman's arm up and down, he began to talk about his wife and his own excitement at the prospect of becoming a father.

The other client, the older man, suddenly said, "The best moment of my life was watching my first child being born."

The older man's therapist commented that he was scared as well as happy during the birth of his children.

"Yes, it's also a very scary time," said the older man.

Jake said, "On the way home from Hawaii, my wife said she could feel the baby flutter."

"I know that flutter," said Wellman. "It's the first feeling of the baby inside you."

Jake suddenly remembered something that had happened to him on that recent trip to Hawaii. He and his wife were at the airport talking to a fellow traveler while they waited for their baggage. They had told this traveler their names, but he had unexpectedly addressed Jake's wife as "Helen," which was not her name but the name of her dead sister. "Helen died suddenly when she was thirty-two," Jake explained.

"That was very strange," Jake went on. "Why would he call her Helen?" Then he told us how at Helen's funeral, a butterfly had somehow got into the church and was flying around for some time.

Helen was connected in their minds with butterflies, and in Hawaii they kept seeing butterflies.

"Perhaps Helen's coming to us in the form of a butterfly," he said. Wellman was lying on her back now and Jake was working on her shoulders, so she couldn't see his face.

"There're many things in life we don't know," she said. "Many mysteries."

The older man spoke up to continue the thought. "—at the end of life and at the beginning. For instance, when does life begin in the womb?"

The other therapist repeated his words thoughtfully and a silence fell among them. The sense of mystery and understanding among them—two of them being complete strangers—seemed to deepen. There was a strange hush and feeling of flow throughout this conversation. Every word had come easily and with a kind of poetic rhythm. They felt the tug of each other's thoughts. They spoke almost in a higher language, without slang, or self-effacement, or attitude. Wellman felt her arm, which at other times had been painful during therapy, relax and stretch more naturally. She didn't want this moment to end, this contemplation of life and death between them all. As with other heightened moments, time seemed to stop and the faces and bodies around her seemed to be more defined, more clear, more three dimensional, and more dear. And like those other moments, Wellman could sense that they all knew how far they'd come in acknowledging one another, in touching something fleeting and precious.

Wellman went back the next evening for another therapy session, but the glow and gleam of that moment were not there, and she even felt as though she shouldn't try to regain it. She felt a sort of embarrassment at knowing it was gone. It was her last session and after receiving instructions on further exercises, she said a warm goodbye to the two therapists. She knew she wouldn't forget what passed there. She was healing in both body and mind, and more hopeful about how men see life and death and their own children.

A new article has appeared citing research on human fathers and oxytocin:

> "There is evidence that when men become fathers they undergo biochemical changes that affect their behavior. Ruth Feldman of Bar-Ilan University in Ramat-Gan, Israel, visited 80 couples shortly after childbirth and again after six months, and found that the transition to parenthood was associated with increased oxytocin not only in mothers but also in fathers, compared with single, childless people."[12]

In Wellman's story at the therapist's, the moment took all the men in that room by surprise. The topic was sheer physicality, yet tender. Raising a baby comes with communitas, but there is puzzlement later when the children are going to school. Children really don't like school. Yet isn't education a rite of passage?

Is Education a Rite of Passage?

In a sense, anything that people learn that they did not know before entails the passage from some small level of knowledge to another, slightly better, and it is not ritualized. Also, all through humankind, little kids have tended to cluster together, in wide or narrow family groups, and they constantly advance in intelligence. Nevertheless, to us, the second stage of "man" looks like this:

> And then the schoolboy, with shining morning face,
> Creeping like snail unwillingly to school.
> —William Shakespeare, *As You Like It*, act II, scene VII

Instead of a celebration of an advance in maturity—a rite of passage as in Mukanda—we have the structure of school. So it has been in the urban world for thousands of years, reckoning back to the Sumerians. In all those ages education was a valuable asset employed by the wealthy primarily to keep the wealth in the family. Their sons would need knowledge and learning to be successful—while the children of the poor had little or no education. Even so, all children are betwixt-and-between babyhood and adulthood, and will play the game of communitas wherever they can. They well understand play and its joy when allowed freedom. I add an account that shows something difficult and hated by many children—learning correct reading and writing. Here, though, it has become exciting, desirable, and competed for.

"Communitas does exist in education," said Wellman, who works as reading specialist at a rural school. "You have to create the conditions for learning. A person who is learning has to *discover*. To discover, not to pin down, not overanalyze. We get it wrong," she said. "I'm learning we can capture the 'teachable moment.'" This teachable moment is when the conditions are aligned and communitas can pass through. She explains how when the kids are happy and they like the teacher, they will learn anything, *fast*. She described her growing school project, a little magazine called *The Blueberry Express*. It was in its fourth issue.

The Blueberry Express[13]

Allenstown Elementary School is a rural school that does a moderately good job among the children of the poor, including the children of trailer camp inhabitants. Many have no actual books at home at all. The kids come under-clothed in minus-ten-degree weather, red-nosed, pale-faced, and undersized. Wellman would take them individually where possible. Sometimes in a few hours they could read. She told me, "To see their little faces looking up at me with so much interest when they get it is such a joy."

The wee ones started to write. She'd say, "We'll write poetry. About the ducks. About the sky, and the train that takes the blueberries to town." They'd say their little words, and write down the letters that seemed to be right... and she herself would privately correct the spelling and not scold them for being wrong. By this time, they were writing hard.

"We're going to publish the poems," she told them. "We'll have a school magazine."

Their mouths dropped open.

"We'll call it *The Blueberry Express*, and we'll have the Blueberry Express on the front cover, a picture of that puffer train that used to collect the blueberries. How about that?"

One of them wrote:

> I am cold! I am cold
> I am very very cold.
> I have gloves.
> I have a hat.
> I am still cold.
> I am tired.
>
> Finally, hot chocolate.

Wellman put together the simple magazine on the school copier. When Wellman gave me a draft, I was mesmerized. "Hot chocolate? I know the feeling." We instituted prizes for the best poets; the magazine came out, and the children were beside themselves. Prizes! Every year it was the same. The joy of writing spread right up to the higher grades. They could just write in freedom.

What had been happening in the classroom? How could little kids produce a magazine? Wellman explained.

The Communitas of Writing[14]

This special program found its own form of development. The children created posters advertising it; one child announced it over the intercom; they wrote, designed, published, and distributed it—enough copies for the whole school to take home. Communitas reigned from the start. The children discussed each other's writing and flew to help one another. Parents became involved, teachers came out with memories of the actual Blueberry Express, and a reporter even turned up to write an article for his newspaper.

The children, young and old, got to know each other. They were happily playing with their new roles: editorial assistant, copy editor, researcher, or distributor. On the cover page, they were listed as editorial assistants. I called the writers poets, or authors. The fact that the program was not held during school hours also put it outside the school-work routine and gave it an atmosphere of fun and freedom of expression.

The authors insisted on their own styles.

A theme in one issue of the magazine was the solar system. We created name tags with pictures of different space objects, such as asteroids, on them and handed them out ceremonially. We planned an activity with toilet rolls in the gym, to measure the distances between the planets and the sun. The noise level in the gym was quite high, and there was much excitement and interest in the activity, measuring the solar system with toilet paper. We had a student, Jeb, who had a rare disease that made him appear skinny and oddly pale. We gave him the only sun tag and announced that they all revolve around him. His face lit up at this gesture, and the students cheered. Helpers and students were all absorbed and focused on the activity. The groups, mixed by age, gender, class, and grade, worked well together, but it did not feel like work. When the time was up, the meeting ended with a feeling that time had flown.

When education is good, the children do not want it to stop—for example, the tots at a day center. Theodora Biney-Amissah was one of the helpers at a day center. The little children whom Theodora looked after knew the rules, and because of the love of the teachers, were philosophical about the small punishments they received if they disobeyed the rules. They loved school so much that there were many times when it was difficult to make the children go home.[15]

A generation of people will arise not minding the structures in such circumstances. They will be used to them. Structures are human made. They are actually alive, just as the bones of the body are alive and are responsive just as nerves and muscles are.

Initiation into an Adult Community

In 1994, I went to church in a small American city, where I sat just behind the choir and sang along with them. Although I thought nobody noticed that I wasn't a member, eventually a tall tenor named Andy asked me to join the choir, and I did. I found that the choir did a lot of laughing in church and that most of them belonged to an inner community, which I have called the Small Group.

I went along to join the women's group meeting and found the women amiable and doing a little praying, such as "Come Holy Spirit." That done, they got down to the real work—which consisted of feminist-type encounter-group discussions, along with easy spirituality. After a time, these friends let drop that an initiation ritual was in order. The initiation was simply known as "the weekend," in an understated way.

The weekend was held in a retreat camp in the mountains, and was for women only. The wider group was even more flamingly feminist, mainly consisting of very motivated teachers, health professionals, mothers of families, and one or two artists. Most of the choir had made their weekends already and were earmarked to help.

Our initiators constituted themselves as our spiritual helpers and group leaders. They had chosen an active woman out of their number to be organizer of affairs, Rectora. When we arrived at the retreat camp with sleeping bags and luggage, the spiritual helpers took our bags and showed us our cabins. There was a flower on each bunk. We were asked not to speak much, to be quiet. At that, a lot of the greenhorns began to feel cut off. We were put to work to write down what we thought in a private letter "to Jesus." My letter was sarcastic—the set-up looked too holy. It's true I liked being given flowers. Still. That night I took a long time going to sleep because everything was a negative blank.

The next day at the camp breakfast, which we ate at long plastic-covered tables, we learned a doggerel song with a good tune that we immediately picked up from our guitar player, and then we belted it out ourselves. It was about a chicken. Somehow it took. We fell straight into communitas. We were all in the same odd circumstance of not knowing what was going to happen; we ate a lot and talked a lot.

The helpers, every day of that long weekend, told us various stories about *their* own poor little lives—danger from flood, being divorced from a drunk, a child with a disability, being fired from her job. I got the impression they'd been dying to tell all, and I hoped that somewhere along the line we ourselves would get to talk, because we had all had odd and lurid lives. I certainly had.

What was happening was that the helpers were getting behind us and giving us a leg up into this comradeship. Nothing seemed as heavy as we thought. What was beginning was the magical effect of support, actual hefty support from a group that was creating something spiritual. These helpers were united in creating some kind of element through which our own feelings could pass. One thing was certain: everyone present seemed to have been through hell and nobody was "better" than anyone else.

We had religious services at the chapel and to our surprise we found that everyone was singing the songs as loudly as she possibly could, *belting* them out—almost unknown in white American circles. The music broke the shell of our individuality, and we seemed to accept the validity of each other right there in the flowing notes—and all this was taking place in the mountains far from anything to do with our regular lives.

What happened next was a manifestation of the support that the wider group community miles away was giving us—with a puzzling element about it. Each of us received a brightly colored bag full of letters. Letters? Each woman took her bag and sat down outside under her own tree far away from the others. Friends, and total strangers as well, had written these letters wishing me—*me?*—a marvelous experience; the letters were written in all kinds of handwriting and individually chosen words. It was weird how they hit the mark. I teared up. "Oh god, how did they know?" We all cried at our separate readings. We had begun to "get" this experience.

We came back together and did posters at our tables; we talked like mad. We invented a skit, and someone did a deadly imitation of the bishop. One curious episode was not planned by anyone. We went to the chapel for what is nowadays called the sacrament of reconciliation, the ritual that used to be called "confession." All the forty women went to confession. The priest, a man of about forty-five, had distributed little printed cards with long lists of sins on them, to remind the penitents what their sins were. Liz, who had acted the pseudo "bishop" in the skit, and I were sitting next to each other. She read the little card and looked uneasy.

"I can't do this," she said. She frowned. Tears began. "And I was going to make my first confession for twenty years." She was biting her lip. "I did hope...." Her head sank.

"What's this card say?" I said. "Let's look."

I read it. "Oho," I said. "What a loathsome card! No one will go for that. Masturbation, that's not a sin, it's great. Kissing! My God! Where did that little man get this card from? He probably goes in for this sort of thing because he's celibate! He must be sick. Look, there's necking. No sin at all. What's the matter with the guy? And down here it says gloom." I laughed.

Just then, our chief organizer, Mary, came around; she is a great, tough, open-minded lady whom I love. Liz held up the card. All the other women were goggling at their cards.

"Where'd you get that?" snapped Mary.

"The Father Confessor passed them around," said Liz.

"He did? This should never have been given out," said Mary, and she rapidly went around the circle collecting up all the cards, hoping that they hadn't already made too many of her beloved women feel like Liz.

It came to my turn in the confessional room. I looked back at my friends. I was easily the eldest, at seventy-two; I could take this little forty-five-year-old boy. These supposedly lascivious, depraved, criminal health professionals, these fiendish mothers and teachers needed an angry old woman like me to defend them.

I went in.

"I'm going to be up front with you," I said to the imperfect person sitting in front of me. "You should never have put this card around. These women are actually angels. They are working 1,000 percent all their lives for the good. You have no idea. You have no business...."

"They are in sin," he said. "Many who have taken the Eucharist have not confessed. The numbers who take communion when they are in sin are very many. I am here to teach them."

"Not these women. They're not in sin." I knew their lives.

Then he said, "You're in denial."

Aha! I'd got him. "*You* are creating iatrogenic disease." I translated for him in case he had not heard of it. "These are the troubles caused, *caused* by doctors, psychiatrists, and *priests*! Misery, the suppression of joy, fear...." That stopped him.

"Okay. Here's my confession. I've committed the sin of gloom. That's it," and I said the words of the confession. I sat there.

He rapidly gave me absolution and got rid of me as quickly as he could. I marched out of there grinning to the remaining women. "You'll be okay," I said. We weekenders had a fine time for the rest of the period.

On the last night, when we unsuspectingly entered the wooden dining shack, all the tables were laid out with fine linen and silverware, with wineglasses, tall bottles, grapes and cheeses and dainties and flowers. It was the Agape, the love feast. And there at the wide center table at the end, as in the scene on the TV show *MASH*,[16] appeared the communion vessels of gold. It was the Mass. It was awesome; it was somehow the original last supper, a situation of "paramount reality," or an "actuality," as Michael Harner and I have named such events.[17] After all my troubles and anger and conflicts, the feast was there. As George Herbert put it in 1633:[18]

> Love bade me welcome: yet my soul drew back,
> But quick-eyed Love,
> Drew nearer to me, sweetly questioning
> If I lacked anything.
> "A guest," I answered, "worthy to be here."
> Love said, "You shall be she."
> "I, the unkind, ungrateful? Ah, my dear,
> I cannot look on thee."
> Love took me by the hand, and smiling did reply,
> "Know you not who bore the blame?"
> "My dear, then I will serve."
> "You must sit down," says Love, "And taste my meat."
> So I did sit and eat.

After we had partaken of communion and drunk and eaten all the goodies, the accordions were brought out; we danced the Macarena and made wicked jokes.

The next day we looked again at our original letters to Jesus and saw the difference between our feelings then and now, before and after that bit of experience. How could we have been so mean? We wrote another letter and ritually burned the first one. Then before leaving we were taken—in some state of secrecy—down to the chapel. We entered, and it was jam packed with a huge crowd of supporters—previously initiated people, men and women, who rose to their feet and cheered and yelled to see us.

It was the Fourth Day, the return celebration of this rite of passage. Here, each of the novices stood up and said a piece. By now I was walking on air and goggling. When it was my turn, I said exactly what I was experiencing. "'Thy kingdom come'—right? It's come! *This is* the kingdom of heaven."

These words of ours were the initiation event itself, and after that the larger membership of the Small Group took us to their hearts.

Celebration is of this order—in every religion. This one was fully existential to me, as initiations are. I was initiated. And at the same time, I was surprised to find such a rich example of a rite of passage here on my doorstep in Virginia. I recognized it as one of the major pearls of that kind to be found anywhere in the world, a list that included the Apache girls' initiation, the Ndembu girls' initiation, the Burmese boy monks' initiation with hair shaving and a two-year seclusion period, the Bangladesh wedding, the Nepalese shaman's personal initiatory experience, and others—all conceptions of genius, following the instruction of the spirit.[19]

I wanted to add my weight to the task of reopening the heavy door that has been barred in serious philosophy, anthropology, many aspects of religious studies, and the study of the psyche against the *experience* of religion. What, then, of the Small Group? It gave me, immediately and directly, the knowledge and vivid experience of a spirit power sizzling under my fingers like the power in an old-time overhead trolley bus arm that brought the electricity down into the trolley engine.

Is this material embarrassing? Pseudo? Not good? To me, it is first-class material, existential, solid as rock, and on par with Wordsworth's presences and shamanism and African spirit rituals and the dreaming of the Aborigines and Black Elk and the best in anthropology. Why on earth taboo it from polite society?

What stands out about Small Group initiation is its well-practiced social effectiveness—the effect of deliberate support; the effect of a *group* of people moved by love. This is not a social milieu such as in competitive business, what one might call social I. This is social II, where the souls of a group of people are at one. What is the nature of support, communitas, social II? What is the actual phenomenon of change of consciousness, and how does it differ from the usual understanding of the term so that it can be experienced by a plurality of people at once? Here is an element of ritual that needs more attention.

The goal is to lay together the characteristics of spirit events so as to arrive at a recognizable object, the social human being, social II, found in any culture or religion. Having ventured into all sorts of paths, I saw how they wound around and under each other and into me and out again. The rich complexity one encounters gives an even greater material rootedness to this spirit process going on across humanity.

Old Age: Longitudinal Communitas[20]

If we live a long time, reverberations of communitas occur and something lights up when we come across it again. Wordsworth mentioned it in his poem "Yarrow Revisited." When people have to be apart, threads of memory are created and those threads strengthen in time. They develop into a distinct picture like an artist's completed picture from a sketch, and they become a whole continuous story, a story of a communitas continuing further. You build on it. It then becomes bonded in.

In a curious way, ancestor power comes down. The gift of the spirit comes of itself (as it came to Tumbuka healers in Africa after initiation), without stress and pother. It is simple, and unconsciously dead-on.

Death

The elderly—the anthropologist Dell Hymes (who passed on), my sister, Anna, my hospital neighbor when I was an inpatient, my mother who suffered from aphasia after a stroke, and many others—went into another land for a long time before they died. Through illness and at the final point of death, families and society come around to recognize the communitas with death. I recall loved ones who faced death quietly, in a sense "elsewhere." They had a gentle communitas with death, the same quietness Whitman celebrated in his long poem "When Lilacs Last in the Dooryard Bloomed," written after the assassination of Lincoln. In that country of death, he saw it "gently arriving," with "lilac and star and bird." That was all he needed to say. Rainer Maria Rilke also knew the same country of the early dead, with its willow trees and their heavenly pollinated catkins drooping down. "Death" was the place of happiness, "happiness falling." The breath when it is going out is the visionary one, besides being the strongest.

Dying "rises up and folds over." One can show it with one's hands. There are two moments. They fold into each other. It is solemn—a sort of somersault, a cartwheel—it goes over into something else, its opposite. One senses the opposite. It affects everybody around, everyone is smoothed—at the same time. It is like being on the same side as a moebius strip—a moment of understanding. One may not notice it, but still, it is there.

An extraordinary phrase arises from the Celtic vision of "the hollow hills," the home of the *tuatha de danaan*, the holy ones. Their inside is outside. If you stamp on the rocks on the stone lands in the Irish Burren in County Clare, you hear an echo below your feet. Could it be a place in and out of time where the dying and those who have passed away find themselves, where we may visit and listen for them?

To describe communitas as ephemeral uses a wrong word. Communitas folds over and back; it is not on our time scale. It is solemn. It is marked; we are aware of its serious nature.

I hear of the extraordinary happiness of working in a hospice, where people are dying all the time. The helpers' happiness? It is true. Something marvelous is going on, helping people to reach a strange new world.

Some of these methods of homing in on the sense of communitas need attention. There are several methods. The methods are almost like science, in their great attention to the "I get it!" syndrome—Archimedes's shout, "I've found it! Eureka!" The next chapter, therefore, opens up to us the way a key unlocks a door, using the principle of alignment.

Chapter 10

Alignment: Turn the Key and the Door Opens

> *Everything is going right with the rower in the racing skiff. Time stands still. The rower looks for a second at the other oarsmen and sees that the magic has touched them all. In that one peep the oars lift out of the water with the blades perfectly aligned like teeth in a comb. The boat and everything in it seems to be moving of its own accord. It is perfect. They win the race and climb out of the boat without saying a word.*
>
> —Laura Scherberger

George Mentore has said, "When the conditions are aligned, communitas can pass through." And Roy Wagner has said, "Think of parallel beings. When two of them are together they never stop laughing." Why did he say that, and why are they laughing?

In this book we have learned about people "getting the idea," or "getting it." Why does this arise? Why do sudden realizations occur? The answers may become clearer if we look at several simple cases. Then we may grasp what alignment is and what triggers it off—whether we are talking about something in spatial terms, or spiritual, or something as easy as laughing, "getting" a joke. There are circumstances surrounding communitas that suggest that it does indeed have something to do with people finding themselves in a state of alignment. Such a sense of alignment stems from many and various practical experiences. Sometimes one way of experiencing reality, perhaps in irritation or helplessness, becomes overlaid by a different sense of things—perhaps the sense of everybody being in the same boat. Then everybody starts pulling in tandem. They become aligned. In cases of communitas, "something" seems to have pulled human souls right over (like dragging a text with a computer mouse) into a better position where they match. Communitas clicks on. One feels this adjusted position is right, and it works.

I remember studying the physics of light with lenses, finding an image of an object using two lenses and adjusting the angle so that the images converged without parallax. Two images became one. We were focusing correctly and, thanks to the alignment of the lenses, we could see the image clearly. This alignment seems necessary with communitas, as well.

I often take my walks down a steep hill leading to a small creek with a dam and a pond. There are two overflow pipes through the dam bank that send water down into the creek below. When you first come down the road toward the stream and arrive at a point below the level of the dam in front, you can see the outfall end of the pipes, dark and blank inside. You go just a little further on, and at a certain point, you can see right through both pipes at the same time, just at the moment when they are aligned with your eyesight. Then you see the pond, brightly lit, through both of the pipes.

Here is a musical example: there are two violin players; the first playing a note a half tone apart from the second. The first stays firm on her note while the second draws the sound closer and closer to unison with the first. As is well known, when the second is all but in unison, a weird throbbing, or vibrato, breaks out and does not cease until the two sounds become exactly the same. Then the shaking stops.

This vibrato is called beats, or beat frequency, due to the interference of one wave frequency with the other. Finding unison here is through a process of aligning sound, gradually getting the sound waves into one simple line. The recognition of the process goes beyond the mere dislike of an interruption in clarity. The vividness of the beats and the subsequent feeling of resolution is said to send people into trance. I have noted that the resolution flicks some people into happiness, even an experience of blessedness.[1]

A scientific picture of this is the experiment of Thomas Young in 1804; he caused a narrow beam of light to issue from two adjacent holes and then onto a screen. He found the two rays formed bands of brightness and darkness, high crests and dark areas where the two rays interfered with each other. The result was an effect like two stones thrown in a pond, forming exaggerated ups and downs where they crossed, which he called interference fringes. It told him that light consists of waves, not just particles, as in Newton's theory; that they had an identifiable wavelength such as is possessed by all types of physical energy.

A further clue is found on the surface of the Pacific Ocean, where there is always motion, a parade of regular ocean waves right across the vast expanse. However, there are many islands in the ocean, and the regular wave motion is broken by each one. The ancient Polynesians in their outrigger canoes found their way back and forth by their knowledge of the particular broken pattern of the waves with their exaggerated ups and downs that existed around each island, and they could do this when there was no sunlight and without a compass. They were familiar with every aspect of the waves' alignment. This was the way they discovered New Zealand, two thousand miles away.

This puts one in mind of the beauty of moiré, watered silk, where the weave of the material is deliberately woven in a curved and wandering direction, producing in the shiny silk distinct rays and flashes whenever the waves of the silk randomly face the light.

Thinking of these random moiré patterns, we may consider the extraordinary gift given to a watchful soul. We may witness an African diviner with a basket of small and varied figurines and objects. Troubled people ask him the meaning of their bad luck or disease, and what to do about these maladies. In response, the diviner draws his helping spirit close, holds his basket firmly, and tosses the objects. Up fly a tiny trio of embracing figures (a "family"); along with a "jealous deceiver" figure; also a coin; a charred bit of wood, "the funerary fire"; a bit of calabash shell, "property"; a bit of mirror glass—all kinds of things in a quick wave in the air. His mind catches a kind of line of sparkles on the edge of some irregularity in the random mass, sparkles that have meaning. The combination settles in the basket and he "reads" the objects concerned.[2] He has *seen*, and he can tell his petitioners the cause of their troubles and what they ought to do.[3]

Alignment in Art

Steven Friedson in his study of African music and healing likened Tumbuka ritual drumming to another visual effect of alignment. This was the curious now-you-see-it-now-you-don't experience when facing those three-dimensional random-dot stereogram pictures that stand up inches high out of their print when one squints the eye.[4] Then one easily sees the lamb, or raindrop, or whatever it is, high, and hovering above the paper. It becomes quite clear. And then the stereo effect goes away.

Similarly, as Friedson says, once a person can hear the music of the drumming in its rhythmic depth—consciously adjusted with slight changes—then the musical experience is transformed into a kind of multidimensional hearing that transcends acoustical phenomena. The whole becomes an entirely different, stand-out acoustical apparition, showing the spirit presence itself. It gives a sudden sense of expansion that bears a terrific charge of energy, heat, and glory, real, not other-worldly but of this world—belonging to the time and space of the world we occupy. One does not have to believe it—the spirit is simply there. The music has slipped the people out from one level into another, by means of a this-world pattern that uses many things at once with great subtlety. Something in people *can* accomplish this. When we are in that moment, it is pure joy. The shift has taken place.

Friedson effectively translated the visual to the aural. A visual effect similar to the moiré effect is seen in the twentieth-century art world. In the 1960s a school of painting grew up using the moiré effect for the sake of its power. It was led by Victor Vasareli. The painter Josephine Harding explains that Vasareli painted a canvas full of two lines going one over the other so that the viewer might encounter the two passing each other at the same time. This happened in such a way that, where the overlapping occurs and comes to a point of convergence, one has a strong sense of belonging and of absolute oneness.

Extracts from a review of the Vasareli group of painters offer information that may help the reader understand more about the alignment experience in this mode of painting.

Review by Shane McAdams[5] of Work by Artist Liz Deschenes: "Moiré #2: Registration"

These prints are made by exposing film to natural light filtered through a perforated scrim, which gives them the appearance of ultra-concrete, super-flat monochromes. Deschenes uses these discrete circles as a base layer onto which a second exposure is overlaid; the slightest shift of registration during this process produces a surprisingly dramatic array of effects.

As one moves toward the work, the monochromes begin to separate into black and white dots. In turn, one's eye naturally bites at the gestalt produced by the speckled field and begins to pull images from the abstraction. Disturbances created by the moiré patterns inevitably read as hazy landscapes; ghostly accidental shapes floating in a hazy gray atmosphere. At a really close range, the obscured landscape gives way to a nausea-inducing field of vibrating black-and-white dots. In the thrall of such optically hypnotic prints, the viewer is unavoidably drawn closer to escape the enveloping effect of the vibrating visual field. These seemingly straightforward pieces are sirens, beckoning viewers deeper inside a slowly unfolding story; a story that ultimately leads from minimal to maximal. For in all the two-tone surprises of the moiré pieces, they unpack a final colorful twist. Although the nature of the process polarizes dark and light, producing an overall black-and-white image, the prints are developed on color film, which results in a slight tonal variation that reads in the dearth as lush color. The color is barely there, but it lunges forward, exploding with a pop.

Do these provoke a suspicion of the presence of optical illusion in these pictures and in divining? We must not forget there is an artist's mind at work, a person who has discovered visual alignment almost as if she were a Polynesian sea voyager, sensing the islands. But she has also grasped the joy aspect of the finding—how it relates to the discovery of something strange, beyond, "mind-altering." We are granted through these experiences a look in to a surprise, part of life that is pure gift. This sense of alignment/communitas is not religion in the usual sense. I recognize that people see it as a glimpse of god, an amazing presence. The matter is sometimes accompanied by real danger, or sometimes the person will resist the sinking into the oneness. The horror of the pre-event, the "nausea-inducing field of vibrating black-and-white dots," the headache-inducing "beats" in the two-string sound effect, exists in many cultural and natural expressions. It is there in the extraordinary book by the Puritan John Bunyan, *The Pilgrims' Progress,* when his main character Christian, a desperate man, tries to start the journey to the Promised Land. At the beginning gate, his mentor, a character called Good-will, is waiting for him, and as he enters, gives him a tug.

"What was that for?" Christian asks.

"They...shoot arrows at those that come up to this gate, if haply they may die before they can enter in," says Good-will.[6]

It is seen in Dylan Thomas's cry, "Do not go gentle into that goodnight, Rage rage against the dying of the light," and in Rilke's wonder at the Great Death, the enormous resistance of a dying man. Then there is Jesus's final despair on the cross, "Father, Father, why have you abandoned me?" Many women have a similar despair in childbirth—just before the waters break.[7] It feels as though the birth is simply not going to happen. It is *after* one gives up and takes it as hopeless that one somehow relaxes, the waters finally break, and the great successful contractions begin in earnest. Then the child passes along in the tract like an express train and emerges alive.

A similar vein runs through the accounts of near-death experiences, bliss after the struggle, that enormous relief, that sudden color, "lunging forward, exploding with a pop." So it was for the art of Liz Deschenes.

This play of lines and irregularities are what we are drawn to; we need to resolve those beats. We need that true alignment, and we can achieve it.

"Flash" signals; interference patterns; moiré patterns—using such vehicles, the human social element enters, triggering off strong person-to-person connections. This comes out in full force in the following case of a Buddhist monk who was the State Oracle in Tibet. On the monk's annual day as the oracle, his alignment with his god spread to much of the city of Lhasa. Furthermore, the communitas that formed his support was seen in the form of the passionate love of the whole crowd, such as is given to the Dalai Lama. This great ritual has been described and recorded by the anthropologist Ter Ellingson. On such occasions, the Buddhist monk who is also a shaman goes into trance, receives the god, and then, in a state of trance, is burdened with an immensely heavy crown. He bursts from the monastery holding a bow-and-arrow while receiving and giving great psychic power. The crowd presses forward to throw him white scarves, even braving his arrow.

Alignment in Spiritual Traditions: The Oracle of Tibet[8]

Very early in the morning, inside the monastery, drumming starts up and the monks gather around the man who will give himself in this way. High above the altar is a picture of three gods in their palace surrounded by a great mandala. Down at the foot of the picture are depicted the monks, their hands folded in worship; one can see their drums and cymbals on each side and their cones of rice offerings in front on the altar. At the same time, the monks are standing, in reality, surrounding the oracle monk, their hands folded in worship; behind them are the actual rice cones and drums. Men are playing the drums, producing an unforgettable slow, rising, hastening, and thundering sound, right up to a climax, then a fall. Another wave of drum beats gathers force, rises, and fades away. The moment is approaching when the god falls into the world. All present steeple their hands and focus intently on the god who is to come. The oracle monk finds that he is abandoning himself to its presence. He finds the one word to say, a mantra. At once the god and his own heart are joined by a ray of light that fuses the two identities "like water flowing into water." At this moment all the monks feel the strong waves of blessing, an effect that passes to the assembled crowd outside, changing many lives. One more great towering burst of sound is made, and trance overcomes the oracle. From that time onward, the monk remembers nothing.

The assistants array the monk in the god's robes and place a mirror on his chest, a reflector that gives him humility and detachment from the world. The mirror is a membrane, marking where divinity begins. On the monk's head they place the enormous, conical, ornate crown weighing fifty pounds. They steady his head for a moment, then in his trance his muscles grow and he is able to support the crown. Nevertheless, his face is humble and accepting, listening, like a servant, for he has become the oracle. They put a bow-and-arrow in his hand. The drums bellow, the gates open, and he goes out to meet the crowd.

The special consciousness of the Oracle has combined with the special consciousness possessing the other monks, and it passes to the crowd outside. Hundreds and thousands of people have assembled in the predawn darkness before the induction ritual began. All of them have heard the drums thundering from the monastery and have caught the sense of religious energy. The god has entered them, too, through the music.

When the oracle emerges, the crowd is frenzied. Men, women, and children charge forward, reaching for contact with the oracle, trying to present him with white greeting scarves, or simply throwing the scarves at him. They are oblivious of everything, even of the danger from the arrow he is grasping, its fletched end set into the drawn bow.

What has happened is that the oracle has allowed his own consciousness to recede so that he can be the instrument that makes it possible for the whole assembly to become aware of the god. The drums and the moment of the mantra produced the oracle's transformation of consciousness. It was at this particular time that the god fell into the world. This is "alignment"; one recognizes the power of the great mandala picture, the presence of actual rice, the care with which the music is handled, and then its alignment with the spirit, so the exact climax of the vibration releases an opening to bliss. The oracle monk finds he slides away into abandonment to the god's presence, which "fuses the two identities" like water flowing into water. This is the point of activation, the "fall" into the decisive moment that can change a life. And it is at this point that trance overcomes him. Now there can be an invisible presence on earth.

In central eastern Mexico, Victor Turner and I witnessed an example that was both geometric and spiritual.

Two Shamans' Tombs at the Winter Solstice in Mexico

During the winter of 1969, Turner, Chicago graduate student Jorge Serrano, and I took a trip from Mexico City down to the Gulf of

Mexico at Tuxpan. We went on to Tamiahua, where there is a pre-Columbian pyramid near the coast. Jorge, who is also a Jesuit priest, wanted to show us the pyramid. It was a late afternoon toward the end of December. We parked the car and came to the foot of the structure. It was a low, wide-topped pyramid, among trees. We climbed its close-set stairs to the exposed flat summit. Laid into the stone, we saw two tombs, side by side.

"Shamans' tombs," said Jorge. The tombs lay parallel to each other, pointing off into the hinterland, which by now was shadowy with the approaching sunset. We could see the sun slowly moving down along the crest of mountains on the western horizon. As we looked in the direction the tombs were pointing we saw a notch on the horizon that the sun had not yet reached.

Sun? Notch? "What's the date?"

"Twenty-second of December," said Vic, quick, sharp, "And look at that!"

The sun slipped neatly into the notch, then was gone. Between the notch and the pyramid on which we were standing, halfway across the shadowy land, rose two mounds, neatly paired on each side of an exact line from the notch to us. I traced the view with my finger and let my arm fall to my side.

At the Gulf of Mexico, we vividly understood the placing of the pyramid in relation to many miles of the earth's surface in connection with that particular date, the winter solstice. We saw that those two shamans' deaths had been treated very seriously indeed. For one thing, the burial of those visionary beings anchored them permanently into the landscape. It was also an act of honoring the sun—for the Mexicans, the sun was "our father." The placing had recognized as sacred that unseen line from the tombs to the horizon. This Gulf pyramid linked human beings to what we call nature, the sun and mountains, just as Wordsworth in his visionary way saw the burial of young Lucy: "Roll'd round in earth's diurnal course, with rocks, and stones, and trees."[9] The ancient people had used precise alignment to make the point, and it was awesome.

The next illustration tells of a deeply human and personal ritual act, the alignment of light.

The Light Shines on Her Face and She Takes It into Her Heart, by Joseph Whelan[10]

For the women who light the Shabbat candles, it is not only a means by which they connect themselves to a culture, a history, and a family identity, but a way in which they allow their children to establish a relationship with that same culture, history, and family. At the moment of lighting the candles, time disappears or collapses. All the memories of loved ones past, together with one's children, the seed of future generations, collapse into the women of the household who are lighting the candles. Together with their family, and the many thousands of other Jewish families that are also lighting the Shabbat candles as the sun sets gradually across the earth, time disappears, and past, present, and future all collapse into the seventh day when God rested—the moment the world is both destroyed and recreated in one final embrace between God and her people, and the world is healed. We catch elements of this relationship constantly as we go about our day and experience the world.

Here the sun ritual takes place within a home, not on a faraway pyramid involving ancient strangers, but with people we know. This careful alignment made by the mother with a match and a candle contains in it the entire sacred moment and produces obvious communitas—this ritual that is aligned to the sinking of the sun, with candles and prayer. It propels all things into that sacred seventh day, that of God's completion of his work.

The Jewish prophet Elijah might well be sitting there with them.

Alignment in Music

We saw this careful alignment toward creativity in Matt Bierce's experience of jamming described in Chapter 3. He demonstrated exactly how the miracle of composition reaches humanity. At the heart of it we hear how the players collectively align themselves to the new sound, never heard before. Other instruments join in, feeling and harmonizing with the tune. We see co-alignment in action. Moreover, as Jerry Kelly says, "The piece of music and the audience somehow become bonded together in such a way that you, the music, and the audience are merged into one another and form a single whole for a moment."[11]

The same "communitas of music" runs through a passage written from the point of view of drummers. David Azzam, a young Western drummer, also discovered the crisis point between the narrowing of intensity built up in drumming and the breakthrough resulting in flow. He says,

> Flow is a crucial part of the power of music. In order to be able to tap into flow, one must first focus with the greatest sharpness on the task in hand. Focus must be exercised precisely and with determination, going impossibly on with the work, never mind what. Finally, before one realizes it, something "clicks," and suddenly there is no more focus, there is only flow. The two are merged. One becomes a

channel for the flow of musical energy. Everything works, the flow has momentum and will continue as long as we give ourselves to it. The sense of timelessness and loss of self comes into play. When enough people can lose their ego and participate in the energy flow, the music reflects it. The performers and listeners breathe as one entity—the collective energy can flow through the entire crowd.[12]

There is a distinct connection between alignment and communitas here.

In 1953, Maya Deren discovered that the drumming in Haitian Voudoun could take her into another world. She recognized the different plane of consciousness into which she was transported:

> The drummer can "break" to relieve the tension of the monotonous beat and bodily motion, thus interrupting concentration. By withholding this break he can bring the Loa [god] into the heads of the participants or stop them from coming. He can also use the break in another way by letting the tension build to a point where the break does not release tension, but climaxes it in a galvanizing shock. This enormous blow empties the dancer's head, leaving him without a center around which to stabilize. He is buffeted by the strokes as the drummer "beats the Loa into his head." He cringes at the large beats, clutches for support, recapturing his balance just to be hurtled forward by another great beat of the drum. The drummer persists until the violence suddenly ceases, and the person lifts his head, seeming to gaze into another world. The Loa has arrived.[13]

This contrasts with Azzam's gentle searching and Friedman's drummer with his secret revelation, but it is the same endeavor. One is reminded of Deschenes's picture and the violent dots of her reinforced wave effect. Somehow we learn the way of great attention, through our very exaggerations. What we come out to at the end is the wonder, the vision.

In these musical examples, one hears the theme of co-alignment. The whole community sometimes searches for the resonances of its entire group, together, in a celebration of our giving of ourselves to each other. The result of the search by such a body of musicians for the whole group's alignment is overwhelming. Music is rich with these examples of alignment. When the anthropologist Colin Turnbull experienced music with the Mbuti pygmies of Congo it became what the ritual of Christian communion could be and sometimes is—a transfiguration of everything, a person-to-person-and-onward-to-all instant reaction.

The Mbuti ritual, Molimo, far in the tropical forest, is carried out by these relatively untouched human groups. The Mbuti love their forest above all things, and they use music for healing in a social milieu of the greatest communitas. The Molimo ritual is available for all and does not highlight any particular individual.

Turnbull witnessed the ritual and pondered its implications when he lived among the Mbuti in the Ituri Forest in the 1950s. He found that Molimo was a work in which an entire group of people became one in a change of consciousness, for the benefit of all. The people gathered frequently for this to happen, and Turnbull was taught that the ritual was the will of the forest. The people made their way in to the presence of the spirit of the forest, conscious of everything they were doing. Their song was deeply attentive, as Turnbull discovered.

"Making Good": The Pygmies' Song in the Forest

The following are selected passages from Colin Turnbull's account of his experiences.[14]

In my first trip to the Ituri Forest I not only witnessed several dramatic, vitally important central rituals, I experienced one of them in particular as a fully participating (however foreign and temporary) member of that society, the Mbuti pygmies. I had come to the Ituri Forest because of my interest in the music, which was far richer and more complex that anything I had yet heard in Africa. The experience brought about for me a radical change at a deeply personal level.

I quickly found sound, in general, to be a vital factor in distinguishing the two worlds of the Mbuti, the forest and the village. The people said I would have to come into the forest with them, as they only sang their real music there. We set off on the path that led northwards, and we shouted, "We are coming, mother forest, we are coming." The forest rose almost sheer at the edge of the village so that it was literally only a matter of a few steps from the hot, hard, arid village path to the cool, soft, moist, shady trail that ran through the forest to the distant hunting camp. As the Mbuti walked along that medial stretch of firm ground the village world would become obliterated and the forest became the sole, entire, exclusive universe. And speaking for myself, it was in that place of sacred seclusion—"liminal," threshold ground—that the forest and the *molimo* sound that I was to hear became merged—as I entered the one I entered the other....

Molimo was the most complex and the most moving music in the forest. The Mbuti sang these songs at night seated around a fire when there was a felt need to cure someone's sickness, "to make good," as they put it. Because of the curing power of song, it was sung from the very outset with great intensity, all the more intense because the singing was so quiet to start with. One feature of the music was that in any melodic line, each individual note was sung by an individual singer in such a way that no one singer carried the entire melody, but each carried an essential part of it and all were therefore equally necessary. Moreover the song form involved both *canon*, "round"—with overlapping voices—and *counterpoint,* the combining of a new incoming melody line after the others had started that harmonized with the original line. This complexity forced me to concentrate all the harder on what I was hearing. In sharp contrast to the complexity the singers' body positions were as relaxed as were their movements—to be seen when they sometimes rose and performed a few impromptu dance steps before sitting down again. I myself felt a strange mixture of relaxation and intense concentration, and I could not put the two together, they seemed incongruent. On the third occasion, no longer afraid I was going to miss anything, and no longer looking for any explanation, just intent on enjoying myself, I closed my eyes and felt free to join in the singing. And in an instant it all came together: there was no longer any lack of congruence, and it seemed as though the song was being sung by a single singer, the dance danced by a single dancer. Then I made the mistake of opening my eyes and saw that while all the others had their eyes open too, their gaze was vacant.... There were so many bodies sitting around, singing away. Something had been added to the importance of sound, another mode of perception that, while it in no way negated the aural or visual modes of observation, none the less went far beyond them. The *molimo* seemed to incorporate all the elements; the totality of the present, including the singers, dancers, listeners, as well as the central fire, the sound of the ritual *molimo* trumpet, the camp itself, the clearing in which the camp was built, and the forest in which the clearing stood, and whatever, if anything, contained the forest, and it very definitely included whatever is implied by such equally ambivalent terms as God and spirit. The whole outside world, other than the forest surrounding that one hunting camp, ceased to exist. And similarly with time, anything that was in the past or the future simply did not exist. All past and all future were annihilated.

When the time came for me to leave the Mbuti and return home, they cut a leaving mark into my forehead. I felt something very strongly, not so much embarrassment as the touch of power, an awareness that something had happened to me, that some transformation had taken place, that I had lost a certain kind of personal, individual power and freedom while gaining another, infinitely greater. Thus by allowing myself the freedom to feel I had allowed myself to be touched by some power. That was when I felt clean and whole, free of all doubt and worry. It was not that any questions were answered; it was simply that they were removed. At first, at the conscious level, they just became insignificant and inconsequential, then they simply vanished. Here we were safely far beyond the reach of mere reason and that rational form of religious experience known as "belief." The liminal state is well perceived as a timeless state of grace.

To conclude, what is needed for this kind of fieldwork is a technique of participation that demands total involvement of our whole being. Indeed it is perhaps only when we truly and fully participate in this way that we find this essentially subjective approach to be in no way incompatible with the more conventional rational, objective, scientific approach. On the contrary, they complement each other and that complementarity is an absolute requirement if we are to come to any full understanding of the social process. It provides a wealth of data that could never be acquired by any other means.

Turnbull knew the enchantment of achieving perfect flow and alignment with the singers. He saw how flow created a group connection that was able to tap into curing power, so that troubles simply vanished—"the song was being sung by a single singer." It was a moment of alignment when the flash went over.

There is always a special quality in the singing of a round or canon, and it had a powerful effect, far away in the Ituri forest. The Mbuti used this art quite independently from the rounds and canons derived from European and medieval sources from which our own knowledge of canon singing arose. But we can tell from our own knowledge of rounds what the molimo singing felt like. We might choose a round such as "Frére Jacque," or "Row, Row, Row Your Boat," or "Dona Nobis Pacem" to experience a similar sense of alignment. Everybody sits and one person starts up that favorite bit of music, a sweet verse with four lines, each line opening with different words and tune. Only this tune of four lines, in its full consecutive form from beginning to end, is framed so that the melody for each line will agree harmonically with the other three lines. So, one person sings the first line, going on to the second. At that point another singer joins in, singing the first line which overlaps the second line that is already beginning—and finds that the tune of the first line agrees with the second line—and blends beautifully in harmony. Everybody in turn picks up the beginning line one after the other in the same way, delivering just the right sound, each sound in its right place. And so it proceeds, with the second line agreeing with the third line and so on to the last line, until everybody is singing in a beautiful changing harmony in four parts, each person forever beginning again after finishing. There is always some overlapping curl of sound that rises high, yet harmonizes neatly all of its own. The other sounds fit in so well that carefulness with the notes becomes second nature. Then you don't know you're doing it any more, it's doing itself. As far as you can tell it never stops—each person's sound arising, fitting in, growing, rising, and being overlapped again, happy to fall below and carry the others along as they in their turn arise. The whole array glides on in flow. This is eternity, one voice flowing like water, bending and streaming and joining.

How may we access this plane of consciousness in our modern thinking? In order to follow Turnbull's experience of deep attention, I borrow a fictional, allegorical account of the same kind of discovery, in storyland. It is a scene of search and careful alignment to what a person can hardly see—to the point of its realization.

Alignment in a Modern Fantasy: The Way to Obtain Access to Liminal Space by Cutting a Hole

Phillip Pullman[15] has written three novels about a boy, Will, and his friend, Lyra, who escape from danger into another world. The books collectively are known as *His Dark Materials*. In an excerpt from the second book, *The Subtle Knife*, old man Giacomo is teaching Will how he can find access to liminal space, through a hole in the air.

> "You have no choice! Listen to me because time is short. Now hold the knife out ahead of you—like that. It's not only the knife that has to cut, it's your own mind. You have to think it. So do this: put your mind out at the very tip of the knife. Concentrate, boy. Focus your mind.... Think about the knife tip. That is where you are. Now feel with it, very gently. You're looking for a gap so small you could never see it with your eyes, but the knife tip will find it, if you put your mind there. Feel along the air till you sense the smallest little gap in the world...."
>
> Will tried to do it. He put the knife down and cried.... But then he felt Pantalaimon's head on his knee. The dæmon, in the form of a wolfhound, was gazing up at him with melting, sorrowing eyes, and laid his head on Will's knee....
>
> Pantalaimon's gesture worked. Will swallowed hard and stood up again, wiping the tears out of his eyes.
>
> "All right," he said, "I'll try again. Tell me what to do."
>
> This time he forced his mind to do what Giacomo Paradisi said, gritting his teeth.... Lyra knew this process. So did the poet Keats, and all of them knew you couldn't get it by straining toward it....
>
> "Stop," said the old man gently.... "No hurry, go gently, don't force it.... Just wander... to the very tip, where the edge is sharpest of

all. You become the tip of the knife. Just do that now. Go there and feel that, and then come back."

Will tried again.... No less intense, he was focused differently now, and the knife looked different too.... Perhaps it was the way it sat so naturally in Will's hand, but the little movements he was making with the tip now turned purposeful instead of random. He felt this way, then turned the knife over and felt the other, and then he seemed to find some little snag in the empty air.

"What's this? Is this it?" he said hoarsely.

"Yes. Don't force it...." It was easier. Having felt it once, he knew what to search for again, and he felt the curious little snag after less than a minute. It was like delicately searching out the gap between one stitch and the next with the point of a scalpel. He touched, withdrew again to make sure, and then did as the old man had said, and cut sideways with the silver edge....

He kept careful hold of the knife and put it down on the table before giving in to his astonishment...because there in the middle of the dusty little room was a window...a gap in midair through which they could see another world.... They were high above North Oxford.... There were houses, trees, roads, and in the distance the towers and spires of the city....

Giacomo Paradisi said, "So much for opening. Now you must learn to close...."

"For this you need your fingers," he said. "One hand will do. Feel for the edge as you felt with the knife to begin with. You won't find it unless you put your soul into your fingertips. Touch very delicately; feel again and again till you find the edge. Then you pinch it together. That's all. Try.... Just sort of relax your mind...."

"All right," he said. "I'll try that."

And this time it was easier. He felt for the edge, found it within a minute, and did as Giacomo Paradisi had told him: pinched the edges together. It was the easiest thing in the world. He felt a brief, calm exhilaration, and then the window was gone. The other world was shut.

Pullman shows the gift of alignment in this moment-by-moment account. He even quotes Keats's negative capability, a central element of communitas. Negative capability means an emptiness of the hands, willing to wander. Turnbull on his part shows the gift of alignment in the readiness to dare, to go 120 percent for the chance of the moment when it arrives, with its joy. It flourishes where there is a mutual purpose, a mutual experience. In many rituals in Africa, in Umbanda in Brazil, among Iñupiat dancers, in my choir in Charlottesville, a point something like an electrical circuit comes alive throughout the group—suddenly there, in everybody—and we act as one person.

In 1985, I went back to Africa after a thirty year gap and did not know I was to lose my handhold on cold objectivity and would be swept into a flood of spirit showings and magical choreography in the ritual of Ihamba. I lost my footing and had to swim. I saw as the natives saw.

Alignment and Healing: Ihamba[16]

What happens when one searches for communitas for four hours? When all the company knows what is going on and when the stages of the ritual are familiar to them? The process is set going and it is carefully fulfilled. Then, to everyone's satisfaction the spirit comes.

My student Bill Blodgett and I were watching the Ihamba ritual in Zambia. The ritual was intended to draw out an afflicting spirit, an *ihamba* in the form of a tooth, from a sick woman, with drumming to bring power for the discernment of the spirit. Support from the community with singing and clapping was essential to the success of the ritual.

From the first, the ritual power was accumulating. Meru, the patient, was seated in the middle with her palms turned upward in front of her. Now the doctors started to perform. The drums began with a rapid threefold beat and the people sang in plangent harmony. Meru's body was rocking to the music, a sign that the spirit was favorable toward the intentions of the ritual. At this sign, the doctors applied cupping horns to her back to draw out the biting tooth.

The crowd of villagers grew. It was a ritual needing great persistence, aimed to create a throughway for the angry spirit—to grow close and personal with it, exactly what Jung in our culture recommended for those afraid of the forces of life. Collective harmonized singing was of highest value in this ritual. The ritual was a procedure disinhibiting the psyche, designed to open it up and awaken the recognition of a distinct spirit entity.

Meru suddenly started to come out with her grievances: "*I don't agree*! I've got something bugging me on my liver, in my heart. It's my children; all my children are *dead*!" They had left her and gone elsewhere. The people heard the grudge breaking out at last and were pleased, and they sang loudly. They saw something concrete amiss in her physical body and her own group—and they saw it as spiritual.

Singleton Kahona, the medicine man, stood in front of Meru with his eyes shut, quiet. He listened, and then sang loud, above the other voices.

"It must be Kashinakaji," he said: he was right. This turned out to be the source of the biting spirit. Singleton had been tracing the effect of ritual, tracing its delicate tuning in those sensitive psyches who, being kin, knew each other very well. Singleton was aligning himself with those kin of his around him and with the former cause of the trouble, which was a case of indemnity for murder that had resulted in Meru's present sorrows. It was time to have the matter out. For this Singleton used his tiny gazelle horn to do exactly the same work as Will's, feeling for the tooth in Meru's body. The horn was packed with medicines. Singleton passed it up and down Meru's body, feeling it jerk when it passed the hidden tooth. Sometimes the tooth moved, to escape being caught.

Singleton saw the spirit and was addressing it directly. As the drums began again, he savagely addressed the cupping horns on Meru's back, "Twaya! Fuma! Get out!"—as if he were shouting at a thieving dog.

Now the heat was drawing up black clouds above us; Meru fell shaking in the midst of the singing, in the dim light under the shade branches. Singleton worked on the cupping horn on Meru's back but when he took it off it was empty: another disappointment.

The drums began anew. Singleton danced savagely backward, hopping on one foot. "Keep singing," he gasped. The sweat was running down his face. He again addressed the horns, his voice harsh. While the percussion thundered the people sang with throbbing voices. In the midst of the heady rhythm, Meru keeled over again, her body twitching in the dust.

"She's fallen!"

"Get out!" yelled Singleton, working on the body with horn and bag. "We'll show them *chiyanga* [the hunter]!" And the song took up the refrain: "*Wuyanga, Wuyanga, Wuyanga, Wuyanga, Wuyanga, Wuyanga*"—hypnotically, endlessly, in which I joined: "*Wuyanga, Wuyanga*"—shaking my head with pleasure as I sang.

Singleton begged and bludgeoned the spirit: "I've said all my words. Just *listen* to what I've been saying. Can't you hear me? We want this thing to come out. Let's beat those drums; let the drums touch the earth—you've been refusing, I tell you. We want this thing to come out! Now! We're not happy."

"We have every medicine to make Ihamba come out," said Singleton. "We need you to come out with your words. Tell your grudges and help make the Ihamba come out." I myself had my grudges. I was gazing across the crowd at my drunken translator.

"They want me to come out with my words as well," I thought. "I want to participate, so much. But how can I?" It was impossible to speak words against the family of the drunkard, and in accepting it tears came into my eyes. The tears came out and I felt the stab of their pain.

And just then, through my tears, the central figure swayed deeply. All leaned forward; this was going to be it. I felt the spiritual motion—a tangible feeling of breakthrough—going through the whole group. Meru fell; Singleton was very agile amid the bellow of the drums, swooping rhythmically with finger horn and skin bag ready to catch the tooth; Bill beat the side of the mortar in time to the drums, and as for me, I had just found out how to clap. You simply clap along with the beat of the drum, and clap hard. All the rest falls into place. Your own body becomes deeply involved in the rhythm, and everyone reaches a unity. Clap, clap, clap. All of us were on our feet. This was it. In the middle of the commotion, the doctor took his bag of medicines and his receiving can and lifted the cupping horn from Meru's back. Immediately she raised her arm, stretched it in liberation; then I saw a gray spirit form come out, a gray miserable sphere of guck. The doctor caught it in his can, and she was cured. Singleton later showed me the human molar tooth that had come out.

Here was alignment: Singleton had clearly been aligning himself with those present, with his past kin, and with an object inside Meru's body. The moment came when all present were united, when all the grudges were out in the open, his own anger included. It was a moment of birth. He spotted the *ihamba* tooth that had been sucked through the veins into the cupping horn. He knew it was consummation.

Lévinas (Chapter 8) laid out this major sense, that of *being* the other person, a calling to be the other that was infinite because the other person is infinite and utterly complex. In the depth of one's disappearance into the other person there appears this marvelous feeling of coming home, of it being alright; there are many friends around; the universe is okay after all.

In my understanding, the self is a naturally turned-around organism and thus operates naturally in respect to its fellows, like Trevarthen's babies in Chapter 1. Christopher Crocker worked with the Bororo of Brazil[17] in the 1970s and saw that the village moiety system, an elegant kinship arrangement, was enabled by the inversion of the power of each part. In that system of men/women, family spirit/nonfamily spirit, earth shaman/holiness shaman, each side inverted its own ostensible power with respect to its opposite. In the

Amazon rainforest, as in the Congo or Inuit village, the means for a peaceful life in the village work themselves easily into everyday life, with the feeling that things are right in this inversion. This is where the two parallel beings of Wagner can find themselves comfortable together and have their fun. There appears to be Lévi-Bruhl's old law of mystical participation in operation. In a sense, we sometimes accidentally maneuver our lives to a position exactly over that which is ripe for mystical participation, again as if we were dragging them on our computer screens with a mouse and we suddenly "got them." We may never come to know exactly *how* to do this deliberately. We may come nearer to it if we take note when it happens so that we can recognize it when it wants to appear. Whatever happens, we can align with it, and act on it. We can move into harmony with it.

In Chapter 8, Harvey in Guatemala had to be totally focused, of one heart, for him to be able to help the sick man, as the healer Miriam pointed out. Harvey the anthropologist saw this in a human way, and called it sympathetic entanglement.

Sliding Off Alignment

Finally, we encounter certain untimely interruptions of communitas. Yet the cases that I am going to show demonstrate the people's even stronger loyalty to communitas.

Sliding off alignment is hard. Among Iñupiat shamans, a man in trance is "dead" and in the spirit world—therefore he would literally die if he were suddenly disturbed by the banging of pots in his vicinity. Alignment is alignment. One has to be able to listen for it. Those in trance need supporters. It follows that those who get used to prayer and communing with God should be treated tenderly. There may be communitas and flow afoot; people are very lucky when it comes.

The 2004 Olympic marathon perfectly illustrates the effects of the sudden disruption of alignment. Vanderlei de Lima, a Brazilian, was set to win. Everyone could see he was "on a cloud." His running gait was perfect, set to go for ever in true alignment. It was magical.

Vanderlei de Lima and the Olympic Marathon in Athens, 2004[18]

...As expected, not until mile 11 did any runner try to break from the very large pack. It was Vanderlei de Lima of Brazil who decided to make a break—beginning at mile 12 while the rest of the pack of 60 runners just watched. By mile 17, de Lima had built a 40 second lead. Only three men were chasing de Lima: Stefano Baldini of Italy, Paul Tergat of Kenya and Meb Keflezighi. At mile 21 de Lima saw he could hold on for the final 5 miles. But just after 21 miles, a fan ran across the road and grabbed de Lima, pulling him off the course—this was incredible. The spectator pulled de Lima completely off the road before other fans were able to free de Lima from his grasp. This lost de Lima almost ten seconds, but psychologically, it was devastating—and perhaps he was somewhat injured. De Lima was now a dozen seconds behind Keflezighi, but ran a strong second and finished with a bronze.

The lingering question remained—what would have happened had that crazed spectator not thrown de Lima off the course? He was the gutsiest runner in the field and led through 6 miles, and from 12 miles through most the whole course of 26.2 miles. However, he looked quite happy with his bronze (the first marathon medal ever for a Brazilian), and smiled as he did his own victory lap.

The God Jagannath with No Hands[19]

At Puri in Orissa in India is a temple that houses the sacred statue of Jagannath, the very statue that is yearly enshrined in an enormous car and dragged by worshipers down the main street of Puri. There is an interesting story associated with this deity. It tells how Krishna appeared to his great devotee, King Indradyumna, and ordered him to carve a deity from a log he would find washed up on the sea shore at Puri. He searched for a carpenter to make the deity and found a mysterious old Brahmin carpenter who appeared and took the responsibility to accomplish it in a few days. Surprisingly the carpenter insisted that he should not be disturbed while he was carving the deity, and started working behind a closed door. Everyone, including the King and Queen, was very anxious and came every day to the closed door. They usually heard sounds of working. After six or seven days of anxious waiting outside his room, all sound stopped. Indradyumna's impatient queen was worried about what had happened. Assuming the worst, they opened the door—only to find the deity half-finished and the carpenter vanished.

The mysterious carpenter was none other than Vishvakarma, the heavenly architect. The king was distraught, because the deity had no hands and feet. Utterly repentant that he had interrupted the carving, the king was only pacified when Narada, the sage, appeared and explained that the form the king now saw was a legitimate form of the supreme personality of godhead.

I visited Puri in 1979 and saw the crowd outside the temple door and the people busily obtaining favors around the water fountain. I was not able to enter the temple, but I peeked in through the door.

Jagannath was facing outward with two large circular eyes that gazed on me hypnotically, and sure enough, his arms came to an end in blocked-off circles. The people told us that for long ages that fact had bothered no one.

The Norse God Thor, Whose Hammer was Too Short[20]

The story of the creation of Thor's hammer, Mjöllnir, is well-known. The mischief god of the Norsemen, Red Loki, had a bet with the dwarf brothers Eitri and Brokkr that they could not make Thor a worthy gift on their forge. Loki bet his own head on it. The brothers set up the forge and Eitri put iron in it, telling Brokkr to pump the bellows and never stop blowing. But Loki was determined to stop him. He turned himself into a stinging fly. The fly came and bit Brokkr on the arm, but Brokkr continued to blow. The fly bit him on the neck twice as hard. But, as before, nothing happened. Loki bit Brokkr on the eyelid much harder than before and the blood made him stop blowing for a short while to clear his eye. When Eitri came to take out Mjöllnir, the handle was a bit short (making it one-handed). Yet Eitri and Brokkr won the bet, which was to be paid with Loki's head. But the bet could not be honored since they would need to cut the neck as well, which was not part of the deal. So Brokkr sewed up Loki's mouth to teach him a lesson. Thor proceeded to work wonders with his great hammer.

Kut for a Korean Shaman by *Laurel Kendall*[21]

When Laurel Kendall with D. S. Lee made the film *Kut for a Korean Shaman*, we saw a scene of careful alignment when the teacher shaman showed the novice shaman how to receive her spirit helper. The novice had to balance barefoot on two knives set with their blade edges upright. The poor novice was struggling like young Will with his knife, afraid of failure. But one could see in the story how she took courage, stood on the knives, and actually touched on the spirit's presence for a moment. The labor of teacher and novice was that of alignment to something other than the ordinary, and it mattered to them and to the viewer. Many know the unity that gently lifts them over the sharp edge and deposits them in the haven.

Then what is this exactness, somehow involved in the mystery of communitas? Alignment is an ordinary word for an ordinary physical matching up of parts to fit perfectly—to reinforce each other, like car wheels. In social life, this is how people come to terms with each other, and they like it. In communitas, one viewpoint actually slips into that of another. What I have done here is to show alignment from the smallest case onwards. This phenomenon, like an autonomous independent organism, will not agree to be assimilated into something else but obstinately exists in its own right, a recognizable process.

This is the key to communitas; the flashes in an elusive curve; flashes that speak to the diviner as he performs; the joy when the Mbuti perfect the trick of "making good" by means of the interweaving of their round singing.

It is the exactitude, the precision with which the listeners catch the tune; the search and the sensitive touch needed for venturing through the membrane, which is extraordinary. This is something we become so avid for that we elbow our way through the gap, over or through the wall, flinging ourselves into the arms of the one-time enemy.

We see that our world is real, in company with the spirits who are comrades proposing ideas and marching ahead of us. Here I have allowed the spiritual dimension into the material one, which social scientists are not supposed to do. I am stating I have one heart, and I have found that this does not disqualify me from speaking in the friendly forum of anthropology. For these are *findings*, findings encountered in research. *Nihil humanum alienum puto*—I consider nothing human to be alien to me. We respond to the up-and-doing nature of energy and set our caps to the future, especially for our children, even great-grandchildren, who will soon, maybe, want to invent a living computer.

Conclusion

A Natural History of Collective Joy

> Communitas is precisely plural reflexivity, the self actively bending back on itself. It is intersubjective reflexivity, where each one is the true mirror of all. Not "binary" oppositions but permutations and combinations of relationships between varying numbers of entities, and the flashing signals from cluster to cluster on different planes and levels.
>
> —Victor Turner[1]

The richness, the naturally occurring communitas described by Turner implies an open readiness without preconceived ideas. There is a democracy and humility about communitas: no one can claim it as their own. In 1996 in Africa, the anthropologist Roy Willis saw this with his own eyes and experienced the permeability of the human soul. It took place in a ritual where the Lungu people of Zambia had gathered to cure a sick woman. The woman sat among them quivering to the rhythm of the drummer, while the seekers tried to divine her spiritual helper:

> "Mbita!" someone cried, triumphantly repeating the newly uttered name of the patient's *ngulu* spirit, along with four other names. A moment later the spirit-filled body of the patient ceased its convulsive quivering, the wordless cries of pain or ecstasy ceased, and, amazingly, the figure rose to its feet, suddenly whole, reborn from suffering and chaos. And now, in its new, changed state and moving with the continuing rhythm of the drums, the spirit danced before us all, visible, revealed.
>
> It was the spirit dancing, in a slow languorous way, a smooth gliding movement, sensual too, with simultaneously gyrating hips as the human-spirit-body turned through a wide arc, then a spiraling movement along the cleared dancing space, going through this sequence of gliding, swooping movements several times. Now the whole group was

dancing with "Mbita-who-was-the-patient," the new spirit, in a dance of spontaneous joy at her epiphany. All were filled with divinity.

To end the session the medicine woman went to the patient and twisted the hair on the top of her head to bring her around from her trance. The patient had no recollection of her altered-state experience. She literally had no words to describe it, nor had the medicine woman....

For us all, the drumming and the movement had pleasantly dissolved the boundaries of ordinary selfhood. Now I felt in a spaced-out state. There had been a hard-to-find "gentleness" about the night's performance. I was lifted out of normal consciousness into a state where ordinary perceptions of time and space were drastically altered. I knew that we are all related, different versions of each other, but that there were no fixed boundaries to selfhood; there was a permeability and flexibility between self and other, an infinite flexibility, and again this sense of everything flowing within the all-encompassing rhythm of the drum. I experienced the dissolution of the ordinary sense of time and space, the coordinates of ordinary selfhood, the sense that "I" am a person with a particular inventory of social characteristics, including a "position" in society, living at a particular time—all these defining and localizing criteria temporarily vanished. I was indeed in Victor Turner's state of *communitas*, intensely aware of myself in relation to my fellows. Interestingly, I could "see" myself more clearly than in ordinary reality, when self-perception is typically more fragmentary, tied to one or other fleetingly relevant social role. Then, in the moment of *communitas*, I saw myself whole and objectively. I was "at home" and among, as it seemed, "kinsfolk." I discovered that the state of *communitas* provides access to those transpersonal entities or forces commonly called "spirits."[2]

Here, where we seem to be following the very electron in its path and movement, we watch how the scene develops from that one person dancing in her holy trance. Soon the entire group dances, and is in it, and we see how its ending is carefully brought about with the attention of the medicine woman.

Communitas—what it is? Trying to answer is like trying to locate and hold down an electron. It cannot be done. Communitas is activity, not an object or state. Therefore, the only way to catch these "electrons" in the middle of their elusive activity, in process, is to go along with them in the very rush of their impossible energy, "kissing the winged joy as it flies."

Again and again come those precise indications of elusiveness—if that can be said, "precise." When we come across references to God as if God were equated with communitas, we encounter characteristics that are rarely mentioned by theologians. We are puzzled because it is the *space between things* that makes communitas happen.[3] Structure tightens, but communitas suddenly happens in the space between structure. It plays "hide and seek" with us. It is like the whale for which we once watched—its playful aspect. "It plows the upside down, leaves foam images—photographic, phosphorescent—to fool you where it is."[4] The spiritual does not want to be defined, so it plays with us to dodge definition. Communitas resists analysis.

Turner said:

> Spontaneous communitas is always completely unique, and hence socially transient. It can never be adequately expressed in a structural form, but it may arise unpredictably at any time between human beings in any kind of social grouping. The phase structure of social life in complex societies is punctuated—without any institutionalized provocations and safeguards—by innumerable instants of spontaneous communitas.[5]

The anthropologist Joanna Overing said this about Native Amazonians: "I challenge the reader to use the language of Western modernist theory to successfully say anything with a ring of authenticity to it about Amazonian egalitarianism, or aesthetics, or poetics, or sociality, or polity."[6] Yet communitas appears obvious to those who experience it. It is my hope that the ethnographic accounts given here and the reader's own perception will provide the understanding that cannot be confined to words on the page.

There is even a desire to keep communitas from ending. The desire for continuation was present with the bunch of children in afterschool activities, building a solar system. It was time to go home, but the students did not want to go. Inevitably one thinks of Solzhenitsyn and the builders in the icy Gulag, a curious but valid comparison. They did not want to stop. Communitas reveals itself through tricks. In 1928, Alexander Fleming was working with a row of bacteria cultures and found that one of them was a dud. Something had gotten into it, and he would have to throw that culture out. But *what was that?* Something had *killed bacteria!* The trouble turned out to be an immense gain: it was penicillin, and through it came a whole range of antibiotics.

Communitas was discovered similarly. When it finds its way into a situation, it seems to kill the bacteria of money and power and makes any culture of "sins" look unimportant.

Peter Ochs's Experiment with Scholars of Three Religions: A Close-Up View of the Development of Communitas[7]

Peter Ochs told how he had been running an interfaith workshop in the religious studies department at the University of Virginia, whereby groups of people from different religions met—Judaism, Christianity, and Islam. He organized them into groups of six, with two Jews, two Christians, and two Moslems in each. They were encouraged to have their own religious texts with them as desired. They met for several days, and Ochs watched the process.

During the first day, they carried on nice civil conversations with one other. On the second morning, some aspect of the engagement caught their attention, but they were not sure what it was. By the second afternoon, they realized what it was: they felt a great interest in each other—and the communitas suddenly flared into being. Ochs's face was grinning all over when he told me this. "It happened precisely during the second afternoon! There it was. They saw each other as themselves. It happened with all the groups of six I tried it with."

One can see it—those scholars catching hints from each others' texts, and then there it was. Within two days, they had come to find the same communitas.

Coda

> When the soul wants to have an experience of something, she throws an image of the thing ahead of her and then enters into it.
> —Meister Eckhart[8]

This book is obviously incomplete. There is a whole world of examples and pointers to communitas that I have overlooked, much work and theory that I honor, yet could not include. I hope—with excited interest—that other books will appear setting this right. Furthermore, I have not dealt with the negative aspects of communitas, nor do I show tough realism: for instance, there are no statistics about how much good or harm communitas may do to people. Communitas is concerned with the delicate and permeable energy zone that surrounds people, that invisible film to be snagged with the tip of the sharpened knife of consciousness. So my work has been devoted to presenting the faculty of perception. I say "Look!" I have presented the insights of many whose passages are included here. From these come real sparkles—flashes, as Bob Dylan called them—all the way through the book. Communitas itself is the uniting thread in the book. Something, some agent—like the harpist by herself with her beloved instrument, bending her head to the music's message—is using the connections, the alignment, to words or sounds of the soul. At this delicate level, there is wholeness and knowledge of communitas.

Notes

Introduction

1. Excerpted from the mission statement of the journal *Anthropology and Humanism*.
2. Victor Turner 1969, 128.
3. Ibid., 133.
4. Colin Turnbull 1990.
5. Steven Friedson 1996.
6. Roy Willis 1999.
7. Tenibac Harvey 2006.
8. Joan Koss-Chioino and Philip Heffner 2006.
9. William Powers 1982.
10. Then Northern Rhodesia.
11. Victor Turner 1975, 255, quoting Sartre in *New Left Review* 58, 59–60.
12. Dawn Hunt, personal communication, June 27, 2009.
13. We may follow the birth of the consciousness of communitas from early studies of ritual. Its first glimmerings were found in the work of many great anthropologists of the past. Perhaps the most fundamental of these glimmerings appeared in van Gennep's [1960 (1909), 15–18] discovery of the literal "transitionland" of liminality between two countries, the anomalous "marches," the no-man's-land territory between them. Thus, having enlarged the notion of passage through unowned territory, van Gennep applied "liminality" to the phenomena accompanying changes in social position—that is, initiations—and documented this from various ethnographies of the time. Later, Victor Turner (1969) took up the concept of liminality, "threshold-ness," as the curious sense that prevails in the rites of passage that accompany the betwixt-and-between of social positions. The very anomalies of this phase of rites of passage release the initiates who pass through it from the normal dictates of society and tend to highlight, in contrast, their basic humanity. Thus, we have the notions of "being under the dictates of society" and of "common humanity," the two as contrasted, as the reverse of each other.

14. Bronislaw Malinowski 1989, 158.
15. Ernst Cassirer 1961.
16. Arnold van Gennep 1960 (1909).
17. Victor Turner 1974, 231.
18. Urban Holmes 1974.
19. Tom Driver 1991, 152–165.
20. Edward Bruner 1984.
21. James Fernandez 1984.
22. Miles Richardson 1990.
23. Barbara Tedlock 1992, 1995; Dennis Tedlock 1990.
24. Timothy Knab 2003.
25. Duncan Earle 2007.
26. Bruce Grindal 1992.
27. Don Mitchell 2009.
28. Margaret Trawick 1990.
29. Nadia Seremitakis 1991.
30. Jean-Guy Goulet 1994.
31. Steven Friedson 1996.
32. Edith Turner 1996, 2005, 2006.
33. Roy Willis et al. 1999.
34. Stephen H. Sharp 2001.
35. George Mentore 2005.
36. Laura Scherberger 2005.
37. Tenibac Harvey 2006.
38. Mieka Brand 2007.
39. Jill Dubisch and Raymond Michalowski, 2001.
40. Pedro Pereira 2008.
41. Sónia Silva 2009.
42. Joan Kiss-Chioino, ed., *Do Spirits Exist? Ways to Know* (special issue), *Anthropology and Humanism* 35 (2), 2010.[43] Jo Thobeka Wreford 2008.
43. The structural order of states and big business can be likened to "hydrogenated oil," natural food oil that manufacturers have treated under high pressure and changed, so that it can never go rancid and cannot be destroyed. It is trans-fat, and neither can it be got rid of from the human body; it is dangerous. It can be seen as analogous to the way states and corporations construct systems to be indestructible and therefore convenient.
44. Some of the knowledge, such as dates, names, and bare facts, is taken from Wikipedia. The author uses the Web generally, with caution—and gratitude—much as one uses a library.
45. See also Chinua Achebe 1996 (1958).
46. The method of showing communitas by its opposite was first proposed for the book by Rose Wellman, personal communication, August 2005.

1 Contrasts: Communitas and False Communitas

1. Excerpted and paraphrased from Colwyn Trevarthen 1980, 83–85. (Braselton et al. 1975; Papousek and Papousek 1975.)
2. Excerpted and paraphrased from Colwyn Trevarthen and L. Murray 1985, 180–195.
3. Colwyn Trevarthen, personal communication, 1982.
4. Stories derived from an account by Kelli Nash and Courtney Stafford-Walter, personal communication,, April 26, 2007.
5. Excerpts from Carl Lindahl 2007, 1526–1538. See also http://muse.jhu.edu/journals/callaloo/v029/29.4jasper.html. Pat Jasper and Lindahl are co-directors of the Surviving Katrina and Rita in Houston project and may be reached via e-mail at hurricaneshtown@aol.com. Lindahl, an American Folklore Society fellow, is the Martha Gano Houston Research Professor of English at the University of Houston.

2 Festivals: July 4th, Carnival, and Clown

1. Edith Turner 2008, 77–78.
2. Edith Turner 1993, 225–252.
3. Derived from Laura Scherberger 2005, 55–69.
4. Clifford Geertz 1973, 416.
5. Don Handelman 1977, 116–118. I have liberally paraphrased his story and reframed it.
6. Excerpts from Mikhail Rabelais 1965, 7–11.
7. See Victor Turner 1982a, 27; Roger Abrahams 1982.
8. Excerpts from Patrick Sawer 2008.
9. Derived from Don Handelman 1990, 238–243.
10. This wedding custom seems to belong to the category of rites of passage, as the term is used in Chapter 8. However, the custom also has strong calendrical associations, as we shall see.
11. Pnina Werbner 1986, 240.
12. Ibid.
13. Derived from Don Handelman 1990, 238–243.
14. Victor Turner 1969, 201.
15. Claire Farrer 1991, 112–115.
16. *Black Elk*, quoted in Neihardt 1932, 1959, 160. Available at: http://en.wikipedia.org/wiki/Heyoka. Accessed April 27, 2009.
17. John Fire Lame Deer 1972, 250.
18. It will be noticed that this list is not organized into types and eras. I have allowed it to form itself of its own accord, because each item seemed to have its own way of propelling another item before it. The

reader may try to organize it rationally, but the material will dodge out of her scholarly grasp.

3 Music and Sport: Being in the Zone

1. The Chinese annuals are in *The Descent of Man* 1871 New York: D. Appleton.
2. Attendees at a top neurobiology conference on music have agreed that musical sounds were the forerunners of speech in humans (Trevarthen et al. 2006).
3. The Ihamba extraction ritual is distinct from the Chihamba sacrifice ritual mentioned in Chapter 2.
4. Presented at the International Conference on Mind, Brain, and Culture: The Neuroscience of Music, Crete, 2006.
5. Colin Turnbull 1990.
6. See Robert Desjarlais 1992, 206–210.
7. Robert Desjarlais 1992, 183–184.
8. Roy Wagner 2001, 160.
9. Ibid., 168.
10. Ibid., 166.
11. Mickey Hart et al. 1990.
12. The following comments are from David Stang's notes, personal communication, April 2002.
13. I use "in the zone" in the sense that athletes and musicians have used it, to be "in a mental state of dissociation of consciousness from skilled performance." Available at: en.wiktionary.org/wiki/in_the _zone See also the following: "Where every player wants to be. When players are in the zone, they're not thinking; they're just playing at the highest level they can possibly play. When everything they do is right they are out of their mind."Available at: www.life123.com /sports/golf-tennis/tennis/tennis-terms.shtml.
14. This is the essence of altruism, the sacrifice of the self for the other, also known as altruism. See Chapter 7.
15. Matt Bierce, personal communication, December 5, 2000.
16. Rory Turner, personal communication, 2001.
17. See also Edith Turner 1992.
18. See also Even Ruud 1995.
19. Mihaly Csikszentmihalyi 1975, 1988, 1991.
20. Zen, see http://en.wikipedia.org/wiki/Zen.
21. Andrew Cooper 1998, 29.
22. Ibid., 33.
23. Ibid., 38.
24. Ibid., 42.
25. Ibid.
26. Ibid., 62.

NOTES

27. Ibid., 64.
28. Ibid., 44–47.

4 The Communitas of Work: Surprising Conclusions

1. Emile Durkheim 1965 (1915).
2. Victor Turner, personal communication, 1945.
3. Aleksandr Solzhenitsyn 1991 (1961), 61, 97–180.
4. The worker is alienated from the product—since its design and production are appropriated by the capitalist class and escape the worker's control—and also alienated from the act of production itself, so that work is reduced to an endless sequence of discrete, repetitive, trivial, and meaningless motions, offering little, if any, intrinsic satisfaction. See http://en.wikipedia.org/wiki/Marx%27s_theory_of_alienation#In_the_labour_process.
5. Aleksandr Solzhenitsyn 1961, 61.
6. Ibid.
7. Ibid., 98–101.
8. Ibid., 98–113.
9. Comment added from personal communication, Irene Wellman, July 2008.
10. Quotations from the mowing scene are taken from Leon Tolstoy 1995 (1877–1879), 250–256.
11. Quotations from Tolstoy's account are taken from Leon Tolstoy 1995 (1877–1879), 786–788.
12. Van Griffiths, a condensed version, December 5, 2007.
13. Martin Buber 1947, 42.
14. Ashleigh Elizabeth Shepherd was familiar with the concept of communitas and saw it in her work as a bus driver around the streets of Charlottesville, Virginia. April 26, 2007.
15. Martin Buber cited in Victor Turner 1969, 127. Turner tells us that Buber is referring to the idea of communitas more than community when he makes his observation.
16. William Blake, see http://www.brainyquote.com/quotes/authors/w/william_blake.html.
17. Bronislaw Malinowski 1922; see also in Chapter 7. Trobriand tribesmen in Melanesia celebrate giving by traveling between the islands in a circle, giving and receiving wealth articles.
18. Turner 1996a.
19. Mentore 2005, 86.
20. Many remember the movie *Babette's Feast*, a story of appealing communitas where food seems to work magic.
21. John Bunch, personal communication, September 2007.

22. Naomi Shihab Nye, passed on as personal communication by Kate Adamson, April 13, 2007. With thanks.

5 The Communitas of Disaster

1. Claudette Bethune, personal communication, January 2008.
2. Derived from Linda Jencson 2001, 46–58. Names of Red River Valley residents are changed to protect anonymity. Names of famous persons, politicians, government leaders, and city officials are unchanged.
3. Like the courtesies of the bus drivers in Chapter 4.
4. The death toll cannot be verified. There were 4,081 deaths according to Dr. Lindsay. See http://robertlindsay.wordpress.com/2009/05/30/final-katrina-death-toll-at-4081/. The losses in housing units amounted to 850,791. See http://www.scribd.com/doc/265292/Hurricane-Katrina-Fact-Sheet.
5. Derived from Carl Lindahl 2007, 1526–1538. Available at: http://muse.jhu.edu/journals/callaloo/v029/29.4jasper.html
6. Ibid.
7. Paul Stoller 2004: 184.
8. Derived from Diana Collins's account, May 5, 2008.
9. As a matter of formality, all names are pseudonyms and physical descriptions are not provided in order to prevent possible identification.
10. Paul Stoller 2004, 185.
11. Victor Turner 1969, 138.
12. Bozidar Voljc (on the spirituality of the doctor–patient relationship) 1997, 81.
13. Paul Stoller 1987.
14. Paul Stoller 2004, 199.
15. From the anthropologist Roberta Culbertson, personal communication, February 2008.

6 The Sacredness of the People: The Communitas of Revolution and Liberation

1. Aristide Zolberg 1971.
2. Yajurveda, see http://en.wikipedia.org/wiki/Ahimsa. This also led to Gandhi's political nonviolence—see Chapter 7.
3. Isha Upanishad, verses 6, 7, and 8, see, http://en.wikipedia.org/wiki/Upanishad.
4. Luke 1, 51–53.
5. Matthew 5, 38–48.
6. Victor Turner 1969, 140–154.

7. Available at: http://en.wikipedia.org/wiki/Francisco_Su%C3%A1rez. Accessed April 15, 2007.
8. Available at: http://en.wikipedia.org/wiki/Francisco_Su%C3%A1rez. Accessed April 15, 2007.
9. Thomas Paine 1986 (1776), 77.
10. Thomas Paine 1976, 87–88.
11. See http://www.ushistory.org/declaration/document/rough.htm.
12. Robert Burns 1797 (1795).
13. William Wordsworth 1995 (1805), 440, 442.
14. Sadly, there has been something in our own times before our eyes, comparable to that state of things: the fate of Haiti after the earthquake, January 13, 2010.
15. Jules Michelet 1973 (1845).
16. Ibid.; Darline Gay Levy 1979; George Rude 1988.
17. Crane Brinton 1934, 2–3
18. See also George Rude 1995.
19. Jules Claretie 1906, 329–331.
20. Jules Michelet 1972 (1845), 10, 25.
21. Claude Lévi-Strauss 1963, 209–210.
22. Available at: http://en.wikipedia.org/wiki/Fran%C3%A7ois_Guizot.
23. Aristide Zolberg 1971, 13.
24. Gustave Flaubert 1969, 292–293.
25. Enactments also included the right to vote for women; the remission of rents owed for the entire period of the siege (during which payment had been suspended); the abolition of night work in the hundreds of Paris bakeries; the granting of pensions to the unmarried companions and children of National Guards killed on active service; the free return, by the city pawnshops, of all workmen's tools and household items valued up to twenty francs that were pledged during the siege. There was concern that skilled workers had been forced to pawn their tools during the war. There was also the postponement of commercial debt obligations, abolition of interest on the debts, and the right of employees to take over and run an enterprise if it was deserted by its owner, who was to receive compensation. Available at: http://en.wikipedia.org/wiki/Paris_Commune.

    These were highly intelligent ways to set a city aright after a siege, and similar enactments could well have been allowed during hurricane Katrina. Not many of these lesser laws remained permanently as increments from the Commune period, but the separation of church and state and the general ethical theory remained.
26. Aristide Zolberg 1971, 9.
27. Elizabeth Gilbert 2006, 329–330.
28. Derived from Aristide Zolberg 1971, 9–11.
29. Peter Kropotkin 1895.
30. Quoted in Aristide Zolberg 1971, 5–6.

31. Ibid., 6.
32. Available at: http://www.britannica.com/eb/article-9060859. Accessed April 10, 2007. Also abridged from http://en.wikipedia.org/wiki/Popular_Front_%28France%29. Accessed February 25, 2007.
33. Aristide Zolberg 1971, 23.
34. The following passage is based on Maurice Brinton 2008 (1968). (An eye-witness account of two weeks spent in Paris during May 1968.) Also compare Alexander Cockburn and Robin Blackburn 1969, 320. Cockburn and Blackburn had no words in their entire collection about what might be called communitas.
35. List from Maurice Brinton 1968.
36. From Maurice Brinton, live witness, 1968.
37. Ari Zolberg 1971, 2–3. Personal communication with Victor Turner, 1972.
38. Ibid., 20–21. Personal communication with Victor Turner, 1972.
39. Ibid., 37.

7 The Communitas of Nonviolence

1. This general sense is felt in the ideals embedded in the human rights movement. Concerning human rights, Nelson Mandela and Desmond Tutu go further and declare that *individual* rights are not enough. They call for respect for *ubuntu*, fellowship, a communitas that goes beyond human rights.
2. Henry David Thoreau 1849.
3. Leon Tolstoy 2006 (1902), 132.
4. Martin Green 1986, 3.
5. Available at: http://www.infinisri.com/stories/Gandhistories.htm.
6. Extracts from Sri Sridharan 2006.
7. Bayard Rustin was a member of CORE, Congress of Racial Equality, the first explicit civil rights organization in the United States, founded in 1943 by a biracial Gandhi study group in Chicago. Rustin was secretary of the Fellowship of Reconciliation for twelve years. He protested the internment of Japanese during WWII and was in prison for twenty-eight months. After his release, he helped organize the Free India Committee and led sit-ins at the British Embassy in Washington, D.C.
8. See also *Richard H. Ackerman* and *Pat Maslin-Ostrowski* 2002, 494.
9. Rosa Parks 1994, 17, 18, 22–23.
10. Martin Luther King 1955.
11. Description of applause from Taylor Branch 1988, 139–141.
12. Martin Luther King 1955. Reverend King's address to the newly formed Montgomery Improvement Association. See King Estate for copyright.

13. Joe Azbell, "5,000 at Meeting Outline Boycott; Bullet Clips Bus," *Montgomery Advertiser* (December 6, 1955), http://www.archives.state.al.us/teacher/rights/lesson1/doc2.html
14. Bayard Rustin 1971.
15. Martin Luther King 1956.
16. Rosa Parks 1994, 17, 18, 22–23.
17. King 1963.
18. Lisa Cozzens Website. 1997.
19. Ibid.
20. Steven Kasher 1996.
21. Available at: tp://en.wikipedia.org/wiki/Martin_Luther_King,_Jr.#Assassination.
22. Available at: http://en.wikipedia.org/wiki/This_Land_Is_Your_Land. Accessed August 2008.
23. Ibid.
24. Lines selected from music and lyrics by Bob Dylan, released on his 1964 album, *Another Side of Bob Dylan*. "Chimes of Freedom" is a song written and performed by Bob Dylan. It was written in early 1964 and was influenced by the symbolist poetry of Arthur Rimbaud, who himself was associated with the Paris Commune in 1871.
25. The whole of the account of Nicholaikirche was derived in 2007 from a leaflet available at the Lutheran church of St. Nicholas at Leipzig, written by Sup. F. Magirius and Rev. C. Führer. I visited the church on Sunday, February 4, 2007. See also http://www.nikolaikirche-leipzig.de//content/blogcategory/0/100/.
26. Ibid.
27. Shortened from Andreas Ramos 1989. Available at: andreas.com/berlin.html. Accessed April 18, 2007. The piece has been included in four American history books or English textbooks, an Australian school history book, and a Canadian school history book. It is also part of the Berlin Wall historical archives.
28. See Bakhtin's insight into carnival: "...We have here a characteristic logic, the peculiar logic of the 'inside out,' of the 'turnabout,' of a continual shifting from top to bottom, from front to rear." Mikhail Bakhtin 1968, 11.
29. More than 80 percent of East Germany, nearly thirteen million people, visited family and friends in the West. After a week, nearly all returned home.
30. David Johnston, "C.I.A. Tie Reported in Mandela Arrest." *New York Times* (June 10, 1990).
31. Excerpts from Alan Thorold 1995, 4–36.
32. Ibid., 4–5.
33. Available at: http://en.wikipedia.org/wiki/Ubuntu_(philosophy).
34. Derived from http://unitedforpeace.org.
35. Some material derived from http://unitedforpeace.org.
36. Derived from http://www.actupny.org.

37. Adapted from the brief article "Civil Obedience Training," by Markley Morris. Available at: http://www.actupny.org/documents/CDdocuments/NVResponse.html. Accessed September 7, 2011.
38. Derived from http://unitedforpeace.org.
39. Personal communication, February 22, 2008.
40. Personal communication, September 21, 2007.
41. Victor Turner et al. 1966.
42. Victor Turner 1969, 143–154.
43. Ibid., 142–143. Also derived from the "Foreword" by Edith Turner to the Finnish translation of Victor Turner 2006c.
44. Martin Buber 1966, 137.
45. Victor Turner 1969, 143.
46. Edith Turner 2006c; Martin Buber 1966.
47. Martin Buber 1962.
48. See the Maurice Brinton pamphlet quoted in Chapter 6 describing the Popular Front.

8 The Communitas of Nature

1. Robert Turner, personal communication, spring 2008.
2. See Matthew Fox 1983.
3. William Wordsworth 1992 (1797–1800), 309.
4. Henry Stephen Sharp 1996, 183.
5. Ibid., 182.
6. Ibid., 173.
7. John Lame Deer Fire and Richard Erdoes, paperback edition, 1972, illustrations, 128–129.
8. Ibid., 276.
9. Ibid., 39–40.
10. Rex Tuzroyluk, personal communication, June 17, 2007.
11. George Mentore, personal communication, January 4, 2007.
12. Selected passages from George Mentore 2007, 192–201.
13. Aldo Gargani 1998, 120.
14. Emmanuel Lévinas 1979.
15. Victor Turner 1969, 137.
16. Irene Wellman, personal communication, November 11, 2007.
17. A shortened version derived from Shankar Vedantam 2007
18. Robert Turner, personal communication, April 2010.
19. The passages on Emmanuel Lévinas are derived from:http://ehttp://en.wikipedia.org/wiki/Emmanuel_Lévinasn.wikipedia.org/wiki/Emmanuel_Lévinas. Accessed January 15, 2009.
20. It is likely that the baby in the womb has its hand around the pumping umbilical chord—possibly a major stimulus to its consciousness.
21. Andrius Valevičius 1987. Derived from: http://www.lituanus.org/1987/87_1_02.htm. Accessed January 15, 2009.
22. Derived from Emmanuel Lévinas 1998, 265.

23. Dawn Hunt, personal communication, June 2008.
24. Tshiamalenga Ntumba 1985, 57–59. See also www.lianes.org/Francophonie-et-cosmopolitisme_a117.html.
25. Society as "given," that is, an exterior system imprinted by the elders onto the tabula rasa of children since babyhood.
26. *Biso*, the common word for "we" among the Lingara people of Congo.
27. Thomas Fowler 2008, 589.
28. George Mentore 2005, 86, 147.
29. Ibid., 147.
30. Ibid., 309.
31. Lucien Lévy-Bruhl 1985 (1910).
32. From a passage on evolution in Mircea Eliade 1972, xii–xx.
33. See Zerka Moreno, Leif Dag Blomkvist, and Thomas Rutzel 2000, 4.
34. Derived from Tenibac Harvey 2006, 1–10.
35. Elena Hurtado and Eugenia Sánenz de Tejada's article on the relationship between the Guatemalan government and indigenous midwives in Brad Huber and Alan Sandstrom's edited volume on Mesoamerican Healers (2001) is a good source for readers interested in some of the issues surrounding cross-cultural medical care in Guatemala.
36. *Perfidia* roughly translates from Latin to English as "treachery" or "faithlessness."
37. The term "theurgical herbalist" is used to describe the therapeutic practices of Miriam and Xper because the medicinal herbs involved divine or supernatural agency in curative affairs.
38. This insight of culture moving from distant object to personal experience comes from Michael Agar 1996.
39. Servando Hinojosa (2002), though not dealing directly with the role of sympathy in healing, focuses on the hands and the role of bodily engagement in Maya healing.
40. The lives of Maya townspeople were not primarily public or particularly communal. On the contrary, they were mostly lived privately, though shared among intimate companions.
41. Roy Wagner, personal communication, October 12, 2005.

9 Rites of Passage: Communitas in Times of Change

1. Arnold van Gennep 1902.
2. Victor Turner 1964.
3. Derived from Barbara Myerhoff 1982, 117.
4. From author's field notes 1953.
5. This account is partly my own experience and partly from personal communication, Victor Turner, 1953.
6. Victor Turner 1967, 255.
7. Ibid., 151–298.

8. Victor Turner 1962, 124–173.
9. Victor Turner had been trained at the University of Manchester, England. I remember as if it were today and not fifty-five years ago, the typewritten sheets of his PhD dissertation, minutely and patiently corrected by Max Gluckman. Gluckman had edited out any phrases showing passion or feeling. What remained was simply the style of academic writing of the time.
10. The domination system has been well identified in Walter Wink's book, *Engaging the Powers: Discernment and Resistance in a World of Domination* 1992 Minneapolis, MN: Fortress Press. The Biblical term for the domination system is Mammon, forever grabbing power for itself. Its modern form is the domination of the world by the principles of business, profits, and greed. Wink relates numerous accounts of nonviolent resistance to the domination system. People exist, even inside the big corporations, and they can be reached. Wink tells how we can engage the powers and release the people inside.
11. Irene Wellman, personal communication, March 2008.
12. "Fathers Aren't Dispensable Just Yet." *New Scientist* (July 22, 2009), http://www.newscientist.com/article/mg20327184.000-fathers-arent-dispensable-just-yet.From a poster session at the Biennial Meeting of the Society for Research in Child Development, April 2–4, 2009 in Denver, Colorado: "Maternal and Paternal Bonding in the Postpartum: Hormones, Parenting Behavior, and Mental Representations," Ilanit Gordon, Ruth Feldman, James F. Leckman, Aron Weller, and Orna Zagoory-Sharon.
13. Wellman, personal communication, August 2005.
14. Extracts from Wellman's master's thesis, Keanes College, New Hampshire, 2007.
15. From the term paper of Theodora Biney-Amissah, who was one of the helpers and who attended the class on communitas, April 25, 2008.
16. As in the classic film *MASH*, about a medical unit in the Korean War, showing a kindly but spoofed Last Supper scene put on by the crew for the sake of a tormented gay fellow worker.
17. The shaman Michael Harner, and Edith Turner over breakfast, American Anthropological Association meetings, circa 1990.
18. Shortened from George Herbert 1975b (1633), 300.
19. Claire Farrer 1991, 128–183 (Apache girls' initiation); Lina Fruzzetti 1982 (Bangladesh wedding); Larry Peters 1981 (Nepalese shaman initiation).
20. In conversation with Wellman, Fall 2006.

10 Alignment: Turn the Key and the Door Opens

1. The resolution of a musical discord occurs with great effectiveness in Mozart's work. It could also be suggested that the famous

NOTES

near-death experience comes at a time when a person is half out of, and half in a state of unison with all creation. The jarring on-off approach of death and its initial blanking off and separation from beauty is followed by a peculiar delight and vividness in the experience once it breaks into the "through vision," so that one can see God, or the figure so many people see when in this state, whether among the Inuit, the Nepalese, ancient Hebrews, modern Westerners, or many others.

2. The African example is from Victor Turner 1975, 292–321, with Edith Turner as observer. See also the outstanding work of Sónia Silva 2011.
3. Connor Lacey and Rowan Webster supplied this interpretation, personal communication, November 2007.
4. See Stephen Friedson 1996, 134, 156–158.
5. Shane McAdams 2007.
6. John Bunyan 1964 (1678–1684), 30.
7. Many women do go through that despair at some point in labor, at transition, near the end of labor, or in the middle. The practice of artificially rupturing of the membranes by physicians is so common these days that most women do not experience labor in its natural progression.
8. Based on Ter Ellingson 1998, 51–76.
9. William Wordsworth's poem, "Lucy." Available at: http://www.poetry-archive.com/w/lucy.html.
10. Extracts from Joseph Whelan, 2006, "The Light Shines on her Face and She Takes It into her Heart," student paper, 10–11.
11. The comment is from David Stang's notes, personal communication, April 2002.
12. David Azzam, personal communication, April 2003.
13. Maya Deren 1953, 242.
14. Extracts from Colin Turnbull 1990, 50–81.
15. Extracts from Phillip Pullman 1997, 182–186.
16. The detailed account of Ihamba, found in Edith Turner 1992, 103–213, includes a discussion of "the tooth in the vein" difficulty, 200–203.
17. Christopher Crocker 1985.
18. Available at: http://www.marathonguide.com/news/exclusives/Olympics2004/MensOlympicsMarathonRace.cfm. Accessed April 15, 2009. Also see http://en.wikipedia.org/wiki/Vanderlei_de_Lima. Accessed August 15, 2009.
19. Extracts from http://en.wikipedia.org/wiki/Jagannath#Traditional_stories. Accessed April 15, 2009. A shortened form was related to Victor Turner and Edith Turner in Puri in 1979.
20. "The Third Gift—An Enormous Hammer" (1902) by Elmer Boyd Smith, from Rose Edda. Available at: http://en.wikipedia.org/wiki/Mjolnir. Accessed April 15, 2009.
21. D. S. Lee and Laurel Kendall 1991.

Conclusion

1. Victor Turner 1990, 107.
2. Extracts from Roy Willis 1999, 120.
3. See Jay Ruby 1982.
4. Irene Wellman, personal communication, July 2006.
5. Victor Turner 1969, 137.
6. Joanna Overing 2006, 11–40.
7. Peter Ochs, personal communication, March 23, 2007.
8. Meister Eckhart, see http://quote.robertgenn.com/getquotes.php?catid=105.

References

Abrahams, Roger. 1982. "The Language of Festivals: Celebrating the Economy." In *Celebration: Studies in Festivity and Ritual*, edited by Victor Turner, 161–177. Washington, D.C.: Smithsonian Institution Press.

Achebe, Chinua. 1996 (1958). *Things Fall Apart*. Oxford: Heinemann Educational Publishers.

Ackerman, Richard H., and Pat Maslin-Ostrowski. 2002. *The Wounded Leader: How Real Leadership Emerges in Times of Crisis*. Hoboken, NJ: John Wiley & Son.

Babcock, Barbara. 1990. "Mud, Mirrors, and Making Up." In *Victor Turner and the Construction of Cultural Criticism*, edited by Kathleen Ashley, 86–107. Bloomington: Indiana University Press.

Baggett, Jerome P. 2001. *Habitat for Humanity: Building Private Homes, Building Public Religion*. Philadelphia: Temple University Press.

Bakhtin, Mikhail. 1965 (1993). *Rabelais and his World*, translated by Helene Iswolsky. Cambridge: MIT Press. Reprint, Bloomington: Indiana University Press

Barnard, Henry. 2005. *Enchanting Books: Redeeming Fetishism*. Thesis for PhD, Massey University, New Zealand.

Barona, Josep Luis. 1997. "Cancer Patients and Medical Practice: Some Historical and Cultural Considerations." In *Communication with the Cancer Patient: Information and Truth*, edited by Antonella Surbone and Matjaz Zwitter, 17–29. Vol. 809. New York: Annals of the New York Academy of Sciences.

Beer, Frances. 1992. *Women and Mystical Experience in the Middle Ages*. Woodbridge, UK: Boydell.

Benjamin, Walter. 1969. *Illuminations*. New York: Schoken.

Benzon, William. 2001. *Beethoven's Anvil: Music in Mind and Culture*. New York: Basic Books.

Bierce, Matthew. 2010. mattbierce@hotmail.com.

Bilu, Yoram. 2000 (1993). *Without Bounds: The Life and Death of Rabbi Ya'aqov Wazana*. Detroit: Wayne State University Press.

Biver, Maris Louise. 1979. *Fetes Revolutionaires à Paris*. Paris: Presses Universitaires de France.

Blake, William. 1970. *The Poetry and Prose of William Blake (1757–1827)*, edited by David Erdman, 461. Garden City, NY: Doubleday.

———. 2006 (c. 1793). "Eternity is in love with the productions of time." *The Columbia World of Quotations*, edited by Robert Andrews, Mary Biggs, and Michael Seidel. Columbia University Press. eNotes.com. 2006. Accessed Dec. 06, 2008. http://www.enotes.com/famous-quotes/eternity-is-in-love-with-the-productions-of-time. From *The Marriage of Heaven and Hell*, "Proverbs of Hell," Plate 7.

Bodin, L., and J. Touchard. 1961. *Front Populaire 1936*. Paris: Armand Colin; "Kiosque."

Boehme, Jacob. 1621. *Signatura Rerum*. London: John Ellistone, Giles Calvert.

Bourgois, Philippe. 1995. *Search of Respect: Selling Crack in El Barrio*. Cambridge: Cambridge University Press.

Brand, Mieka. 2007. "Making Moonshine: Thick Histories in a U.S. Historically Black Community." *Anthropology and Humanism*, 32 (1): 52–61.

Branch, Taylor. 1988. *Parting the Waters: America in the King Years, 1954–1963*. New York: Simon & Schuster.

Brinton, Crane. 1934. *A Decade of Revolution 1789–1799*. New York: Harper & Row.

Brinton, Maurice. 2008 (1968). "Introduction." In *Paris: May 1968*. Paris: Dark Star Press and Rebel Press. Available at: http://www.geocities.com/cordobakaf/maya.html. Accessed August 14, 2008. Original,Paris: Solidarity.

Bruner, Edward. 1984. "Introduction: The Opening Up of Anthropology." In *Text, Play, and Story: The Construction and Reconstruction of Self and Society*, edited by Edward Bruner, 1–18. Washington, D.C.: American Ethnological Society.

Buber, Martin. 1947. *Between Man and Man*. New York: Routledge.

———. 1958. *I and Thou*. New York: Scribner.

———. 1962. *Thoreau in Our Season*. Boston: University of Massachusetts Press.

———. 1966. *Paths in Utopia*. (tr. R.F.C. Hull.) Boston: Beacon.

Bunyan, John. 1964 (1678–1684). *The Pilgrims' Progress*. In modern English by James Thomas. Chicago: Moody Press.

Burns, Robert. 1797. "Is there for honest poverty." *Glasgow Magazine*. Available at: http://www.lyricstime.com/robert-burns-a-man-s-a-man-for-all-that-is-there-for-honest-poverty-lyrics.html. Accessed January 2009.

Cassirer, Ernst. 1961. *The Myth of the State*. New Haven: Yale University Press.

Chariots of Fire. 1981. Burbank: Enigma Productions.

Chishti, Shaykh Hakim Moinuddin. 1985. *The Sufi Book of Healing*. New York: Inner Traditions International.

Cockburn, Alexander, and Robin Blackburn, eds. 1969. *Student Power, Problems, Diagnosis, Action*. Harmondsworth, UK: Penguin.

REFERENCES

Cooper, Andrew. 1995. "In the Zone: The Zen of Sports." *Shambhala Sun Online* (March 1995). Available at: http://www.shambhalasun.com.

———. 1998. *Playing in the Zone: Exploring the Spiritual Dimensions of Sports*. Boston: Shambhala.

Cortes, Ernesto, Jr. 1993. "Reweaving the Fabric: The IAF Strategy for Power and Politics." Reprinted from *Interwoven Destinies: Cities and the Nation*, edited by Henry G. Cisneros, 295–319. New York: W.W. Norton & Company.

Cozzens, Lisa. 1997. "The Civil Rights Movement 1955–1965: Selma." *African American History*. Available at: http://fledge.watson.org/~lisa/blackhistory/civilrights-55-65. Accessed August 20, 2008.

———. "The Montgomery Bus Boycott." http://www.watson.org/~lisa/blackhistory/. Accessed August 2008.Crocker, Jon Christopher. 1985. *Vital Souls: Bororo Cosmology, Natural Symbolism, and Shamanism*. Tucson: University of Arizona Press.

Csíkszentmihályi, Mihály. 1975. *Beyond Boredom and Anxiety*. San Francisco: Jossey-Bass.

———. 1988. *Optimal Experience: Psychological Studies of Flow in Consciousness*. New York: Cambridge University Press.

———. 1991. *Flow: The Psychology of Optimal Experience*. New York: HarperPerennial.

Damasio, Antonio. 1994. *Descartes' Error: Emotion, Reason, and the Human Brain*. New York: Putnam.

Darwin, Charles. 1871. The Descent of Man [1871] Philip Appleton New York: Norton.

Davies, Douglas J. 2002. *Anthropology and Theology*. Oxford: Berg.

Deikman, Arthur J. 1975. "Deautomization and the Mystic Experience." In *The Psychology of Consciousness*, edited by Robert Ornstein, 200–220. New York: Penguin Books.

Deschenes, Liz. 2007. *Time Out New York*, (May 3–9). Available at: http://www.timeout.com/newyork/articles/art/55/liz-deschenes. Accessed February 11, 2009.

Desjarlais, Robert. 1992. *Body and Emotion: The Aesthetics of Illness and Healing in the Nepal Himalayas*. Philadelphia: University of Pennsylvania Press.

Dilthey, Wilhelm. 1914–1974. *Gesammelte Schriften*. Vol. 6. Stuttgart: Teubner.

Douglas, Mary. 1966. *Purity and Danger: An Analysis of Concepts of Pollution and Taboo*. London: Routledge.

Douglass, James. 1993. *The Non-Violent Coming of God*. New York: Maryknoll.

Drewal, Margaret. 1992. *Yoruba Ritual*. Bloomington: Indiana University Press.

Driver, Tom. 1992. *The Magic of Ritual: Our Need for Liberating Rites that Transform Our Lives and Our Communities*. San Francisco: Harper San Francisco.

Dubisch, Jill, and Raymond Michalowski. 2001. *Run for the Wall: Remembering Vietnam on a Motorcycle Pilgrimage*. Piscataway, NJ: Rutgers University Press.

Durkheim, Emile. 1965 (1915). *The Elementary Forms of the Religious Life*. New York: Free Press.

Dylan, Bob. 2007. Available at: http://movies.nytimes.com/2007/11/21/movies/21ther.html. Accessed Aug. 10, 2008.

Earle, Duncan. 2007. "Dog Days: Participation as Transformation." In *Extraordinary Anthropology: Transformations in the Field*, edited by Jean-Guy Goulet and Bruce Granville Miller, 310–320. Lincoln: Nebraska University Press.

Ehrenreich, Barbara. 2006. *Dancing in the Streets: A History of Collective Joy*. New York: Metropolitan.

Eliade, Mircea. 1959. *The Sacred and the Profane: The Nature of Religion*. New York: Harcourt, Brace & Jovanovich.

———. 1970 (1964). *Shamanism: Archaic Techniques of Ecstasy*. Translated by Willard R. Trask, xi–xxi. Princeton: Princeton University Press.

Ellingson, Ter. 1998. "The Arrow and the Mirror: Interactive Consciousness, Ethnography, and the Tibetan State Oracle's Trance." *Anthropology and Humanism*, 23 (1): 51–76.

Erdoes, Richard. 1972. "Introduction." In *Lame Deer, Seeker of Visions*, by John Lame Deer Fire and Richard Erdoes. New York: Washington Square Press.

Evans-Pritchard, E. E. 1976 (1937). *Witchcraft, Oracles, and Magic among the Azande*. Oxford: Clarendon.

Fast, Howard. 1943. *Citizen Tom Payne*. New York: Grove Press.

Fernandez, James. 1984. "Convivial Attitudes: The Ironic Play of Tropes in an International Kayak Festival in Northern Spain." In *Text, Play, and Story: The Construction and Reconstruction of Self and Society*, edited by Edward Bruner, 199–229. Washington: American Ethnological Society.

Farrer, Claire. 1991. *Living Life's Circle: Mescalero Apache Cosmovision*. Albuquerque: University of New Mexico Press.

Ferro, Marc. 1980. *October 1917*. London: Routledge & Kegan Paul.

Fields, Tina. 2009. "*Kumu Pohaku* (Stones as Teachers): Awakening to the Spiritual Dimensions of Ecosystems." In *So What? Now What? The Anthropology of Consciousness Responds to a World in Crisis*, edited by Matthew Bronson and Tina Fields, 317–359. Newcastle-on-Tyne, UK: Cambridge Scholars.

Fire, John Lame Deer, and Richard Erdoes. 1972. *Lame Deer, Seeker of Visions*. New York: Touchstone Books, Simon & Schuster, Washington Square Press.

Fowler, Thomas. 2008. "Sentient Intelligence: Consciousness and Knowing in the Philosophy of Xavier Zubiri." In *Ontology of Consciousness: Percipient Action* Edited by Helmut Wautischer, 549–575. Cambridge: MIT Press.

REFERENCES

Flaubert, Gustave. 1964 (1869). *Sentimental Education*. Harmondsworth, UK: Penguin.
Friedson, Stephen. 1996. *Dancing Prophets: Musical Experiences in Tumbuka Healing*. Chicago: University of Chicago Press.
Fruzzetti, Lina. 1982. *Gift of a Virgin: Women, Marriage, and Ritual in a Bengali Society*. New Brunswick: Rutgers University Press.
Gargano, Aldo. 1998. "Religious Experience as Event and Interpretation." In *Religion*, edited by Jacques Derrida and Gianni Vattimo, 111–135. Stanford: Stanford University Press.
Geertz, Clifford. 1972. *The Interpretation of Cultures: Selected Essays*. San Francisco: Harper-Collins.
Gennep, Arnold van. 1960 (1909). *The Rites of Passage*. Translated by Monica Vizedom. London: Routledge and Kegan Paul.
Ghosh, Indu Mala. 1988. *Ahimsa: Buddhist and Gandhian*. Delhi: Indian Bibliographies Bureau.
Gilkey, Langdon. 1993. *Nature, Reality, and the Sacred: The Nexus of Science and Religion*. Minneapolis: Fortress Press.
Gluckman, Max. 1955. *The Judicial Process among the Barotse of Northern Rhodesia*. Manchester, UK: Manchester University Press.
Goulet, Jean-Guy. 1994. "Ways of Knowing: Towards a Narrative Ethnography of Experiences Among the Dene Tha." *Journal of Anthropological Research* 50 (2): 113–139.
Grass, Günter. 1978. *The Flounder*. Translated by Ralph Manheim. New York: Harcourt Brace Jovanovich.
Green, Martin. 1986. *The Origins of Nonviolence*. University Park: Pennsylvania State University Press.
Grindal, Bruce. 1983. "Into the Heart of Sisala Experience: Witnessing Death Divination." *Journal of Anthropological Research* 39 (1): 60–80. 1992. "Immortality Denied." *Anthropology and Humanism Quarterly* 17 (1): 23–32.
Handelman, Don. 1977. *Work and Play among the Aged: Interactions, Replications, and Emergence in a Jerusalem Setting*. Amsterdam: Van Gorcum, Assen. 1990. *Models and Mirrors: Towards an Anthropology of Public Events*. Cambridge: Cambridge University Press.
Hart, Mickey, Jay Stevens, and Fredric Lieberman. 1990. *Drumming at the Edge of Magic: A Journey into the Spirit of Percussion*. San Francisco: Harper.
Harvey, Tenibac. 2006. "Humbling, Frightening, and Exalting: An Experiential Acquaintance with Maya Healing." *Anthropology & Humanism* 31 (1): 1–10.
Hemingway, Ernest. 1968. *For Whom the Bell Tolls*. New York: Scribner.
Herbert, George. 1975b (1633). "Love (III)." In *The Norton Anthology of Poetry*, edited by Alexander Allison et al., 300. New York: W.W. Norton.
Holmes, Urban Tigner. 1976. *Ministry and Imagination*. New York: Seabury Press.

Itzkin, Eric. 2000. *Gandhi's Johannesburg: Birthplace of Satyagraha*. Johannesburg: Witwatersrand University Press.
James, William. 1985 (1929). *The Varieties of Religious Experience*. Cambridge: Harvard University Press.
Jencson, Linda. 2001. "Disastrous Rites: Liminality and Communitas in a Flood Crisis." *Anthropology and Humanism* 26 (1): 46–58.
Jones, Ernest. 1989 (1855). *The Bard*. In *An Anthology of Chartist Poetry: Poetry of the British Working Class, 1830s–1850s*, edited by Peter Scheckner, 214. Madison, NJ: Fairleigh Dickinson University Press.
Junod, Henri Alexandre. 1962 (1927). *The Life of a South African Tribe*. New Hyde Park, NY: University Books.
Kapferer, Bruce. 1983. *A Celebration of Demons: Exorcism and the Aesthetics of Healing in Sri Lanka*. Bloomington: Indiana University Press.
Kasher, Steven. 1996. *The Civil Rights Movement: A Photographic History, 1954–68*. New York: Abbeville Press.
Keeney, Bradford, ed. 2000. *Gary Holy Bull, Lakota Yuwipi Man*. Philadelphia: Ringing Rocks Press.
Kelly, Kevin. 2006. Available at: http://www.kk.org/thetechnium/archives/2008/06/scenius_or_comm.php. Accessed August 2008.
King, Martin Luther, Jr. 1955. Address to First Montgomery Improvement Association (MIA) Mass Meeting, Dexter Avenue Baptist Church, Montgomery, Alabama, December 5, 1955. Available at: http://www.stanford.edu/group/King/publications/speeches/MIA_mass_meeting_at_hol_street.html. Accessed February 21, 2009.
———. 1956. Quoted in Wayne Phillips, "Negroes Pledge to Keep Boycott: 2,000 at Montgomery Rally—Bus Arrests Continue." *New York Times* (February 24). Available at: http://proquest.umi.com/pqdweb?index=13&did=313808222&SrchMode=1&sid=1&Fmt=10&VInst=PROD&VType=PQD&RQT=309&VName=HNP&TS=1248838914&clientId=3507.
———. 1963. "I Have a Dream" speech, August 28. Available at: http://www.mlkonline.net/dream.html. Accessed July 28, 2009.
Kipling, Rudyard. 1927. *Stalky & Co*. Garden City, NJ: Doubleday.
Koss–Chioino, Joan, and Philip Heffner, eds. 2006. *Spiritual Transformation and Healing: Anthropological, Theological, Neuroscientific, and Clinical Perspectives*. New York: Altamira.
Kramnick, Isaac, ed. 1986. "Editor's Introduction." In *Common Sense*, by Tom Paine, 7–60. London: Penguin Books.
Kropotkin, Peter. 1895. "The Commune of Paris: II, How the Commune Failed to Realize its True Aim and Yet Set that Aim before the World." *Freedom Pamphlets*, 2. London: W. Reeves. Available at: http://www.paris.org/Kiosque/may01/commune.html. Accessed March 20, 2007.
Krupskaya, N. K. 1979. *Reminiscences of Lenin*. New York: International Publishers.

REFERENCES

Lahood, Gregg. 2008. "Paradise Bound: A Perennial Tradition or an Unseen Process of Cosmological Hybridization?" *The Anthropology of Consciousness* 19 (2): 155–189.

Laidler, Keith J. 1998. *To Light Such A Candle*. Oxford. Available at: www.secondlaw.com/ten.html and http://www.2ndlaw.com.

Lau, Kwok-ying. nd. *War, Peace and Love: The Logic of Lévinas*. Chinese University of Hong Kong. Available at: http://74.125.47.132/search?q=cache:60rpUDdBGSsJ:www.europhilosophie.eu/mundus/IMG/doc/LauKY-ar_Peace_Love_the_logic_of_Levinas.doc+levinas+love&hl=en&ct=clnk&cd=2&gl=us. Accessed January 15, 2009.

Leach, Edmund. 1976. *Culture and Communication*. Cambridge: Cambridge University Press.

Leach, Edmund, and Jerry W. Leach. 1983. *The Kula: New Perspectives on Massim Exchange*. Cambridge: Cambridge University Press.

Lee, D. S., and Laurel Kendall. 1991. *Kut for a Korean Shaman*. Video. Honolulu: University of Hawaii Press.

Lévinas, Emmanuel. 1979. *Totality and Infinity*. Pittsburgh: Duquayne University Press.

Lévi-Strauss, Claude. 1963. *Structural Anthropology*. New York: Basic Books.

Levy, Darline Gay. 1979. *Women in Revolutionary Paris, 1789–1795*. Urbana: University of Illinois Press.

Lévy-Bruhl, Lucien. 1985 (1910). *How Natives Think*. Princeton: Princeton University Press.

Lewis, C. S. 1973 (1951). *Prince Caspian: The Return to Narnia*. New York: Collier Books.

Lindahl, Carl. 2007. "Storms of Memory: New Orleanians Surviving Katrina in Houston." *Callaloo* 29 (4): 1526–38. Available at: http://muse.jhu.edu/journals/callaloo/v029/29.4jasper.html.

Malinowski, Bronislaw. 1922. *Argonauts of the Western Pacific*. London: Routledge.

———. 1989. *A Diary in the Strict Sense of the Term*. London: Athlone.

Marx, Karl. 1998 [1845]. *The German Ideology:Including Theses on Feuerbach*. In *Marx/Engels Selected Works*. Great Books on Philosophy. New York: Prometheus Books..

Mauss, Marcel. 1954 (1925). *The Gift: Forms and Functions of Exchange in Archaic Societies*. New York: Cohen and West.

McAdams, Shane. 2007. "Moiré #2: Registration": Review of the artist Liz Deschenes at Miguel Abreu Gallery April 6–-May 20. Accessed Feb. 22, 2009.

McGuire, Meredith. 1988. *Ritual Healing in Suburban America*. New Brunswick: Rutgers University Press.

Mentore, George. 2005. *Of Passionate Curves and Desirable Cadences: Themes on Waiwai Social Being*. Lincoln: University of Nebraska Press. 2007. "Spiritual Translucency and Pornocratic Anthropology: Waiwai and Western Interpretations of a Religious Experience." *Anthropology and Humanism* 32 (2): 192–201.

Metzger, Deena, and Barbara Myerhoff. 1980. "The Journal as Activity & Genre: On Listening to the Silent Laughter of Mozart." *Semiotica* 30 (1–2): 97–114.

Michelet, Jules. 1973 (1845). *The People*. Urbana: University of Illinois Press.

Milbank, John. 1990. *Theology and Social Theory*. Oxford: Blackwell.

Moreno, Zerka T., Leif Dag Blomkvist, and Thomas Rutzel. 2000. *Psychodrama, Surplus Reality, and the Art of Healing*. New York: Brunner-Routledge.

Murray, L. and Colwyn Trevarthen. 1985. "Emotional Regulation of Interaction Between Two-Month-Olds and Their Mothers." In *Social Perception in Infants*, edited by M. Field and N. A. Fox, 177–98. New Jersey: Ablex Publishing Corporation.

Myerhoff, Barbara. 1982. "Rites of Passage: Process and Paradox." In *Celebration: Studies in Festivity and Ritual*, edited by Victor Turner 109–35. Washington, D.C.: Smithsonian Institution Press.

Narayan, Kirin. 1989. *Storytellers, Saints, and Scoundrels*. Philadelphia: University of Pennsylvania Press.

Neihardt, John. 1932. *Black Elk Speaks: Being the Life Story of a Holy Man of the Oglala Sioux*. As told by John G. Neihardt. New York: Morrow.

Ntumba, Tshiamalenga. 1985. "Langage et socialité: Primat de la 'bisoité' sur l'intersubjectité." ("Language and Sociality: The Primacy of 'Bisoity,' 'We-ness,' over Intersubjectivity.") *Philosophie Africaine et Ordre Social*, 2: 57–59.

Obama, Barack. 2006. *The Audacity of Hope*. New York: Vintage.

O'Neill-Butler, Lauren. 2007. Review of the artist Liz Deschenes, at Miguel Abreu Gallery, through May 20, 2007. *Time Out New York* (May 3–9). *Available at:* http://www.timeout.com/newyork/articles/art/55/liz-deschenes. Accessed Feb. 11, 2009.

Overing, Joanna. 2006. "The Backlash to Decolonizing Intellectuality." *Anthropology and Humanism* 31 (1): 11–40.

Paine, Thomas. 1986 (1776). *Common Sense*. London: Penguin.

———. 1992 (1791). *The Rights of Man*. London: Woodstock Books.

Parks, Rosa, with Gregory J. Reed. 1994. *Quiet Strength: The Faith, the Hope, and the Heart of a Woman Who Changed a Nation*. Grand Rapids, MI: Zondervan Publishing.

Paul, William. 2006. "Force: The Midwife of Revolution." *Labour Monthly* 2 (2). http://www.marxists.org/archive/paul-william/articles/1922/force.htm.

Pereira, Pedro Paulo Gomes. 2008. "Anthropology and Human Rights: Between Silence and Voice." *Anthropology and Humanism*, 33 (1–2): 38–52.

Peters, Larry. 1981. *Ecstasy and Healing in Nepal: An Ethnopsychiatric Study of Tamang Shamanism*. Malibu: Undena Publications.

Preston, James. 1992. *Mother Worship*. Chapel Hill: University of North Carolina Press.
Pullman, Phillip. 1995. *The Golden Compass*. New York: Ballantine.
———. 1997. *The Subtle Knife*. New York: Random House.
———. 2000. *The Amber Spyglass*. New York: Yearling.
Putnam, Robert D. 2000. *Bowling Alone: The Collapse and Revival of American Community*. New York: Simon & Schuster.
Rappaport, Roy A. 1999. *Ritual and Religion in the Making of Humanity*. Cambridge: Cambridge University Press.
Richards, Audrey. 1982 (1956). *Chisungu: A Girl's Initiation Ceremony among the Bemba of Zambia*. London: Tavistock.
Richardson, Miles. 1990. *Cry Lonesome and Other Accounts of the Anthropologist's Project*. New York: State University of New York Press.
Rodríguez, Havidán, Joseph Trainor, and Enrico L. Quarantelli. 2006. "Rising to the Challenges of a Catastrophe: The Emergent and Prosocial Behavior following Hurricane Katrina." *The Annals of the American Academy of Political and Social Science* 604 (3): 82–101.
Rosaldo, Michelle. 1984. "Toward an Anthropology of Self and Feeling." In *Culture Theory: Essays on Mind, Self, and Emotion*, edited by R. A. Shweder and R. A. LeVine, 137–157. Cambridge: Cambridge University Press.
Ruby, Jay, ed. 1982. *A Crack in the Mirror: Reflexive Perspectives in Anthropology*. Philadelphia: University of Philadelphia Press.
Rude, George. 1988. *The French Revolution*. New York: Grove Weidenfield.
Rustin, Bayard. 1971. *Down the Line: The Collected Writings of Bayard Rustin*. New York: Quadrangle-New York Times Books.
Ruud, Even. 1995 "Improvisation as a Liminal Experience: Jazz and Music Therapy as Modern 'Rites de Passage.'" In *Listening, Playing, Creating: Essays on the Power of Sound*, edited by Carolyn Bereznak Kenny, 96–98. Albany: State University of New York Press.
Samanta, Suchitra. 1998. "The Powers of the Guru: Sakti, 'Mind,' and Miracle in Narratives of Bengali Religious Experience." *Anthropology and Humanism* 23 (1): 30–50.
Sartre, Jean-Paul. 1969. "Itinerary of a Thought." *New Left Review* 58: 57–59.
Sawer, Patrick. 2008. "Cambridge University's '1958 car on roof prank' secrets revealed." *The Daily Telegraph* (June 28, 2008). Available at: http://en.wikipedia.org/wiki/Senate_House_(University_of_Cambridge). Accessed Mar. 2009.
Scheckner, Peter. 1989. *An Anthology of Chartist Poetry: Poetry of the British Working Class, 1830s–1850s*. Madison: Fairleigh Dickinson University Press.
Scherberger, Laura. 2005. "The Janus-Faced Shaman: The Role of Laughter in Sickness and Healing among the Makushi." *Anthropology and Humanism* 30 (1): 55–69.

Scott, A. O. 2007. Review of the film *I'm Not There*. *New York Times* "Critics' Pick" (November 21). Available at: http://movies.nytimes.com/2007/11/21/movies/21ther.html. Accessed August 10, 2008.
Seremitakis, Nadia. 1991. *The Last Word: Women, Death, and Divination in Inner Mani*. Chicago: University of Chicago Press.
Sharp, Stephen H. 1996. "Experiencing Meaning." *Anthropology & Humanism* 21 (2): 171–186.
———. 2001. *Loon: Memory, Meaning, and Reality in a Northern Dene Community*. Lincoln: University of Nebraska Press.
Shawki, Ahmed. 1997. "80 Years since the Russian Revolution." *International Socialist Review* 3.
Silva, Sónia. 2009. "Mothers of Solitude; Childlessness and Intersubjectivity in the Upper Zambezi." *Anthropology and Humanism* 34 (2).
———. 2011. *Along an Africa Border: African Refugees and Their Divination Baskets*. Philadelphia: Pennsylvania University Press.
Sobrino, Jon. 2009. *The Eye of the Needle: No Salvation Outside the Poor: A Utopian-Prophetic Essay*. London: Darton, Longman & Todd.
Solzhenitsyn, Aleksandr Isaevich. 1990 (1962). *One Day in the Life of Ivan Denisovich*, translated by Max Hayward and Ronald Hingly. New York: Bantam Books.
Sridharan, Sri. 2006. *A Garland of Stories*. Available at: http://www.infinisri.com/stories/Gandhistories.htm. Accessed July 28, 2008.
Stoller, Paul. 1987. *In Sorcery's Shadow*. Chicago: University of Chicago Press.
———. 1989a. *The Taste of Ethnographic Things*. Philadelphia: University of Pennsylvania Press.
———. 1989b. *Fusion of the Worlds: An Ethnography of Possession among the Songhay of Niger*. Chicago: University of Chicago Press.
———. 2004. *Stranger in the Village of the Sick: A Memoir of Cancer, Sorcery, and Healing*. Boston: Beacon Press.
———. 2007. "Ethnography/Memoir/Imagination/Story." *Anthropology and Humanism* 32 (2): 178–91.
Suarez, Francisco. c. 1600. Available at: http://en.wikipedia.org/wiki/Francisco_Su%C3%A1rez. Accessed April 15, 2007.
———. 1613. Available at: http://en.wikipedia.org/wiki/Francisco_Su%C3%A1rez, page 4. Accessed April 15, 2007.
Suchitra, Samanta. 1998. "The Powers of the Guru: Sakti, 'Mind,' and Miracles in Narratives of Bengali Religious Experience." *Anthropology & Humanism* 23 (1): 30–50.
Taussig, Michael. 2006. *Walter Benjamin's Grave*. Chicago: University of Chicago Press.
Tedlock, Barbara. 1992. *The Beautiful and the Dangerous: Dialogues with the Zuni Indians*. New York: Penguin Books.
———. 2005. *The Woman in the Shaman's Body: Reclaiming the Feminine in Religion and Medicine*. New York: Bantam Books.

Tedlock, Dennis. 1990. *Days from a Dream Almanac*. Urbana: University of Illinois Press.
Thoreau, Henry David. 2005 (1849). "The Duty of Civil Disobedience," published as *Walden and Civil Disobedience*. New York: Barnes and Noble Classics.
Thorold, Alan. 1995. "Miracle in Natal: Revolution by Ballot-Box." *Prickly Pear Pamphlet No. 7*: 4–36.
Todd, Jane Marie. 1998. *La trace de l'infini*. Ithaca: Cornell University Press. Available at: http://www.mythosandlogos.com/Levinas.html. (Translation of the 1998 work) Accessed Jan. 15, 2009.
Tolstoy, Leon. 2002 (1865–1869). *War and Peace*. New York: Modern Library.
———. 1995 (1877–1879). *Anna Karenina*. Oxford: Oxford University Press.
———. 1984 (1893). *The Kingdom of God Is Within You*. Lincoln: University of Nebraska Press.
———. 2006 (1902). *Spiritual Writings*. Maryknoll, NY: Orbis Books.
Tolstoy and Thoreau. 2007. Available at: http://peaceguru.wordpress.com/2007/06/25/tolstoy-and-thoreau/trackback/.
Trawick, Margaret. 1990. *Notes on Love in a Tamil Family*. Berkeley: University of California Press.
Trevarthen, Colwyn. 1980. "Neurological Development and the Growth of Psychological Functions." *Developmental Psychology and Society*, edited by J. Sants, 46–95. London: Macmillan.
———. "The 'Communicative Musicality' of Childhood: Seeking Harmony in Companionship." Paper presented at the International Conference on Mind, Brain, and Culture: The Neuroscience of Music, Crete. 2005
Trevarthen, Colwyn, and L. Murray. 1985. "Emotional Regulation of Interaction Between Two-Month-Olds and Their Mothers." In *Social Perception in Infants*, edited by M. Field and N. A. Fox, 177–198. Norwood, NJ: Ablex Publishing Corporation.
Turnbull, Colin. 1990. "Liminality: A Synthesis of Subjective and Objective Experience." In *By Means of Performance*, edited by Richard Schechner and Willa Appel, 50–81. Cambridge: Cambridge University Press.
Turner, Edith. 1987. "Drums of the Thunder." In *The Spirit and the Drum* 117–147. Tucson: University of Arizona Press.
———. 1992. *Experiencing Ritual: A New Interpretation of African Healing*. Philadelphia: University of Pennsylvania Press.
———. 1993. "Rabbi Shimon Bar Yohai: The Creative Persona and his Pilgrimage." In *Creativity/Anthropology*, edited by Smadar Lavie, Kirin Narayan, and Renato Rosaldo, 225–252. Ithaca: Cornell University Press.
———. 1996a. *The Hands Feel It: Healing and Spirit Presence among a Northern Alaskan People*. DeKalb: Northern Illinois University Press.

Turner, Edith. 1996b. "Communitas: We Shall Know What It Is." Paper presented at the American Anthropological Association annual meeting, San Francisco, November.

———. 1997. "There are No Peripheries to Humanity: Northern Alaska Nuclear Dumping and the Iñupiat's Search for Redress." In special issue on Globalization and Fieldwork, edited by Sandra Bamford and Joel Robbins. *Anthropology & Humanism* 22 (1): 95–109.

———. 2004a. Keynote speaker, "Acts of Women's Collective Power in Three Rituals." Conference on "Women Healing Women: Empowering Women Healers to Enhance Women's Health." Center for the Study of World Religions, Divinity School, Harvard University, March 22.

———. 2004b. "Communitas." In *The Encyclopedia of Religious Rituals*, edited by Frank Salamone, 97–101. Great Barrington, MA: Berkshire/Routledge Religion and Society Series.

———. 2005. *Among the Healers: Spiritual and Ritual Healing across the World*. New York: Praeger.

———. 2006a. *Heart of Lightness*. New York: Berghahn.

———. 2006b. "Advances in the Study of Spirit Experience: Drawing Together Many Threads." *Anthropology of Consciousness* 17 (2): 33–61.

———. 2006c. "Foreword." In Finnish translation of *The Ritual Process*, by Victor Turner, translated by Maarit Forde. Helsinki: Finnish Anthropological Society.

———. 2006d. "Discussion: Altruism, Spiritually Merging with a Fellow Human Beings' Suffering." *Zygon* 41(4): 933–939.

———. 2008. "The People's Home Ground." In *The National Mall: Rethinking Washington's Monumental Core*, edited by Nathan Glazer and Cynthia Field, 69–78. Baltimore: Johns Hopkins University Press.

Turner, Edith and Victor. 1978. *Image and Pilgrimage in Christian Culture: Anthropological Perspectives*. New York: Columbia University Press.

Turner, Victor. 1962. "Three Symbols of Passage in Ndembu Circumcision Ritual: An Interpretation." In *Essays on the Ritual of Social Relations*, edited by D. Forde, M. Fortes, M. Gluckman, and V. Turner, 124–173. Manchester: Manchester University Press.

———. 1964. "Betwixt-and-Between: The Liminal Period in Rites de Passage." *Symposium on New Approaches to the Study of Religion*, edited by June Helm, 4–20. Paper presented at the annual spring meetings of the American Ethnological Society, Chicago.

———. 1967. *The Forest of Symbols*. Ithaca: Cornell University Press.

———. 1968. The *Drums of Affliction: A Study of Religious Processes among the Ndembu of Zambia*. Oxford: Clarendon Press.

———. 1969. *The Ritual Process: Structure and Anti-Structure*. Chicago: Aldine.

———. 1974a. *Dramas, Fields, and Metaphors: Symbolic Action in Human Society*. Ithaca: Cornell University Press.

REFERENCES

———. 1974b. "Pilgrimage and Communitas." *Studia Missionalia.* 23: 305–327. Rome: Gregorian University.

———. 1975. *Revelation and Divination in Ndembu Ritual.* Ithaca: Cornell University Press.

———. 1977. "Variations on a Theme of Liminality." In *Secular Ritual,* edited by Sally Falk Moore and Barbara Myerhoff, 36–52. Assen, Netherlands: Van Gorcum.

———, ed. 1982a. *Celebration: Studies in Festivity and Ritual.* Washington, D.C.: Smithsonian Institution Press.

———. 1982b. "Liminal to Liminoid in Play, Flow, and Ritual." In *From Ritual to Theatre: The Human Seriousness of Play,* by Victor Turner, 20–60. New York: Performing Arts Journal Publications.

———. 1985. *On the Edge of the Bush: Anthropology as Experience,* edited by Edith Turner. Tuscon: University of Arizona Press.

———. 1992. *Blazing the Trail: Way Marks in the Exploration of Symbols,* edited by Edith Turner. Tuscon: University of Arizona Press.

Turner, Victor, Mark Swartz, and Arthur Tuden, eds. 1966. *Political Anthropology.* Chicago: Aldine.

Valevičius, Andrius. 1987. "Emmanuel Lévinas: Some Basic Facts." *Lituanus. Lithuanian Quarterly Journal of Arts and Sciences* 33 (1).

Vedantam, Shankar. 2007. "If It Feels Good to Be Good, It Might Be Only Natural." *Washington Post* (May 28, 2007): A, 1, 9.

Voljc, Bozidar 1997. "On the Spirituality of the Doctor-Patient Relationship." In *Communication with the Cancer Patient: Information and Truth,* vol. 809, edited by Antonella Surbone and Matjaz Zwitter, 80–82. New York: Annals of the New York Academy of Sciences.

Wagner, Roy. 2001. *An Anthropology of the Subject: Holographic Worldview in New Guinea and Its Meaning and Significance for the World of Anthropology.* Berkeley: University of California Press.

Waking Ned Devine. 1998. Beverly Hills: Fox Searchlight Pictures and Tomboy Films.

Watts, Alan. 1969. *The Book: On the Taboo Against Knowing Who You Are,* 5–11, 113–114. London: Jonathan Cape.

Werbner, Pnina. 1986. "The Virgin and the Clown: Ritual Elaboration in Pakistani Migrants' Weddings." *Man.*New Series 21(1)

Willis, Roy, with K. B. S. Chisanga, H. M. K. Sikazwe, Kapembwa B. Sikazwe, and Sylvia Nanyangwe. 1999. *Some Spirits Heal, Others Only Dance: A Journey into Human Selfhood in an African Village.* Oxford: Berg.

Wilson, Monica. 1951. *Good Company.* Boston: Beacon.

Wordsworth, William. 1992 (1797–1800). *Lyrical Ballads.* Ithaca, NY: Cornell University Press.

———. 2006 (1798–1799). "There is an active principle" In *Romanticism: An Anthology,* Duncan Wu, ed. Maiden, MA: Blackwell.

Wordsworth, William. 1967 (1802–1804). "Ode on Intimations of Immortality from Recollections of Early Childhood." *The Poetical Works of William Wordsworth.* Vol. 4. Edited by E. de Selincourt, 279–285. Oxford: Clarendon Press.

———. 1995 (1805). *The Prelude: The Four Texts (1798, 1799, 1805, 1850).* Text 1, book XI, 440, 442. London: Penguin Books.

———. 1995 (1805). *The Prelude: The Four Texts (1798, 1799, 1805, 1850).* Text 1, book XIII, 512–516. London: Penguin Books.

Wreford, Jo Thobecka. 2008. *Working with Spirit: Experiencing Izangoma Healing in Contemporary South Africa.* New York: Berghahn.

Yokoyama dos Anjos, Anna Claudia, and Marcia Maria Fontao Zago. 2005. "The Cancer Chemotherapy Experience in a Patient's View." *Review Latino-am Enfermagem* 14 (1). Available at: www.eerp.usp.br/riae.

Zolberg, Aristide. 1972. "Moments of Madness." *Politics and Society*, 2 (2): 183–207. Available at: http://pas.sagepub.com/cgi/pdf_extract/2/2/183.

Index

AIDS quilt, 25
Alaska, ix–xii
Alcoholics Anonymous, 2
alignment, a key to communitas, 197–218
alignment and healing, 212–14
alignment interrupted, 215–18
alignment with god, 203
Amazonia, 148–51, 221
analysis, 1, 155
Animals, ix–x, 146, 148–51
Anna Karenina, 61
Anthropology and Humanism, 1
Apache clowns, 39–41
Aroha unconditional love, 55
Azzam, David, 205–6

Bakhtin, Mikhail, 2, 32–4
ballot box, South Africa, 132–4
Bar Yohai Day, Israel, 26–7
basket divination, 199
beats, interference fringes, 198
Benwa, Fideli, 212–14
Benzon, William, 45
Berlin's wall, 128–31
Bethune, Claudette, 73
betwixt and between, liminality, 4, 7
Bierce, Matt, 47
Biney-Amissah, Theodora, 189
bisoity, We-ness, 157–8
Blake, William, ix, 67, 92
Blodgett, Bill, 212
Blum, Leon, of the Popular Front, 105

Bo Tree, 146
boat, blessing of, ix–xii
Bob Dylan, 124–5
Bond Gang in World War Two, 57
Bororo of Brazil, 214
boundary occasions and liminality, 38–41, 207
Brand, Mieka, 8
Brinton, Crane, 97
British Army, 6, 55
Brokkr, 217
Bruner, Edward, 7
Buber, Martin, 2, 65, 139–40
Buddhism, 5, 111, 136
Bunch, Elaine, 83
Bunyan, John, 201
Burma protests, 141
Burns, Robert, 66
bus driving, 64–8

Caius College, 35–7
Cambridge prank, 35–7
Camp, 4, 20
cancer, 78–81
canon in music, 209
carnival, 32–4
Cassirer, Ernst, 6
chayanga, huntsmanship, 213
chemical affinity, 161
childbirth, 201
Christianity, 88–9
circumcision, 173–82
Civil Rights Movement, 117–22
clairvoyance, 161
Clem, 9

clowns, 38–41
Collins, Diana, 78–81
commercialization, xii
communitas, 1–3
  and anthropology, 7–8
  Anthropology and Humanism, 1
  characteristics of, 1–3
  classification, 1
  and commercialization, xii
  its contrasts, 13–21
  definition, lack of, 1
  in disasters, 73–84
  of the earth, 203–4
  experience of, 8
  extraordinary, xii
  the eye of communitas, 22–3
  of food, 68–72
  and humanism, 1
  ineffable, provenance is universe, 3
  or "in-group versus out-group," 5
  interruptions in, 216–18
  language of communitas, stories, 9
  and liminality, xi, 4
  plural, 1
  potential of, 3
  of sex, 184
  and stories, 1–9
  and structure, 4–5
  of work, 55–68
conscientious objectors, 6, 57
consciousness, 159
Cooper, Andrew, on the Zone, 50–2
counterpoint, 209
"courtesy," 66–8
Crocker, Christopher, 214
Csikszentmihalyi, Mihaly, 50, 51
cupping ritual, 212–14

Daladier, Edouard, 105–7
Dalai Lama, 5, 202
Damasio, Antonio, 153
dancing, 219–20
death, 195–6, 201

Declaration of Independence, 93–6
democracy, 2, 85
Department of Philosophy and African Religion, Kinshasa, 157
Deren, Maya, 206
Deschenes, Liz, 200
Desjarlais, Robert, 45
disasters, 73–84
divination, 199
donkey tree, 29–31
Driver, Tom, 7
drumming, 47–8, 199–200, 202–3
drumming and flow, 50, 205–6
Dubisch, Jill, 8
Dunkirk, 2
Durkheim, Émile, 5, 55
Dylan, Bob, 124–5

eagle, 146
Earle, Duncan, 7
earth-communitas, 203–4
Eckhart, Meister, 222
Edinburgh School of Neurobiology, 13–15
education, 187–9
"The Effectiveness of Symbols," 8
ego, loss of, 3, 50, 220
ekatï, spirit, 159–60
electron, 220
Eliade, Mircea, 160
Ellingson, Ter, 202
Ellis Ashleigh, 47
empathy, 44, 154–8, 203
energy, 49, 160
Erdoes, Richard, 145–6
Essays on the Ritual of Social Relations, 182
Événements de Mai in Paris, 106–8
experience, xii

fatherhood, 184–7
February Revolution, 101–3
Fernandez, James, 7
festivals, 23–42
Fiddler on the Roof, 5
fieldwork, xii, 170–2

INDEX

"flashes," 63, 124–5, 209, 218, 220, 223
floods of Dakota, 73–6
flow, 50, 62, 205–6, 220
flow and zone, 49–50
food, 68–72
Fowler, Thomas, 159
Francis, Saint, 4, 89, 153
Friedson, Stephen, 4, 8, 199–200

Gandhi, Mahatma, 2, 114–17
Geertz, Clifford, 8
Gennep, Arnold van, 7, 167
Gilbert, Elizabeth, 104
global warming, 147
Gluckman, Max, 6
Gospels, 2
Goulet, Jean-Guy, 8
Grafman, Moll and Jordan, 151–4
Grateful Dead, 45
Griffiths, Van, 64–5
Grindal, Bruce, 7
Guthrie, Woody, 122–3

Habitat for Humanity, 64–5
hammer, Thor's, 217
Handelman, Don, 37–8
Hart, Mickey, 46
Harvard Yard, 135–6
harvesters of Kansas, 68
harvesters of Russia, 61–2
Harvey, Tenibac, 4, 8, 162–4
Hasidism, 5
healing 28–9, 45, 162–4
heart, 8
hearts, one or two, 161–2
Heffner, Philip, 4
Herbert, George, 193
Heyoka clowns, 41
His Dark Materials, 210–11
Hitler, Adolf, 6
Holmes, Urban, 7
Holy Thursday, 25–6
hospice, 196
Human Rights, 2, 157
humanism, 1

"I-Thou," 2
Ihamba ritual, 212–14
ineffable, 1
infants and communitas, 13–15
    and song, 44–5
initiations, 7, 167–96
intercultural concepts of power, 49
interference fringes, 198
interrupted alignment, 216–18
intersubjectivity, 157–8, 219
Iñua, soul, 46, 166
Iñupiat, 11, 44, 68
Iñupiat, change weather, ix–x
Inversions, 87–9
    Bororo, 214–15
    and the Buddha, 87–9
    in the chemo-therapy ward, 80
    clowns, 40
    in disaster, 73
    at festivals, 34
    Holy Thursday, 25
    of rank, 78
Islam, 5, 136, 222
Israel, 26–7

Jagannathi, 216–18
Jefferson, Thomas, 93, 95
Jencson, Linda, 73–6
Jenitongo, Adamu, 82
Jesus, 88–9
Judaism, 5, 136, 222
Jung, Carl, 212

Kahona Singleton, 212–14
Kashinakaji, a spirit, 212–14
Katrina disaster, 76–8
Kelly, Jerry, 205
Kendall, Laurel, 217–18
key to alignment, 11, 98, 196
Kickapeg, 31
Kierkegaard, Søren, 64
King, Martin Luther, 118–22, 137
Kipling, Rudyard, 37
Knab, Tim, 7
Knock shrine, 2
Knupp, Eckhart, 47

Korea, 217–18
Koss-Chioino, Joan, 4, 8
Krishna, 5, 216
Krupp, Eckhart, 47
Kut for a Korean Shaman, film, 217–18

Lag B'Omer, 26
Lakota, 41, 161
Lame Deer, 145–6
Land, 144, 165, 204
language of communitas, stories, 9
laughter, 27–32
law of mystical participation, 160
Leipzig, "Nikolaikirche, Open to All," 126–8
Lévinas, Emmanuel, 150, 154–6, 214
Lévi-Strauss, Claude, 8, 100
Lévy-Bruhl, Lucien, 160, 215
Lhasa oracle, 202–3
Lima, Vanderlei de, 215–16
liminality, 4, 7, 38, 181–184, 207, 252
"Liminality: A Synthesis of Subjective and Objective Experience," 206–10
liminality and boundary occasions, 38–41, 169, 207, 210
Lincoln Memorial, 32–4
Lindahl, Carl, 76–8
Living Wage Protest, 136–9
loa, spirits, 206
Loki, 217
Lungu of Zambia, 219–20

MacAloon, John, 50
Machi Benzangani, 133
Makushi of Guyana, 27
Malinowski, Bronislaw, 6, 55
Manchester, and the anthropology of process, 6
mandala, 202–3
Mandela, Nelson, 2, 132–6
Mardi Gras, 35
marginals, 183

Mbuti, 206–10
McAdams, Shane, 200–1
Meron, 26–7
Molimo, music, 206–10
Moreno, Jacob Levy, 161
Marx, Karl, 2
Max Planck Institute, 154
Mdlovu, Seraphina, 134
mechanical solidarity, 5
Meister Eckhart, 222
Mentore, George, 148–51, 159–60, 197
Meron, Israel, 26–7
Merton, Thomas, 2
Meru, 212–14
Methodism, 2
Mexican pyramid, 203–4
Michelet, Jules, 99
Miriam, healer, 162–3
Mitchell, Don, 7
Mjöllnir, Thor's hammer, 217
Moebius strip metaphor, 216–18
moiré, 199
Moses, 2
mowing, 61–2
Mukanda, Ndembu boys' circumcision, 173–82
music, 43–50
 in Ihamba ritual, 48
 in Molimo, 209
 as "seed," 46
musical rounds, 209
Myerhoff, Barbara, 83, 168–9

naked unaccommodated human being, 1, 184
Nash, Kelli, 10, 15–19
Natal, 132–6
nature communitas, 143–65
nature/culture dyad, 143–4
Ndembu of Zambia, fieldwork, 170–2, 212–14
Ndembu song, 44
Necker, Jacques, 97
negative capability, 3, 210–11
Nepal, Yolmo, 45

INDEX

nonviolence, 112–41
nonviolence versus intransigence, 113–14
Norsemen, 217
Novak, Michael, 50
Ntumba, Tshiamalenga, 9, 157–8

ocean wave patterns, 198–9
Ochs, Peter, 221
old age, 194–5
Olympic Games, 5, 215–16
One Day in the Life of Ivan Denisovich, 7, 48–61
Ontology of Consciousness, 159
Oracle in Tibet, 202–3
Orissa, 216–17
Osborne, Scott, 51
Overing, Joanna, 221

Paine, Thomas, 92–3
Pakistani migrants, 37
Parks, Rosa, 118–19
Peccary hunt, 148–51
Pentecost, 156–7
Pereira, Pedro, 8
permafrost, 147
permeability of the soul, 220
Peters, Larry, 8
Piaroa, 27
Piaroa people of Amazonia, 27
Pilgrims' Progress, 201
pizza, 70–1
Playing in the Zone, 51
Pohjola's daughter, 2
Polynesians' seamanship, 198–9
poor, the, 3
Popular Front, 105–6
Porch, Bernie, 20–1
power, 49, 145–6
Powers, William, 4
prank Cambridge, 35–7
psyche, 159, 161
psychodrama, 161
Pullman, Phillip, 210–11
Puma, John, de, 66
pygmies, 206–10

Rabbi Shimon Bar Yohai, 26–7
Rabelais, Mikhail, 32
Ramos, Andreas, 128–31
revolutions, 84–110
    American, 91–5
    by ballot box in South Africa, 132–6
    Événements de Mai, 106–8
    French, 96–100
    Paris Commune, 103–4
    Popular Front, 105–6
    Second Republic, 101–3
Richardson, Miles, 7
Rilke, Rainer Maria, 201
Rites de Passage, Les, 7, 167
rites of passage, 167–96
Ritual Process, The, 2, 3
Robin Hood Looters, 76–8
Rosette, Benetta Jules, 8
rounds in music, 209
Rustin, Bayard, 116–17

Sargeant, Phil, 57
Sartre, Jean-Paul, 4–5
Scherberger, Laura, 8, 187
second sight, xi
Sephardim, 26
Seremitakis, Nadia, 7
Serrano, Jorge, 203
Shabbat candles, 204–5
shamanism, xi, 217–18
    Iñupiat, ix–x
    Korean, 217
    at Llasa, 202
    Makushi, 28
Shangase Ntombikayise, 132–3
Sharp, Stephen Henry, 8, 144–5
Shekhinah, 26
Shepherd, Ashleigh, 65–8
Sibelius, 2, 49
Silva, Sónia, 8
Small Group initiation, 189–91
soccer, 51
social brain, 154
social nature of communitas, 156
solstice in Mexico, 204

Solzhenitskin, Aleksandr, 7, 58–61
song, African, 44, 206–10
Songhay, Niger, 82
Songhay of Niger, 82
soul, 146, 159, 161
South Africa, 132–6
spirit, 3, 143
  in Guyana, 148–51
  in Haiti, 206
  Lungu, 219–20
  in Zambia, 212–14
Stafford-Walter, Courtney, 10, 15–19
Stang, David, 45, 47
status, 16–21
Staviski, Alexandre, 105–6
Stoller, Paul, 46, 81–2
stories, language of communitas, 9
structure, 4–5
Suarez, Francisco, 89–90
Subtle Knife, 210–11
Sufi brotherhoods, 5
sympathetic clairvoyance, 161
sympathetic entanglement, 161–4

Tahrir Square, 105
Tamiahwa, 204
Tedlock, Barbara and Dennis, 7
Thomas, Dylan, 201
Thor, 217
Thoreau Henry David, 110, 111–12
Thorold, Alan, 132–6
three-dimensional drum rhythm, 199–200
three-dimensional stereogram, 199
Tibet, 202–3
Tolstoy, Leon, 4, 61–2, 112–13
trance, 202–3, 215
Trawick, Margaret, 7
Trevarthen, Colwyn, 10, 13–15, 44–5, 154
Turnbull, Colin, 4, 206–10
Turner, Victor, xii, 203, 219
  "Betwixt and Between," 2
  at circumcision camp, 203–4
  communitas and its potential, xii, 3
  and liminality, 78, 169
  at Lincoln Memorial, 23–4
  on local level politics, 139
  and process, 6
  The Ritual Process, 2, 3
  and social scientists, 7
  and Suarez, 90
  work and its communitas, 55
Tutu, Desmond, 135

Ubuntu, humanness, 134, 135, 157

Vasareli, Victor, 200
Vedantam, Shankar, 153–4
Vilakazi Nozipho, 133

wedding, 37–8
Wagner, Roy, 46, 164, 197
Waiwai, 148–51
Wakantanka, power, 145–6
Walaker, Dennis, 75–6
washing feet, 25–6
Washington Mall, 23–5
wedding, 37–8
Weil, Simone, 105–6
Wellman, Irene, 184–9
whales, ix–xi
Whelan, Joseph, 204–5
Willis, Roy, 4, 8, 219–20
Wordsworth, William, 96, 144
work, 55–68
World War II, 2, 6
Wreford, Jo Thobeka, 8

Yohai festival, Israel, 26–7
Young, Thomas, 198

Zambia, 212–14, 219–20
Zen, 50
Zolberg, Aristide, 86–110
Zone, 49–54